# In Action:

*Measuring Return On Investment*

## ASTD

**AMERICAN SOCIETY
FOR TRAINING AND
DEVELOPMENT**

1640 KING STREET
BOX 1443
ALEXANDRIA, VIRGINIA
22313-2043

703/683-8100
FAX 703/683-8103

**Ordering information:** Books published by the American Society for Training and Development can be ordered by calling 703/683-8100.

Library of Congress Catalog Card Number: 94-78503

ISBN: 1-56286-008-9

# Table of Contents

# Preface

Few topics generate as much interest among human resource development (HRD) professionals as the return on investment (ROI) in HRD. In almost every list of high-priority issues in HRD, ROI ranks near the top. At least one presentation at every HRD conference is usually devoted to this topic. Professional journals and research-based publications regularly devote space to this important area.

HRD professionals around the world are seeking practical information about ROI and measurement and evaluation. Specifically, they want to see examples of successful applications of HRD measurement and evaluation at the business-results level. Although a few case studies are available, they are loosely scattered in the literature and often hard to locate. A comprehensive collection of cases is needed—cases that illustrate the successful application of measurement and evaluation to identify the results from HRD programs.

This book represents a successful fulfillment of this challenge by providing a unique collection of 19 cases from a variety of settings involving a wide range of HRD programs. Each case covers the strategy, techniques, and methodologies utilized to measure the results of the program. The book fills a literature void by providing high-impact examples from real-world situations. It should bring a ray of hope to people who are struggling with this process and provide encouragement and satisfaction to those who have implemented similar methodologies.

Few books have received as many favorable comments as this book when it was announced by the American Society for Training and Development (ASTD). I received dozens of telephone calls and letters from individuals all over the world congratulating us for tackling such a tough topic and wanting to purchase the book when it is published. Several colleagues are eager to adopt it. This is convincing evidence that we are on the trail of a very hot topic and that this publication represents a long-overdue contribution to the literature.

## The Seed for this Book

This book grew from a series of seminars I conduct on ROI in training and development. At these seminars, I present examples from my own work, as well as a few cases from colleagues. I noticed, however, that seminar participants were eager for more practical examples. "Show us more cases" was a familiar request.

On my way back from a trip to South Africa, where I had conducted three of these workshops and received requests for more cases, I decided it was time to identify, develop, and publish cases on this important topic. As a long-term member of ASTD, I had been pleased with its programs and publications. I suggested my ideas to them, and their approval for publication came quickly.

## Target Audience

This book should interest anyone involved in HRD. The primary audience is the practitioners who are struggling to determine the value of HRD programs and to show how the programs contribute to an organization's goals. They are the ones who request more examples from what they often label "the real world." This same group also complains that there are too many models, methods, strategies, and theories, and too few examples to show if any of it has really made a difference. This publication should satisfy this need by providing successful models of how the process works. Also, this book should encourage additional practitioners to tackle this important topic, and help them avoid some of the problems that are inherent in the measurement and evaluation process.

The second audience is HRD instructors. Whether in university classes with students who are pursuing degrees in HRD, internal workshops for professional HRD staff members, or public seminars on HRD implementation, this casebook will be a valuable reference. It can be used as a supplement to a standard HRD textbook or complement a textbook on measurement and evaluation, such as the second edition of the *Handbook of Training Evaluation and Measurement Methods* (Phillips, 1991). In my seminars on ROI in training and development, the handbook and casebook will be standard requirements. As a supplemental text, this casebook will bring practical significance to training and development, convincing students that the process does make a difference and that it represents an important function in the organization.

A third audience is the researchers and consultants who are seeking to document results from programs. This book provides additional insight into how to satisfy the client with impressive results. It shows the application of a wide range of models and techniques, some of which are based on sound theory and logical assumptions and others of which may not fare well under the scrutiny of close examination. Unfortunately, the HRD measurement and evaluation process does not have a prescribed set of standards and techniques.

The last, but certainly not least, audience is those managers who must work with HRD on a peripheral basis—managers who are participants in HRD programs to develop their own management skills, who send other employees to participate in HRD programs, and who occasionally lead or conduct sessions of HRD programs. In these roles, managers must be comfortable and have a true understanding of the value of the HRD process. This casebook should provide evidence of this value.

Each audience should find the casebook entertaining and engaging reading. Questions are placed at the end of each case to stimulate additional thought and discussion. One of the most effective ways to maximize the usefulness of this book is through group discussions, using the questions to develop and dissect the issues, techniques, methodologies, and results.

## The Cases

The most difficult part of putting this book together was to identify case authors for a topic that represents a process that does not exist in many organizations. Where it does exist, HRD staffers are not always willing to talk about it. With a lot of hard work from the ASTD staff, however, we were able to identify more cases than needed. In the search, letters were sent to more than 2,000 individuals who have an interest in evaluation. In order to tap the global market, 1,000 of the people contacted were outside the United States. ROI in HRD is a global topic, with no boundaries. We were pleased that more than 100 individuals requested copies of detailed case guidelines and 40 made the commitment to develop a case. In the end, 19 case studies have been accepted for publication.

Cases for this publication had to meet some very tough guidelines. They had to focus on the business results of training, usually at Level 4 in Kirkpatrick's evaluation levels (Kirkpatrick, 1975). It was more than 30 years ago that Kirkpatrick developed what has become a very popular framework for evaluating training at four levels: reaction, learning, behavior, and results. Most of the cases in this book use these levels of evaluation or some modified version of them.

In addition to focusing on results, cases had to have data that could be converted to a monetary value so that ROI could be calculated. In almost all the cases, this quantitative analysis is a part of the presentation. There was some concern that this requirement alone would eliminate too many potential cases. Fortunately, it did not, and the cases contain business results and monetary benefits.

Although there was some attempt to structure cases similarly, they are not identical in style and content. It is important for the reader to experience the programs as they were developed and identify the issues pertinent to each particular setting and situation. The result is a variety of presentations with a variety of styles. Some cases are brief and to the point, outlining precisely what happened and what was achieved. Others provide more detailed background information, including how the need for the program was determined, the personalities involved, and how their backgrounds and biases created a unique situation.

There was no attempt to restrict cases to a particular methodology, technique, or process. It is helpful to show a wide range of approaches. We have resisted the temptation to pass judgment on the various approaches, preferring to let the reader evaluate the different techniques and their appropriateness in their particular settings. Some of the assumptions, methodologies, and strategies might not be as comprehensive and sound as others.

In some cases the name of the organization is identified, as are the individuals who were involved. In others the organization's name is disguised at the request of either the organization or the case author. In today's competitive world, and in situations where there is an attempt to explore new territory, it is understandable why an organization would choose not to be identified. Identification should not be a critical issue, however. Though some cases are slightly modified, they are based on real-world situations faced by real people.

## Case Authors

It would be difficult to find a more impressive group of contributors to an HRD publication than those for this casebook. For such a difficult topic, we expected to find the best, and we were not disappointed. If we had to describe the group, we would say they are experienced, professional, knowledgeable, and on the leading edge of HRD. Collectively, they represent practitioners, consultants, researchers, and professors. Individually, they represent a cross section of HRD. Most are experts, and some are well known in the field. A few are high-profile authors who have made a tremendous contribution in the HRD field and have taken the opportunity to provide an example of their top-quality work. Others have made their mark quietly and have achieved success for their organizations.

## Best Practices?

In our search for cases, we contacted the most respected and well-known organizations in the world, leading experts in the field, key executives in HRD, and well-known authors and researchers. We were seeking examples that represent best practices in measurement and evaluation. Whether they have been delivered, we will never know. What we do know is that if these are not best practices, no other publication can claim to have them either. Many of the experts producing these cases characterize them as the best examples of measurement and evaluation in the field.

## Now for Volume II

The initial reaction to this publication has been outstanding, both from the potential audience and from the contributors who have provided cases. Consequently, we have decided to develop a second volume. The number of cases submitted for this volume exceeded our expectations for both quality and quantity. We also discovered during our search for cases that there were many planned or ongoing projects that would not be completed in time to include in this publication. We would like to capture those, and others, in a volume to be published in either late 1995 or early 1996. Anyone interested in submitting a case or needing additional information can contact me at Performance Resources Organization, P.O. Box 1969, Murfreesboro, TN 37133-1969.

## Suggestions

As with any new publication, we welcome your input. If you have ideas or recommendations regarding presentation, case selection, or case quality, please send them to the above address. All letters will be not only appreciated, but also acknowledged. Your opinions about Volume I will help to improve Volume II.

## Acknowledgments

Although a casebook is the collective work of many individuals, the first acknowledgment must go to all the case authors. We are grateful for their professional contribution. We also want to acknowledge the organizations that have allowed us to use their names and programs for publication. We realize this action is not without risk. We trust the final product has portrayed them as progressive organizations interested in results and willing to try new processes and techniques.

Two of my assistants deserve special recognition. Treva Hall, a former training manager with NationsBank, was extremely helpful with the editing process. She has a keen insight into HRD and provided many helpful suggestions to improve this publication. She has recently completed her M.B.A. at Middle Tennessee State University, where she provided assistance on this project. Tammy Bush has served as my assistant for this project, and without her untiring efforts this publication would not have been developed or delivered within a reasonable time frame. With her experience in human resources, she was able to make important contributions and offer useful input throughout the process. Thanks for a job well done.

Finally, I owe continued appreciation to my spouse, Johnnie, who has tolerated my hectic and demanding schedule during the development of this book. She is a very understanding, thoughtful, and patient partner.

Jack J. Phillips
Birmingham, Alabama
May 1994

## References

Phillips, J.J. (1991). *Handbook of training and evaluation and measurement methods* 2d ed. Houston: Gulf Publishing.

Kirkpatrick, D.L. (1975). Techniques for evaluating training programs. *Evaluating Training Programs* (pp. 1-17). Alexandria, VA: ASTD.

# How To Use This Casebook

These cases present a variety of approaches to measuring the return on human resource development (HRD). The vast majority of the cases focus on evaluation at the ultimate level: business results. Collectively, the cases offer a wide range of settings, methods, techniques, strategies, and approaches, representing manufacturing, service, and government organizations. Target groups for the programs vary from all employees to managers to technical specialists. Although most of the programs focus on training and development, others include organization development, total quality, performance management, and employee selection. As a group, these cases represent a rich source of information on the thought processes and strategies of some of the best practitioners, consultants, and researchers in the field.

Each case does not necessarily represent the optimum or ideal approach for the specific situation. In every case, it is possible to identify areas that could benefit from refinement and improvement. That is part of the learning process—to build on the work of other people. Although the evaluation approach is contextual, these methods and techniques can be used in other organizations.

Table 1 presents basic descriptions of the cases in the order in which they appear in the book. This table can serve as a quick reference for readers who want to examine the evaluation approach for a particular type of program, audience, or industry.

## Using the Cases

There are several ways to use this book. In essence, it will be helpful to anyone who wants to see real-life examples of the business results of training. Specifically, four uses are recommended:

- This book will be useful to HRD professionals as a basic reference of practical applications of measurement and evaluation. A reader can

*These cases were prepared to serve as a basis for discussion rather than to illustrate either effective or ineffective administrative or managerial practices.*

analyze and dissect each of the cases to develop an understanding of the issues, approaches, and, most of all, refinements or improvements that could be made.
- This book will be useful in group discussions, where interested individuals can react to the material, offer different perspectives, and draw conclusions about approaches and techniques. The questions at the end of each case can serve as a beginning point for lively and entertaining discussions.

**Table 1. Overview of the case studies.**

| Case | Industry | HRD Program | Target Audience |
|------|----------|-------------|-----------------|
| Penske Truck Leasing Company | Truck leasing | Supervisory skills training | First-level supervisors |
| International Oil Company | Petroleum | Customer service training | Dispatchers |
| Magnavox Electronic Systems Company | Electronics | Literacy training | Electrical and mechanical assemblers |
| North Country Electric and Gas | Electric and gas utility | Productivity and quality improvement program | All supervisors and managers |
| Yellow Freight System | Trucking | Performance management system | Managers |
| Midwest Banking Company | Banking | Sales training | Consumer loan officers |
| National Paper Company | Paper products | Organizational development | All employees |
| Causeway Corporation | Direct sales | Total quality management | Employees in financial services |
| U.S. Government | Federal government | Supervisory training | New supervisors |

- This book will serve as an excellent supplement to other training and development or evaluation textbooks. It provides the extra dimensions of real-life cases that show the outcomes of training and development.
- Finally, this book will be extremely valuable for managers who do not have primary training responsibility. These managers provide support and assistance to the HRD staff, and it is helpful for them to understand the results that HRD programs can yield.

**Table 1 (continued). Overview of the case studies.**

| Case | Industry | HRD Program | Target Audience |
|------|----------|-------------|-----------------|
| Insurance Company of America | Insurance | Technical skills training | Underwriters |
| Coca-Cola Bottling Company of San Antonio | Soft drink | Supervisory training | All supervisors |
| Information Services Inc. | Information services | Interpersonal skills training | All employees |
| Multi-Marques Inc | Bakery | Work process analysis and training | Administrative supervisors |
| Metropolitan Health Maintenance Organization | Health care | Organizational development | All employees |
| Litton Guidance and Control Systems | Avionics | Self-directed work teams | All employees |
| Financial Services Inc. | Financial services | Selection and training | District managers |
| Arthur Andersen and Company | Accounting and consulting | Comprehensive technical skills training | Tax consultants |
| Midwest Automotive Plant | Automotive manufacturing | On-the-job training | Production employees |

It is important to remember that each organization and its program implementation is unique. What works well for one may not work for another, even if they are in similar settings. It is not recommended that an approach or technique necessarily be duplicated. The book does, however, offer a variety of approaches and provides an arsenal of tools from which to choose in the evaluation process.

## Follow-Up

Space limitations have resulted in some cases being shorter than both the author and the editor would prefer. Some information concerning background, assumptions, strategies, and results had to be omitted. If additional information on a case is needed, the lead author can be contacted directly. The address is listed at the end of each case.

# Measuring ROI: Progress, Trends, and Strategies

By Jack J. Phillips

*For readers new to the topic, the following discussion provides an introduction to measuring return on investment in HRD programs. For others, it provides a framework for reviewing and analyzing the case studies that follow.*

## Important Strategic Initiatives

The human resource development (HRD) field has changed significantly in recent years. It has enjoyed increased attention, its role has been enhanced, and it is now positioned to have a tremendous influence. Although there is no consensus among the experts of where the field is going, there are three important strategic initiatives that HRD professionals must continue to pursue.

The first initiative is the integration of HRD into the overall strategic framework of the organization. Among the competitive strategies of organizations is the use of the HRD function to implement change, build skills for the future, and retain a capable workforce. From a bottom-line perspective, HRD programs enhance profitability, increase productivity, develop new markets, and create business opportunities. The chief training officer is now an important participant in the strategic planning process.

The second major strategic initiative involves building effective partnerships with management. For HRD to be successful and produce the desired results, there must be an effective partnership with primary internal customers, usually the line management group. Through collaborative efforts, the HRD staff must continue to work productively with line management to help them solve problems, improve operational performance, and enhance the organization's effectiveness.

The third strategic initiative is the continuing need to measure the effectiveness of HRD. Although there has been a measurement imperative for years, only recently has measurement become essential for survival of HRD within some organizations. The HRD staff can no longer afford to operate in a world without accountability. HRD must meet the challenge of showing its contribution and measuring the effects of programs.

These three strategies should continue to be integrated into each HRD function and should command attention for the remainder of this decade. The extent to which they are implemented will ultimately determine the success of the HRD function within an organization.

## Uncomfortable Realities of Evaluation

As most experts agree, measuring the return in HRD is difficult and will challenge even the most sophisticated and progressive HRD departments. As shown in Table 1, one publication on ROI has offered 11 barriers to successful measurement and evaluation, described as myths that prevent effective evaluation (Phillips, 1991). Although they are myths, they point to realistic barriers and actual problems with this process. Three uncomfortable realities of measurement and evaluation are that the variables are complex, effects can only be estimated, and economic benefits cannot be calculated precisely.

**Table 1. Measurement and evaluation myths (from Phillips, 1991).**

1. I can't measure the results of my training effort.
2. I don't know what information to collect.
3. If I can't calculate the return on investment, then it is useless to evaluate the program.
4. Measurement is effective only in production and financial areas.
5. My chief executive officer does not require evaluation, so why should I do it?
6. There are too many variables affecting the behavior change for me to evaluate the impact of training.
7. Evaluation will lead to criticism.
8. I don't need to justify my existence, I have a proven track record.
9. The emphasis on evaluation should be the same in all organizations.
10. Measuring progress toward objectives is an adequate evaluation strategy.
11. Evaluation would probably cost too much.

## Complex Variables

Human performance in organizations can be influenced by a variety of factors with complex interactions. Consequently, the output of the interaction of these factors is complex as well. The relationship of input to output almost never can be established without considerable effort. The challenge for the HRD staff is to tackle the issue with all the techniques available. Waiting for a simpler relationship is fruitless. It will never happen. With assumptions and appropriate methodology, however, some of the variables affecting performance can be isolated, or at least approximated, to a confidence level adequate for a program's sponsors and supporters.

### Unknown Program Impact

Regardless of the approach taken, the effects of an HRD program cannot be pinpointed with complete accuracy (although the control-group design comes very close). Short of the control group, the various approaches and strategies can only estimate the effects. Two questions arise: Why is such precision needed? Is it necessary to know the exact amount of HRD's influence, or is an approximation sufficient? After all, many business output variables are approximations or estimations attributed to certain events or activities. An estimation of HRD's effects will usually be sufficient.

### Imprecise Economic Benefit

The economic benefits of HRD are not precise. Even if the relationships between input variables and output performance have been determined and the effects of an HRD program have been isolated, there still remains the problem of converting the benefit derived from the program to an economic value. To measure the ROI, the monetary value of the net benefit must be compared with the cost of the program. The conversion of an improvement to a monetary value is not always an exact process. It often requires estimates or subjective input of individuals or groups. The process is not really different from making other calculations, however. In many financial transactions, such as depreciation, cost allocation, transfer pricing, and inventory adjustments, the values are estimates, sometimes based on subjective opinions.

### Confronting Reality

These three uncomfortable realities are present in most situations, leaving some HRD professionals and executives uncomfortable measuring ROI. Too often, these realities become barriers to evaluation and keep even the most progressive organizations from measuring the effects of HRD. These difficulties should not inhibit an organization's attempt to measure the return, however.

This project—identifying and presenting cases on ROI in HRD—has resulted in hundreds of conversations, inquiries, and comments on the topic from some of the best professionals in the field. One conclusion that resulted from this exercise and that has the support of veteran HRD professionals is that

---

A Comprehensive Evaluation Effort Is Essential
for Process Improvement and Funding Increases.

---

Evaluation is in part formative, designed to improve the process. Evaluation is also designed to show the ultimate results of the process. Measurement and evaluation are necessary to provide evidence of the contribution of HRD programs to the organization's goals and output variables. Without such evidence, it is difficult for organizations to continue to fund or increase funding for the programs.

## ROI: The Pressure Is Increasing

In any direction one chooses to take in the HRD field, the pressure to measure ROI is increasing. In developing countries as in fully developed nations, the issue is a hot topic. At some time or another, virtually every organization will face this important issue. The pressure to measure the results from training may come from line managers, the internal customers of HRD who must support HRD, or from top executives who must allocate resources to those functions in the organization that are contributing to the bottom line. Five important trends are visible on the HRD horizon. Collectively, they provide evidence of the pressure for increased use of ROI.

### Training and Development Budgets Are Increasing

There is clear evidence of the increase in training and development budgets. In the United States, budgets for 1993 were up 7 percent over 1992, and the number of individuals trained increased 15 percent, one of the largest increases in recent history ("Industry Report," 1993). Budgets are also increasing in other countries, particularly where training expenditures are tied to government legislation. As budgets increase, so does the need for accountability. Large (and growing) budgets become big targets for critics. When HRD receives significant funding increases, it is usually at the expense of other parts of the organization that have not received similar increases. As the percentage of operating expenses allocated to HRD continues to increase, the HRD budget will continue to be a target of people who question its existence or its ability to enhance organizational effectiveness. This situation places pressure on the HRD staff to show that the function is achieving results.

## HRD Is Linked to Competitive Strategies

Many organizations are utilizing HRD as a competitive weapon to create a distinct advantage. In some situations, training is seen as the most critical competitive weapon. Whether the organization is experiencing tremendous growth, restructuring, right-sizing, or changing markets and locations, training is seen as an important vehicle to implement these changes. HRD has become a powerful change management tool to help organizations successfully meet the challenges of the future. Ambitious HRD efforts, linked with competitive strategies, enable organizations to increase market share, introduce new products, improve delivery and customer service, reduce cost, become more efficient, improve response times, and increase productivity. When training takes on a highly visible role, such as implementing parts of the strategic plan, there is pressure for accountability. Top executives and other significant groups want to ensure that all competitive tools are accountable and measurable.

## HRD Is a Critical Part of Total Quality Management Programs

Total quality management (TQM) programs have been introduced at a fast pace in recent years. Almost all progressive organizations now have some version of TQM, although some programs are more effective than others. A variety of HRD programs form an important part of TQM, and measurement and evaluation are at the heart of the entire process. When emphasis is placed on measuring quality, productivity, cost, and time, there is also increased pressure to measure the primary vehicle to implement TQM, namely, HRD.

## Accountability of All Functions Is Increasing

Virtually every function in an organization is being subjected to increased demands for accountability. Functions previously taken for granted as necessary and unmeasurable (e.g., public relations) are now required to show a contribution. This is especially true for staff support functions. Even internal auditors, who several years ago never dreamed of being held accountable for their success, are now adapting measurement processes and in some cases turning audit functions into profit centers. In this respect, HRD is just one of many functions responding to pressures to show their contribution in measurable terms.

### Top Executives Require ROI Information

Chief executives, struggling to make their organizations lean, profitable, and viable, are demanding accountability with all expenditures. They are encouraging, and sometimes requiring, the HRD staff to measure ROI. In some cases, executives issue ultimatums to show the value of HRD or take a budget cut, as happened at IBM (Gallagan, 1989). In other cases, top executives use subtle hints and suggestions.

These five trends are occurring in all types of organizations and are placing renewed demands on HRD staffs to show their contribution in measurable, quantitative terms. This pressure creates a need to calculate the ROI for at least a few programs, so that management will have confidence that there is an adequate return on all programs. Even executive education programs offered by universities, which were previously untouchable on the accountability issue, are now facing tremendous pressure to show their results. A recent comprehensive report in the *Wall Street Journal* (Fuchsberg, 1993) revealed many problems with executive education and asked, "Would you spend millions of dollars without knowing what, if anything, you are going to get for it?" The HRD staff must meet the challenge and find ways to measure ROI, at least on a limited basis.

## The Ultimate Level of Evaluation: Business Results

Perhaps it is helpful to review briefly the different levels of evaluation developed more than 30 years ago by D.L. Kirkpatrick, and modified by various organizations and individuals. The concept of different levels of evaluation is instructive for understanding how ROI is calculated (Kirkpatrick, 1975). The first level of evaluation is measurement of reaction to an HRD program; and addresses program participants' attitudes and level of satisfaction. At the second level, measurements focus on what participants learn during the program. The third level is the measurement of behavioral changes and on-the-job applications of the training material. The fourth level, which represents the ultimate outcome, is the measurement of business results. This level focuses on the actual results the program achieves in the organization when the program objectives have been met successfully.

Figure 1 shows the relationships and characteristics of these four levels. The value of information derived from this process is highest at Level 4 and lowest at Level 1. The power to show business results is greatest at Level 4 and decreases at lower levels, with almost no possibilities at the reaction level. Almost all organizations conduct reaction evaluations to measure customer satisfaction, but very few conduct evaluations at the results level—perhaps because reaction evaluation is easy, whereas business results evaluation is very difficult. The ROI in HRD usually rests with this infrequently used, valuable, and difficult fourth level of evaluation.

**Figure 1. The four levels of evaluation.**

| Chain of impact | Value of information | Power to show results | Frequency of use | Difficulty of assessment |
|---|---|---|---|---|
| Reaction (Level 1) | Least valuable | Least power | Frequent | Easy |
| Learning (Level 2) | | | | |
| Behavior (Level 3) | | | | |
| Results (Level 4) | Most valuable | Most power | Infrequent | Difficult |

Although business results are desired, it is very important to evaluate the other levels, as well. There is some evidence of a chain of impact among the levels, which indicates that if measurements are not taken at each level, it is difficult to conclude that the results achieved were actually caused by the HRD program (Alliger and Janak, 1989).

## ROI Strategy

Although it is important to produce business results with HRD programs, it is difficult to measure at that level. This fact leads to two important questions. What is the appropriate strategy? Is anything short of Level 4 evaluation acceptable? The answers are not easy. Level 4 evaluations are not appropriate for every program; the calculation of an ROI should be reserved for only a few types of programs. Some organizations, wrestling with this issue, develop specific strategies for ROI calculations. These strategies often hinge on four specific actions, outlined in this section.

### Set Targets for Each Evaluation Level

Recognizing the varying complexity of the evaluation levels, as described in Figure 1, some organizations attempt to manage evaluation by setting targets for the percentage of HRD programs measured at each level. For example, it is easy to measure reaction, and many organizations require 100 percent evaluation at that level. The second level, learning, is another relatively easy area to measure and the target is high, usually less than 100 percent but greater than 50 percent. This decision is specific to the organization, based on its desire to measure learning and the nature and types of programs. At the ultimate level, business results, the target is relatively small because of the difficulty of the ROI process, which commands significant resources and budgets. Table 2 presents an example of evaluation targets from a large electric utility.

**Table 2. Targets for percentages of programs to be evaluated.**

| Level | Percentage |
|---|---|
| Participants' satisfaction | 100 |
| Learning | 70 |
| On-the-job applications (behavior) | 50 |
| Results | 10 |

Setting evaluation targets has several advantages. First, it provides measurable objectives for the HRD staff. Second, adopting targets focuses more attention on the accountability process, communicating a strong message to the HRD staff about the commitment to measurement and evaluation. Finally, focusing on targets at all levels helps realize the benefits of the chain of impact. There is usually a requirement that all Level 4 evaluations involve evaluations at the previous three levels. This requirement enhances the organization's ability to show that the results obtained at Level 4 are caused by the HRD program and not other factors.

### Evaluate at the Micro Level

Measurement and evaluation usually focus on an individual program or a few tightly integrated courses. Attempting to evaluate a series of courses scattered over a long period becomes quite difficult. The cause-and-effect relationship becomes more confusing and complex. Evaluation is more effective when applied to an individual program, possibly consisting of several modules, that can be tied to a direct result or payoff. In situations where a series of courses that are tied to the same objectives must be completed before the objectives can be met, an evaluation of the series of courses may be more appropriate. This decision should take into consideration the objectives of the program, the timing of the courses, and the cohesiveness of the series. It is inappropriate to attempt to evaluate an entire function, such as management development, career development, executive education, or technical training. For this reason, it is recommended that evaluation be conducted at the micro level.

### Use Sampling for ROI Calculations

If organizations need ROI calculations for some—but not all—courses, each organization must attempt to find that desired level of ROI calculations. There is no prescribed formula, and the number depends on many variables, including
- staff expertise in evaluation
- resources that can be allocated to the process
- the organization's commitment to measurement and evaluation
- pressure from other people to show ROI calculations
- the nature and types of HRD programs
- other variables specific to the organization.

A few organizations use a statistical sampling process to select a small number of programs for ROI calculations. Most organizations, however, settle for evaluating one or two sessions of their most popular programs. For example, the U.S. Office of Personnel Management developed an ROI calculation for one of its most popular courses, Introduction to Supervision. The results of this evaluation are presented in this book. Other organizations pick a program from each major training segment. For example, in one large bank with six academies, ROI is calculated for one program selected from each academy each year. If an organization is implementing ROI for the first time, it is recommended that only one course be selected for a calculation.

Although it is important to take a statistically sound approach to the sampling process, it is more important to consider a trade-off between available resources and the level of sampling and analysis that management will accept for ROI calculations. The primary objective is not to convince the HRD staff that their programs work, but to show top management that HRD makes a difference. Therefore, it is important that the sampling plan be developed with the input and approval of top management. In the final analysis, top management must be comfortable that the selection process yields a satisfactory assessment of the HRD function.

### Make Inferences at the Macro Level

In a few organizations there is pressure to evaluate the total impact of the HRD function. Although this cannot be accomplished accurately, it is possible to develop estimates. If a statistically appropriate sampling plan is adopted for a cross section of programs, ROI calculations can be used to estimate the effects of other programs. For example, suppose an organization offers 120 individual HRD programs annually, and it is determined that 24 represents a statistically significant sample size. Each of 24 HRD programs, selected at random, is evaluated at Level 4 with an ROI calculation. The total return can be estimated from the sample. This inference is not recommended, however, because of the subjective nature of many ROI calculations and the variety of HRD programs usually offered. To have an adequate sample may require measuring almost all programs. It is usually more important to sample at a reasonable level, selecting those courses that are most suited for this type of evaluation. Top management can then draw its own conclusions about all programs.

## A Framework for Developing ROI

The model shown in Figure 2 is offered as an overall framework for developing the ROI. Some of the cases presented in this book follow this framework, but others do not. The framework serves as a simple and useful tool for identifying cases' weaknesses and problems. It tracks the steps in developing an ROI from data collection to calculating the actual monetary return. The model assumes that costs to compare with monetary benefits will be developed. Also, it assumes

# Figure 2. Model for determining the return on HRD.

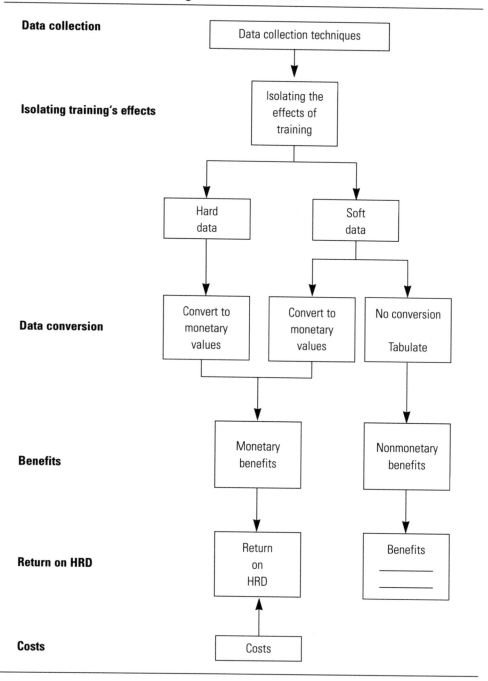

**Data collection** — Data collection techniques

**Isolating training's effects** — Isolating the effects of training

— Hard data — Soft data

**Data conversion** — Convert to monetary values — Convert to monetary values — No conversion / Tabulate

**Benefits** — Monetary benefits — Nonmonetary benefits

**Return on HRD** — Return on HRD — Benefits

**Costs** — Costs

that each program will have intangible benefits that are not converted to monetary values, but nevertheless are reported as benefits.

The ROI process begins with data collection methods, which are at the heart of any evaluation system. Table 3 shows a list of evaluation methods. (For information on the various data collection methods, see Basarab and Root, 1992; Dixon, 1990; Phillips, 1991.)

**Table 3. Data collection methods for evaluation (from Phillips, 1991).**

**Measuring participants' performance during the program by**
- measuring reaction with questionnaires and interviews
- using surveys and tests to measure changes in attitudes, skills, and knowledge.

**Measuring job applications and business results by**
- using a follow-up assignment
- planning a follow-up assessment with surveys, questionnaires, interviews, observations, and focus groups
- integrating action planning into the program
- implementing performance contracting
- conducting a follow-up evaluation session
- tracking performance after the program.

Two formulas are often used to determine the return of a program: the benefit-to-cost ratio (BCR) and ROI:

$$BCR = \frac{program\ benefits}{program\ costs} \qquad ROI\ (\%) = \frac{net\ program\ benefits}{program\ costs} \times 100$$

The BCR utilizes the total benefits and costs. In the ROI formula, the costs are subtracted from the total benefits to produce the net benefits, which are then divided by the costs. For example, if an HRD program has benefits of $600,000 and a cost of $200,000, the BCR is calculated as follows:

$$BCR = \frac{\$600,000}{\$200,000} = 3,\ or\ 3\ to\ 1$$

In other words, for every $1 invested, $3 in benefits are returned. The net benefits are $400,000 ($600,000 - $200,000), so the ROI is

$$\text{ROI (\%)} = \frac{\$400,000}{\$200,000} \times 100 = 200\%.$$

This ROI means that for each $1 invested, there is a $2 return in net benefits.

The benefits are usually annual benefits (the amount saved for a complete year). Although savings may continue after the first year if the program has lasting effects, the amount begins to diminish and is usually omitted from calculations. In the total program cost, it is recommended that development costs be included in the first year of the program. An alternative is to prorate development costs over the projected life of the program.

The values for ROI in HRD are usually quite large, in the range of 150 percent to 400 percent, which illustrates the significant results of successful programs. In this book, ROI values range from 150 percent to 2,000 percent.

## Isolating the Effects of HRD

An area that is often overlooked is the process of isolating the effects of HRD—that is, determining how much credit the HRD program can take for the improved results. At a very minimum, an evaluation report should acknowledge that other factors influenced results and should list those factors. Doing so adds credibility to the process, even if no attempts are made to isolate HRD's influence. Fortunately, several strategies can be helpful to isolate the effects. They are presented briefly here.

### Use of Control Groups

The use of control groups is the most effective way to isolate the effects of an HRD program. In this arrangement, a control group that is nearly identical to the group involved in the HRD program is established. The performances of the two groups are compared and, if the groups are similar and subject to the same external influences, the differences in the performance of the participant group can usually be attributed to the HRD program. Other variations of the control-group paradigm are described elsewhere (Fitz-Gibbon and Morris, 1987; Pedhazur and Sehmelkin, 1991). When control groups are not feasible or practical, other possibilities are available.

### Trend Line Analysis

Sometimes trend lines can predict where an output performance variable would be without the program. A trend line can be drawn using a series of preprogram measures. This is not an exact process, but provides an estimation. The predicted values from the trend line are compared with measures taken after the program, and the differences are attributed to the program.

Figure 3 shows an example of a trend line analysis for a reject rate. As can be seen in the figure, there was a downward trend in the reject rate prior to the program, which took place in July. Although the program apparently had a dramatic effect on the reduction of rejects, the trend line, based on the trend that had been established previously, shows that rejects would have continued to decline anyway. Therefore, comparing the average six months prior to the program with the average six months after the program may be an inappropriate way to measure the improvement. A better approach would be to compare the six-month average after the program with the trend line's value at the midpoint of the six-month period after the program (October value).

**Figure 3. Trend line example.**

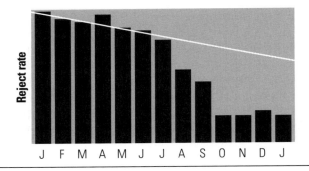

## Forecasting Methods

A more analytical approach to trend line analysis is to use a variety of forecasting methods to determine the expected level of an output that would be variable in the future if the program were not undertaken. There are several forecasting models that can take into account variations such as seasonal and cyclical fluctuations and can develop reasonably accurate predictions of future values of the variable. Although a detailed discussion of forecasting methods is beyond the scope of this book, interested readers can find information on the different models and processes in Makridakis (1989) and Jarret (1991).

## Participants' Estimates of Training's Effects

It may be helpful to have participants estimate the percentage of their improvement attributable to the HRD program. The participants are very close to the improvement and may know how much of the improvement each factor caused. Their collective estimates can be reliable and can carry much credibility with the management group. In one of the cases in this book, involving an HRD program at Yellow Freight System, each participant who achieved an improvement estimated the percentage of the improvement that was related to the HRD program. These values were then approved by three levels of management.

## Management's Estimates of Training's Effects

In some cases, upper management and/or supervisors of participants can estimate the percentage of improvement attributable to the HRD program. Although this process is subjective, the source of the estimate is the group who may be most familiar with the situation and are aware of the other influences that affect performance. In the case involving Litton Guidance and Control Systems, management subtracted out any factors known to have contributed to the improvements in productivity and quality. Then, to arrive at a conservative estimate, management applied a subjective factor, in this case 60 percent, to determine the portion of results that could be attributed to the HRD program. Although this process was subjective, the 60 percent factor was decided on in a meeting of top executives, so the group had confidence in this value and was comfortable with the resulting calculations. Ideally, one should have estimates from both participants and management and combine them in some creative, helpful way.

## Calculating the Effects of Other Factors

When it is possible to isolate the effects of other factors, the HRD program should account for the remainder of the improvement. In the Midwest Banking case, the effects of the other factors that influenced consumer loan volume were determined and subtracted from overall results, leaving the remaining volume increases attributable to the training program.

## What It Means

Although these approaches are subjective (except for perhaps the control-group and forecasting methods), they provide useful information that helps focus on the effects of HRD. The results can be more accurate than the results obtained from evaluating other functions.

Consider, for example, the difficulty of isolating the effects of an advertising program, a public relations function, a new purchasing policy and procedure, a new cost-accounting program, or a new engineering design. In each case, subjective input and decisions are required to estimate the impact. This is an area that will need additional research and application in the future.

## Hard Data versus Soft Data

It is sometimes helpful to divide the collected data into hard data and soft data. Hard data are
- objectively based
- easy to measure and quantify
- assigned dollar values relatively easily
- common measures of organizational performance
- very credible in the eyes of management.

Soft data are
- subjectively based in many cases
- difficult to measure and quantify, directly
- assigned dollar values with difficulty
- less credible as performance measures
- usually behaviorally oriented.

This distinction helps in the data analysis and conversion processes. All hard data are usually converted to monetary values, whereas soft data may or may not be converted, depending on the difficulty of making the conversion and the credibility of the output. Hard data usually involve quantity, quality, cost, and time. Soft data focus more on attitudes, work climate, work habits, and other items that are behaviorally based and subjective.

## Converting Hard Data

Converting hard data is a relatively easy task. The output values are translated into profit units, which are converted to monetary values. Cost savings can usually be transferred directly to the ROI formula, although the money value of time may alter the exact amount. A future cost savings will need to be discounted to obtain a present value to compare with program costs. Quality measures are a little more difficult because there are so many factors that can be affected by quality improvements. Table 4 shows the specific items that may be influenced by a change in quality. The value of a time savings needs some attention, too. Sometimes the salary of the individual whose time has been saved is an appropriate measure. At other times, as shown in

Table 5, the value of time savings derives from any of several different factors.

**Table 4. Factors involved in converting quality data to monetary values.**

- Scrap or waste
- Rework
- Customer or client dissatisfaction
- Product liability
- Inspection and quality control
- Internal losses
- Employee morale

**Table 5. Factors involved in converting time savings to monetary values.**

- Wages or salaries
- Better service
- Penalty avoidance
- Opportunity for profit
- Training time

### Converting Soft Data

Perhaps the most difficult conversion is determining the monetary value of a soft-data improvement, and many organizations do not attempt this process. Several strategies can provide reliable estimates of the value of soft-data improvements, however.

HISTORICAL COSTS. Some organizations track the costs of certain soft-data variables, such as grievances, absenteeism, or turnover. If these costs are available, they should be utilized when developing monetary values for improvements in those variables. Unfortunately, for most soft-data items, historical costs are not available, which creates a need for reliable estimates. The International Oil Company case illustrates the use of costs in soft-data conversion. The value of improvement (reduction, in this case) in customer complaints was converted to a monetary value based on historical records. The time it took to resolve a complaint was monitored, and the cost was derived using the salaries and benefits of the individuals involved. This approach used internal cost data (i.e., salaries) in a soft-data conversion.

EXPERT OPINION. Sometimes the best estimates of the value of a soft-data improvement may come from experts in the field. Experts who have studied, analyzed, and developed these estimates previously may come from within the organization. There may also be external experts who have researched the topic across organizations. For example, information on the cost of a grievance might be obtained from a labor relations staff member internally, or from an external expert who studies the costs of grievances in several organizations and industries.

EXTERNAL STUDIES. For some soft-data items (e.g., turnover, absenteeism, tardiness, and customer complaints), studies that place a value on a unit of improvement are available. When such studies are available, they should be utilized. For example, there have been many studies to calculate the cost of absenteeism both by industry and in specific organizations (Martocchio and Harrison, 1993). The values in the studies may need to be adjusted to apply to a particular organization.

PARTICIPANTS' ESTIMATES. The individuals involved with an improvement may have some sense of the value of the improvement and should be asked directly. Sometimes participants in an HRD program are asked to place a value on a particular unit of improvement that will serve as a measure of the program's success. For example, in a program aimed at reducing absenteeism, the participants, all of whom were supervisors, were asked to estimate the cost of a single absence in their work units. After discussion of the factors that contributed to the cost, the supervisors provided estimates. The average value for the group was used in the final analysis to estimate the value of the reduction in absenteeism. In some cases this approach may not be feasible, because participants are unable to provide estimates. In other cases, however, this may be the richest source of information available

MANAGEMENT'S ESTIMATES. If it is assumed that managers or supervisors of participants have more knowledge of the process than the participants, management can be asked to place a value on a unit of improvement. This approach increases management support and buy-in for the evaluation.

HRD STAFF'S ESTIMATES. The last and probably the least credible source of estimates is the HRD staff. In this approach, the HRD staff uses whatever information is available to estimate the value of the improvement. This is risky because the value may be perceived to be self-serving and not very credible.

## What It Means

A typical reaction to these strategies is that they are so subjective that the conversion is virtually worthless. This is not the case. Subjective assignments appear in all aspects of business. Data deveoped in organizations are often based on estimates or subjective assessments. The HRD staff should not have to apologize for the subjectiveness of soft-data conversion. The best strategy is to use all the input from people who are knowledgeable, clearly identifying the sources and assumptions when the results are communicated to audiences. Program evaluators seem hesitant to use the strategies to convert the values of soft-data improvements to monetary values. This is an area that will need increased attention in the future.

## ROI Challenges: More Standardization and Thoroughness

After researching the literature, seeking cases from more than 2,000 individuals, editing the selected cases, and discussing the issues with colleagues, I have come to several conclusions concerning weaknesses in ROI evaluations. These weaknesses, which appear in some of the cases in this book, are challenges to the profession.

### Cost Standards

The methods organizations use to track costs vary considerably. What one organization assumes is a cost of training, another may not. The HRD field needs standard cost data. Although there have been several attempts at standardization, most of the efforts have failed. It is becoming increasingly difficult to compare costs from different programs. Although the benchmarking project of the American Society for Training and Development may develop some standards, the results will be short of what is needed for the HRD field overall. This issue is particularly important as the U.S. government attempts to require, or encourage, employers to invest more in training. When the specific makeup of an organization's investment becomes a crucial measure, standardization can help. In the interim, presentations of ROI should clearly describe the cost components in the total costs for programs.

### Evaluation Designs

Many organizations do not focus enough attention on evaluation design. Although a control group, the preferred approach, was used in several cases in this book, this paradigm is infrequent in practice. Yet it can be used without the disruption, problems, and inconvenience that are usually feared by practitioners. In addition, the use of pre- and post-course measurements does not appear to be as frequent as it should be. Other design schemes, such as time-series measurements, are also useful, but largely ignored.

### Isolating the Effects of HRD

In far too many situations, the improvement in an output variable after an HRD program is conducted is assumed to be caused by the implementation of the program. In reality, several variables affect output and performance. Many practitioners are not taking the extra step to attempt to isolate the influence of the program on the overall results.

As described earlier, there are a variety of strategies available, but examples of their actual use are very rare. This is an excellent area for future research and is an important challenge for the HRD field.

### Standardized Methodology

Evaluation methods and techniques vary. There are only so many ways in which data can be collected, however, and the number of processes for data analysis is finite. Data collection methods are often used without regard to their advantages and disadvantages. Additional efforts to standardize and publicize these methods would be helpful to the field.

### Statistical Techniques

Although most HRD practitioners want to avoid statistics, many conclusions require statistical analysis. Even top executives who may not understand a sophisticated statistical analysis need to know that conclusions are based on a certain confidence level, supported by appropriate methodology. In several of the cases in this book, as in many other evaluation projects, the concept of statistical power is largely ignored. Some sample sizes are so small that the results cannot be considered to be supported statistically. This factor does not receive enough attention with practitioners.

### Converting Data to Monetary Values

Because of the subjective nature of the conversion, the results from HRD programs are often not converted to monetary values. This is an essential step for an ROI calculation. Although this step was included in most of the cases in this book, many other evaluations do not compare benefits with cost. Conversion to monetary values should be a fundamental requirement.

### What It Means

The challenges described here represent a mandate for the HRD field. Standardization and consistency are needed to continue to make progress with ROI calculations. Perhaps the different groups involved in HRD should attempt to develop standards or generally accepted guidelines. Although development and acceptance of standards will take a long time, the HRD field will be much better off if such an effort is undertaken, and there will be many more successes in the future.

## Conclusion

Although there is almost universal agreement that the ROI for HRD programs merits more attention, there seems to be a small number of successful examples of the calculation of the ROI. In reality, this process is not as difficult as it seems. The approaches, strategies, and techniques are not complex and can be useful in a variety of settings. It will take the combined and persistent efforts of practitioners and researchers to continue to refine the techniques and show successful applications.

## References

Alliger, G.M., and E.A. Janak. 1989. Kirkpatrick's levels of training criteria: Thirty years later. *Personnel Psychology, 42,* 331-342.

Basarab Sr., D.J., and D.K. Root. 1992. *The training evaluation process.* Boston: Kluwer Academic.

Dixon, N.M. 1990. *Evaluation: A tool for improving HRD quality.* San Diego, CA: University Associates.

Fitz-Gibbon, C.T., and L.L. Morris. 1987. *How to design a program evaluation.* Beverly Hills, CA: Sage.

Fuchsberg, G. 1993. Taking control. *Wall Street Journal,* 10 September.

Gallagan, P.A. 1989. IBM gets its arms around education. *Training & Development Journal, 43,* 37.

Industry report. 1993. *Training, 30*(10), 29.

Jarret, J. 1991. *Business forecasting methods* (2d ed.). Cambridge, MA: Basil Blackwell.

Kirkpatrick, D.L. 1975. Techniques for evaluating training programs. In D.L. Kirkpatrick (ed.), *Evaluating training programs.* Alexandria, VA: ASTD.

Makridakis, S. 1989. *Forecasting methods for management* (5th ed.). New York, NY: Wiley.

Martocchio, J.J., and D.A. Harrison. 1993. To be there or not to be there? Questions, theories, and methods in absenteeism research. In G.R. Ferris (ed.), *Research in personnel and human resources management* (Vol. II). Greenwich, CT: JAI Press.

Pedhazur, E.J., and L.P. Sehmelkin. 1991. *Measurement, design and analysis: An integrated approach.* Hillsdale, NJ: Erlbaum.

Phillips, J.J. 1991. *Handbook of Training Evaluation and Measurement Methods* (2d ed.). Houston, TX: Gulf Publishing.

# Interactive Skills Training for Supervisors

## Penske Truck Leasing Company

By Paul R. Bernthal and William C. Byham

*Interactive skills training for supervisors is a very common type of HRD program; almost every organization conducts some sort of program to build supervisory skills. The following case shows an evaluation of a supervisory skills training program developed by an organization with a reputation for delivering effective training programs. The results have been outstanding, and the program has been sustained for several years.*

## Background

In the early to mid 1980s, the truck renting and leasing industry was growing into an increasingly competitive market that today produces over $30 billion in annual revenues. These changes included the merging of Penske Truck Leasing with the Hertz truck division in 1982 to form Hertz-Penske. In 1988, Gelco Truck Leasing (owned by General Electric) merged with Hertz-Penske to form Penske Truck Leasing. This last merger, which involved a buyout of Hertz, produced one of the largest and most successful truck leasing organizations in the world. Today, Penske Truck Leasing has annual revenues of about $800 million, with more than 6,000 customers nationwide. The fleet of more than 50,000 vehicles ranges in size from heavy-duty tractor trailers to parcel vans, and is managed and maintained by almost 5,000 employees at more than 350 locations in the United States.

As can be imagined, the growth spurts of the 1980s, coupled with significant organizational restructuring, necessitated an expanded pool of leaders and administrators. At this stage, however, Penske's training department was in its infancy and not entirely ready to cope with organization-wide supervisory improvement. Faced with these significant challenges, two human resource development (HRD) professionals came forward to help Penske implement a new training program that would change the way supervisors operated.

Robert Carter, the senior vice-president of personnel, had been working at Penske for approximately 10 years. Not only was he asked to assist with the development of a new training program, he was also responsible for a broad range of human resource areas, such as recruitment, employment, salary, labor relations with unions, benefits, and employee development. His experience and vision provided information concerning where the organization had been and where it was going. Fortunately, he was able to delegate much of the responsibility for developing the training program to Randolph Mase, manager of training and development. Mase, who had worked at Penske for about 10 years, was responsible for spearheading the implementation of the training program and its subsequent evaluation. Having worked as a manufacturing manager and as a training manager, he had experience dealing with the important links between management and training.

Unlike some organizations with a history of training, Penske did not have definite preconceptions about what training should involve or how it should be conducted. This situation was especially helpful for Mase and Carter, because they were provided with a receptive and supportive environment in which to try out new ideas. Together they worked out a rationale for why they wanted to take on the challenge of implementing a training program. They noted that the turnover rate at Penske was higher than they wanted, hovering at about 20 percent annually. Actually, this rate was typical of the industry and often considered an expected or even acceptable level of turnover. When turnover rates were questioned, a common response was "Our competitors have high turnover, too. It must be the nature of our industry, so why don't we just accept it?" Mase and Carter were committed to continuous improvement and believed they did not have to settle for the status quo. They thought they could use training as a means for reducing the high turnover rate.

Reducing turnover was not the only motivation for implementing and evaluating a training program. The HRD department also felt that they should strive toward overall organizational improvement by working to make supervisors more effective. Rather than simply stating organizational mandates for performance and then expecting compliance, Penske implemented training to establish a set of core skills and behaviors necessary for supervisory success.

## Defining Training Needs

All good training programs begin with a careful analysis of job requirements and desired end states. The first step in this process involved establishing an inventory of skills necessary for a supervisor to be successful at Penske. Unlike a job description describing areas of competence, this inventory was designed to include a breakdown of which concrete behaviors were necessary for effective performance. To get the ball rolling, a list of 20 to 25 skills was generated and presented to the supervisors, who were asked to review the list and note any additional skills they thought important. Next, the supervisors used two 5-point scales to evaluate the skill list. They rated each skill in terms of its importance for being an effective manager and rated how effective the managers they knew, including themselves, were at addressing each skill. Combining this information and computing importance scores for each of the skills created a practical guide that helped direct training toward meeting needs. Not only did this process avoid the tendency for some trainers to "shoot in the dark" at supposed training needs, it also avoided alienating the trainees themselves. By involving the trainees in the process, the trainers gained valuable buy-in and a sense of trainee ownership that would pay off in enthusiasm and commitment toward making the training work.

After evaluating current levels of skill importance and proficiency, the trainers generated a list of behaviors that should be addressed by training. The trainers used two criteria for evaluating which behaviors should be targeted. First, they did not want to train behaviors that were not important for the job, even if supervisors had low proficiency in those behaviors. Second, they did not want to train behaviors that were deemed important, unless supervisors showed a low level of proficiency in them. These two criteria helped the trainers avoid the common problems of unnecessary training and overtraining. In the end, the list of trainable behaviors was narrowed to include what could be most accurately described as interpersonal skills. For example, supervisors noted that there was room for improvement in the important areas of discipline, giving performance appraisals, providing feedback, and recognizing employees who displayed effective performance. The trainers used this list of interpersonal behaviors to guide their search for an appropriate training product. Their search ended when they selected the five core modules of Interaction Management (IM), an empowerment-based training system produced by Development Dimensions International Inc. (DDI).

IM uses skill-building modules that prepare leaders to manage, empower, and influence other people. The five core IM modules selected for use at Penske were Improving Employee Performance, Improving Work Habits, Maintaining Improved Performance, Utilizing Effective Follow-up Action, and Utilizing Effective Disciplinary/Corrective Action. These training sessions involved video instruction, lectures, individual skill-building exercises, and group activities. IM training sessions are designed to last approximately four hours and typically involve four to 12 participants.

## Setting up the Study

Unlike many organizations, Penske planned from the start to evaluate their training program. With the results of their study, they would be able to evaluate the utility of the training and decide if they should continue with their existing plan. When setting up the training evaluation, Mase and Carter wisely settled on a pretest/posttest control-group design. By using this design, they would be able to draw between-group comparisons to see if trainees were different from a comparable control group. In addition, they would be able to conduct a within-group comparison to look for changes in the training group from pretest to posttest.

### Participants

All program participants were what might be called maintenance supervisors. Each supervised approximately seven to eight mechanics and fuel island attendants who worked in his district. As part of their qualifications for the position, approximately 80 percent had worked as a mechanic at one time. The participants were all male, and most were white. They ranged in age from the mid 20s to early 60s. The trainers used geographic proximity to company headquarters in Reading, Pennsylvania, as a means for selecting participants. This process yielded 13 training sites and 11 control sites. Although there were two or three supervisors taken from each site, the unit of analysis was the location rather than the individual. Therefore, the total sample was 24.

### Measures

Turnover in the experimental and control groups was the primary measure of interest in this study. Turnover was defined as the percentage of people leaving the company per month, not including retirements, deaths, layoffs, or other "uncontrollable" reasons for ending active employment. In addition, although the training was not specifically targeted to affect other variables, absenteeism and overtime were monitored over time, as well. Finally, a simple "smile sheet," or reaction questionnaire, was used to assess the immediate effects of each training session.

Measures of turnover, absenteeism, and overtime were monitored both before and after the training. As shown in Figure 1, pretest, or baseline, measures were tracked from April to December (nine months), and posttest measures were taken from March to September (seven months) of the following year. A single pretest and posttest value for each of the dependent measures was computed by taking the mean monthly value for the period of measurement.

### Figure 1. Measurement design.

| Pretest | | | | | | | | | Training | | Posttest | | | | | | |
|------|------|------|------|------|------|------|------|------|------|------|------|------|------|------|------|------|------|
| Apr | May | Jun | Jul | Aug | Sep | Oct | Nov | Dec | Jan | Feb | Mar | Apr | May | Jun | Jul | Aug | Sep |

### Training Procedure

All training sessions were conducted by the same DDI-certified trainer. Approximately eight to 12 supervisors participated in each training session. Training in the five modules was completed within a two-month period (January and February). All five training modules were delivered during a three-day workshop for each group of trainees.

## Results

For each of the three primary dependent variables—turnover, absenteeism, and overtime—several comparisons were conducted. Ideally, statistical comparisons using inferential methods such as $t$ tests require a minimum sample size of 30. Given that this study based its analyses on 24 test sites, some liberties were taken with these conventions. The researchers felt that, because the measures from each test site were based on the means of two or more participants, the data were more stable than if they were based on individual measurements. Nevertheless, some statistical power for drawing inferences was lost using a sample of this size. In any case, perhaps more attention should be given to the effect size of the observed changes than to strict conventions of statistical significance.

Because the pretest and posttest measures were based on measures of the same set of individuals, change from pretest to posttest was assessed from a correlated-samples (or paired) $t$ test. Comparisons were also made between pretest measures (control vs. experimental) and between posttest measures. Because the two groups comprised different individuals, these comparisons were made by using an independent-samples $t$ test.

## Turnover

Comparisons at pretest did not show a significant difference between the two groups in terms of turnover rates. Therefore, the two groups' turnover rates were considered equivalent at pretest. In the training group, turnover measures at the posttest showed a 46 percent drop from pretest levels ($p < .10$). A similar change did not appear in the control group. Based on these findings, turnover appears to have been affected strongly by the training intervention (see Figure 2).

**Figure 2. Change in turnover rates from pretest to posttest, for the training and control groups.**

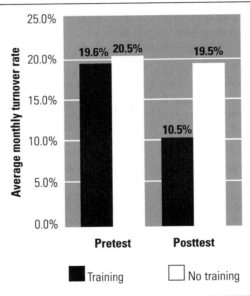

## Absenteeism

Unfortunately, absenteeism data were not available for the control group at the posttest. Therefore, these analyses summarize only the changes in absenteeism for the training group between the pretest and posttest measures. Comparison of the means, although not statistically significant, showed a 16.7 percent reduction in the rate of absenteeism (see Figure 3).

## Figure 3. Change in the training group's absenteeism rates from pretest to posttest.

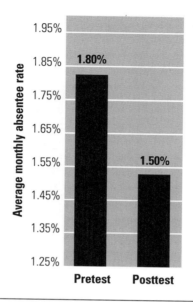

## Overtime

Overtime (see Figure 4) for the training group showed a noticeable, but nonsignificant, drop from pretest ($M = 7.3$ percent) to posttest ($M = 6.8$ percent), a 6.8 percent reduction. A similar but much smaller drop appeared in the control group (2.5 percent reduction).

## Reactions to Training

Overall, reactions to the training sessions were positive. The simple evaluation questionnaire distributed after each training session assessed issues such as satisfaction with training, applicability of skills, and perceived value of training. Almost all means for these measures were near the upper ends of the 5-point scale.

## Discussion

Based on the combined changes in turnover, absenteeism, and overtime, the trainers concluded that the intervention did produce a meaningful reduction in negative outcomes at the organizational level. Limitations in the sample size made it difficult to conduct sound statistical comparisons, but the intended effect of training was achieved. The turnover rate for the training group was almost halved. Depending on

**Figure 4. Change in overtime rates from pretest to posttest, for the training and control groups.**

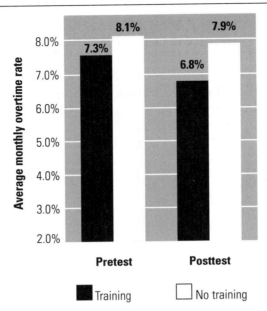

whom in the organization was asked, this change was estimated to pro-duce a savings ranging anywhere from $200 to $20,000. Although a utili-ty analysis was not conducted in this study, one can make inferences about the possible effects on hiring and training costs. For example, because approximately 26 individuals participated in the training group (13 sites), a 19.6 percent turnover rate at pretest represents about five employees lost per month. After training, turnover was reduced to about three (2.7) employees lost per month (10.5 percent). Therefore, training helped Penske avoid the process of hiring and training two new employ-ees per month. As in any profession, new hires often require a lengthy period of orientation before productivity moves to expected levels.

Although changes in absenteeism and overtime were tracked in this study, one should not place too much emphasis on those results. Neither variable showed a large change in value, and analyses of absen-teeism suffered from incomplete data. Similarly, measures of overtime were somewhat contaminated because a companywide push to reduce overtime may have affected both groups. Even so, it is the combined changes of all the organizational-level variables that leads us to draw conclusions about the effects of the training intervention.

Participants' responses to the training indicated both curiosity and positive feelings. The trainer was careful to emphasize that training was being provided to help participants do an even better job than they were already doing. Reactions such as these were common: "Boy, it's about time we did this," "I wish I had had this when I was promoted," and "This is really helpful and I'm able to use it." The introduction of interpersonal skills training where there had previously been none took a bit of adjustment for the organization in general. As the effects of the intervention unfolded over time, many Penske associates expressed shock or disbelief. Anecdotal evidence showed that supervisors had become more effective when dealing with subordinates and were actively applying IM's key principles for interaction. Follow-up telephone interviews conducted six months after training revealed that supervisors were continuing to find uses for their new skills.

## Epilogue

After this initial evaluation, Penske made substantial progress in its fledgling training program. The primary recommendation resulting from the evaluation was that training be extended to all supervisors and managers. Penske planned to have all supervisors and managers in the organization—approximately 700 people—trained by the end of 1993. To help facilitate this process, all regional personnel managers at Penske became IM-certified instructors. The interpersonal skills taught by IM have received organization-wide support and continue to be effective tools for managing employees. A further goal of the training program is to make sure that all new supervisors and managers be trained within three months of assuming their positions.

Although the five core modules first evaluated in this study continue to be effective, several follow-up modules are being introduced to develop and enhance supervisors' skills further. Currently, regional managers are being asked if they will make sure that everyone in each of the regions has been trained in one of the follow-up modules every year. This effort represents an ongoing commitment to continuous improvement.

Many companies have implemented training for years without any hard evidence of organizational results. Too often, posttraining reaction questionnaires are used to justify questionable training programs. By evaluating training as it was first introduced, Penske laid the groundwork for a growing and flexible training program.

## Questions for Discussion

1. Critique the approach used to determine the training needs for the target group.
2. How would you assess the overall approach to the implementation of this program?
3. How can we deal with the issue of a small sample size as reported in this case?
4. Discuss the evaluation design and the data collection methods.
5. Should a monetary value be attached to the reduction in turnover? Explain.
6. Should the improvement in absenteeism be converted to a monetary value? Explain.
7. What recommendations for follow-up would be appropriate here?

## The Authors

Paul R. Bernthal, Ph.D., is a research consultant at Development Dimensions International. He completed his graduate education in social psychology at the University of North Carolina at Chapel Hill in 1992. Currently, he conducts research evaluations of various DDI training products and is developing a multirater tool intended to assess perceived levels of empowerment. His previous work has appeared in publications such as the *Journal of Experimental Social Psychology* and *Group and Organizational Behavior*. Bernthal can be contacted at the following address: Development Dimensions International, 1225 Washington Pike, Bridgeville, PA 15017.

William C. Byham, Ph.D., is president and co-founder of DDI, a leading human resource training and development company. An internationally known educator, consultant, and trainer, Byham is author of more than 100 articles, papers, and books. He is widely regarded as a thought leader in selection, training, and human resource development. He has received numerous awards for his innovative training technologies and his commitment to research on the effectiveness of DDI programs. Recent book titles include *Zapp! The Lightening of Empowerment, Empowered Teams, Zapp! in Education, Shogun Management,* and *Zapp! Empowerment in Health Care.*

# Evaluating an Organization Development Program

## National Paper Company

By Michael Albert

*Organization development programs are among the most difficult HRD programs to evaluate. The following case shows how one such endeavor was evaluated. This program involved all employees and used a variety of HRD activities to significantly improve the participants' performance.*

## Background

Richard Alston, director of organization development (OD) at a major paper products company, was going to present the results of an 18-month OD program to senior management. The quantitative and qualitative analyses he had prepared indicated the program's results were quite positive overall. However, he was concerned about justifying not using a return-on-investment (ROI) analysis for this type of program. Alston felt that some of the major program benefits could not be converted to quantitative results and using ROI for the quantitative data would clearly understate the overall value of the program.

Alston felt confident that most of the executive staff would understand his rationale, but he was concerned about the pressure he would face from Ron Jamisson, vice-president for finance. Jamisson had strongly expressed the view that all major corporate projects and programs—whether financial, human resource, marketing, operations, or new product development—use an ROI analysis during final program evaluation. The corporate stickler for this point, he frequently challenged Bob Robbins, vice-president for human resource (HR), about his "soft programs" and the lack of converting program costs to measurable benefits. Robbins, who was Alston's boss, had made a commitment to the executive team at the yearly planning retreat three months ago that the HR function would begin to focus on a more formal evaluation of HR programs. With about 20 minutes to go before the presentation, Alston began to think about the sequence of events that had occurred over the past year and a half.

Alston worked for the Paper Products Division of one of the major companies in the forestry products industry, which includes Boise Cascade, Kimberly Clark, International Paper, Mead, and Weyerhaeuser. He had been hired specifically to manage the OD function. The president of the division, Larry Beninger, realized that competitive pressures for lowering costs while increasing quality and service meant that traditional organization designs had to be replaced with ones more appropriate for the environment of the 1990s. Because the division had more than 10 geographically dispersed manufacturing plants, the president wanted to implement organizational improvements at one plant that could serve as a model for subsequent programs. A decision was made to implement an OD program in one of the division's smaller plants located in the northeastern United States, about 1,000 miles from divisional headquarters. The primary products manufactured at this plant were cardboard packaging used by major soft-drink and beer companies for beverage six-packs. The plant was an ideal choice for the division's initial OD effort, because it was characterized by a variety of operational and personnel problems, and because it was small enough to use as a pilot program. In this regard, one major outcome of the program would be to learn about improving the implementation of change in the other plants during the decade.

Beninger felt that the decision to implement an OD program at the plant reflected his desire to look at alternative ways of managing operations and employees throughout the division. He felt that there was a need to look at ways of getting employees more involved in and committed to the operations of the organization. Moreover, he wanted to look for a process that would have long-term benefits and could serve as a model for subsequent programs.

## Plant History and Culture

The plant was built in 1980 and was initially headed by an autocratic plant manager. From the beginning, the philosophy and style of the original plant manager conflicted with the changing values of a youthful northeastern workforce. The plant was unproductive, and a wildcat strike was evidence of a high level of employee dissatisfaction. Two years later, the company hired a new plant manager who was not as autocratic as the first, but who also was ineffective in dealing with people. He hired in his own image and developed a cadre of hard-nosed, production-oriented supervisors who continued to fuel, rather than manage, the conflict between the hourly employees and management.

Communications were a continuing problem. In part, a lack of supervisory-employee communication was the result of the plant manager's style—operating without keeping his supervisors informed. No exchange of information meant the employees went over their supervisors' heads to the plant manager, thereby diminishing the supervisors' role and effectiveness.

Furthermore, some of the hourly employees would "negotiate" their merit raises with the plant manager months before the formal review. As a result, the manager lacked credibility with most of the workforce: He was very friendly with some employees and not friendly with others. It seemed there were no rules or regulations that applied consistently to the group as a whole.

The plant manager, who accepted this disregard for the chain of command, caused further problems by periodically responding to employee grievances by chewing out the supervisors in front of their employees. The supervisors, in turn, expressed their hostility in even more destructive ways: Supervisors were involved in such bizarre incidents as shooting car windows in the parking lot with air rifles, dismantling a forklift in the plant, and flicking cigarettes on a worker's head. In addition, the supervisors were not honest with their employees and operated by a "look out for yourself" philosophy.

A high rate of turnover—partly the result of a failure to screen job applicants carefully—added to the unstable situation. Organizational frustration and low morale were expressed among the hourly employees in the form of vandalism and sabotage. Crews did not clean up at the end of their shift and failed to report problem areas to the next shift. Employees lacked discipline and had little pride in what they were doing; many only seemed determined to see how much they could get away with.

These personnel problems were further complicated by technical problems. One important press did not work properly, and production and quality goals were not being achieved. This failure to attain production goals caused considerable frustration in a young, energetic workforce who lacked the skill to respond effectively. In hindsight the decision to hire young people who lacked necessary skills instead of hiring skilled workers could be seen as instrumental in contributing to the intensity of problems experienced at the plant. Furthermore, the most qualified person did not always get the job because of union constraints. Adding to the technical and social problems was the lack of effective administrative systems. Records of plant safety and grievances provided further evidence of organization-wide problems: The plant had the worst safety record for its size in the corporation, and a large number of grievances of a relatively serious nature were filed at the plant.

## Program Description

An OD effort was sanctioned by the division's top management to combat the problems of obviously ineffective social and technical systems. The OD program was undertaken to obtain greater productivity by increasing efficiencies, increasing quality, reducing waste, improving the safety record, and creating an organizational climate characterized by open communication and friendly relations among all employees. Underlying the program was management's belief that plant employees wanted to participate in determining how things could be done differently to improve productivity and relationships among workers.

Robbins and Alston decided to hire external consultants to design and implement the OD program. Based on a recommendation, they selected a consulting firm that had successfully implemented an OD program for a major soft-drink company. Two consultants from the firm worked on designing and implementing the 18-month program for a total fee of $80,000 plus travel expenses. The following specific objectives were developed during the planning phase of the program:

- to give each individual an opportunity for involvement, accomplishment, and recognition
- to develop a positive work attitude
- to maximize utilization of human resources
- to improve cost effectiveness
- to increase productivity
- to improve organizational structure
- to demonstrate bottom-line results.

Phase I of the program was divided into seven major areas. A breakdown of each follows:

- *Group interviews of employees* were conducted to determine the plant climate. In all, approximately 50 percent of the hourly and nonexempt workforce was interviewed. In addition, plant management and key divisional executives were interviewed at length.
- *Employee attitude surveys* were administered to the entire plant workforce on three occasions during Phase I. The first survey was administered

prior to implementing the program and served as a second vehicle in determining the overall plant climate. Subsequent surveys were given every six months to measure attitude changes among the employees.

- *Program introduction workshops* were held to review the program concept with plant employees. Three workshops (by shift) were conducted for plant employees, and a fourth one was held for key divisional managers along with plant exempt employees.

- *Action study committees* were formed as a result of the group interviews and the attitude survey. Each of the committees was charged with the responsibility of discussing, making recommendations for, and implementing ways to improve the organization. Initially, there were four action study committees: Communications and Relations with Divisional Management, Constructive Supervisory/Employee Involvement, Cost Effectiveness and Waste, and Performance and Recognition. A fifth committee, Quality Concerns and Plant Recreation, was formed after the first four committees had completed their assignment. The following guidelines were established to ensure that each committee achieved as much as possible.
  — Each committee was composed of hourly, nonexempt, and exempt employees. In all, approximately 80 percent of the hourly workforce volunteered to serve on a committee.
  — Meetings alternated between 7:30 a.m. and 3:30 p.m. to accommodate all three shifts.
  — Meetings were held every other week and limited to one hour in length.
  — Within 10 weeks (five meetings), each committee was required to submit a final written report covering accomplishments and recommendations.

- *Work teams* were formed to replace the department concept. Work-team members participated in establishing goals and held monthly meetings conducted by the supervisor (i.e., the work-team leader). Meeting topics included a review of the work team's performance charts, corporate announcements, ways to improve the organization, and other employee concerns.

- *Project assignments* were made by plant management. During the group interviews, it became evident that various administrative and operational systems were either lacking completely or in need of revision. Three work teams received assignments, all of which have been completed. The project titles were
  — Warehouse and Shipping Work-Team Project
  — Maintenance Work-Team Project

— Administration Work-Team Project.
- *Training and developmental activities* for both exempt and hourly employees included:
  — Basic Manager/Supervisory Development Workshop (nine sessions)
  — How To Conduct a Meeting (four-hour workshop)
  — How To Instruct (on-the-job training)
  — Planning, Organizing, and Controlling for the Production Supervisor (three sessions)
  — Lift Truck Operator Certification Program (four-hour session attended by 26 hourly employees).

## Program Evaluation

In preparing the program evaluation, Alston had collected and analyzed data from interviews with key divisional executives and plant personnel, attitude surveys of plant personnel, and quantitative measures of plant operations. People interviewed at the Paper Products Division included the president, vice-president for HR, and director of operations; at the plant, the plant manager and two production supervisors were interviewed. Because collective bargaining was scheduled to begin in the very near future, it was decided not to gather data from the union employees at that time, but to interview a sample of plant employees after the contract was settled.

Alston planned to discuss the results to date of the OD program by summarizing the subjective impressions of people interviewed and by presenting objective data to reflect changes in various measures of operations.

## Results from Interviews and Attitude Survey

There was a strong feeling that the program dramatically improved communication throughout the plant. The program resulted in the employees' knowing each other better and helped close the gap between the supervisors and the hourly employees. The supervisors had become much more open, and their ability to communicate was greatly improved. As a result, there was a significant decrease in the number, as well as the severity, of grievances. In addition, the practice of going over the supervisor's head to the plant manager had ended. Hourly employees were able to confront their supervisors, and both parties felt free to discuss problem areas openly. One interviewee stated, "Before the program, it was impossible to review the employees; now, every six months, supervisors and employees have a one-on-one discussion on areas in which they are lacking, where they're effective, and where they need improvement." The supervisors also instituted monthly meetings with their employees to discuss general issues.

There was also the perception that the work-team concept had served to promote the feeling that "I'm part of a team and I'm proud of it." These feelings, in turn, facilitated the perception of common goals with management. As evidence of improved labor-management relations, first-, second-, and third-level grievances were being handled by plant labor relations personnel instead of being referred to divisional staff. The company picnic and Christmas party, for which the costs were shared 50-50 between company and union, were also a reflection of the improved organizational climate. One interviewee stated, "We could never have had this in the past because of the hostility."

Attitude survey data, collected prior to the start of the program and every six months during the 18-month program, indicated clear improvements in such areas as communications, employee involvement, management style, and overall job satisfaction.

An unforeseen but constructive side effect of the program was that the hourly employees elected more open, listening leaders as union officers. Attendance at the union meetings went up, and people felt relations between the union and management had improved.

Plant management felt the improved communications enabled management to recognize key people without creating dissension. They felt they had much better rapport with the division since the inception of the program, stating that the plant personnel could now have input into the schedule and that the division had come to view the plant as a well-run operation rather than an eyesore.

Everyone interviewed acknowledged the role of Jim Parker, who had assumed the position of plant manager one year prior to the OD program, in acting to create an environment that helped initiate and sustain the organizational change process. Upon his arrival, Parker immediately began to establish a more positive environment. One month after he began working, he announced that employees could sign up to be considered for a vacant supervisory position, and, ultimately, an hourly employee was hired for the position. This internal move helped to create the perception among the hourly employees that there were opportunities for them to be promoted.

In an effort to establish management credibility, Parker did away with the prior plant manager's practice of giving hourly employees their merit raises before the requisite time period transpired, and he confronted the issue of undesirable employee behaviors head-on. His firm insistence on uniformly applied and constructive discipline led eventually to the termination of a number of employees, including several union stewards, for such violations as absenteeism, lateness, and insubordination. In one instance, a pressman who threatened a supervisor was fired and subsequently filed a grievance. The company, to demonstrate its support for supervision, pursued the case to arbitration. The employee was reinstated, but lost four months' pay. The employees learned the organization would insist on appropriate behavior, and the supervisors felt real support. This incident was seen by many people in the organization as a turning point in organization-employee relations.

Plant personnel also saw support from the division as very helpful. During implementation of the program, top management accepted some flexibility in meeting deadlines in order to support the high priority of the program. Plant personnel felt this flexibility was very important, especially at the early stages of the OD program when the employees were learning new skills. The plant personnel interviewed definitely felt the program was supported by the division's top management.

One additional benefit of the OD program was that it eased the acceptance of increased production standards. It was known that production standards were being reevaluated and that the new standards were implemented midway through the OD program. Perhaps because of the improved communications resulting from the program, the employees accepted the standards and were able to generate ideas as to how the new standards might be attained.

Despite the positive evaluation of some program results, the evaluation of the consultants was negative overall. Even though there was strong sentiment not to hire the consultants in the future, there was also the feeling that the consultants got the division and plant started on an important process. Following is a sample of typical comments about the consultants:

- "Originally they promised, 'We'll measure you, then you'll set goals relative to where you want to be,' but this was never implemented."
- "The consultants didn't tell the employees when they were not dealing with relevant issues."
- "The process was good, but they didn't follow up, and they lacked continuity."
- "Their attendance at meetings was erratic after the initial meetings."
- "They did provide a framework for change and direction to start the change process."
- "They didn't use the attitude survey data to back up their recommendations."

The evaluation of Phase I of the program also led to the design and implementation of a revised Phase II program, the details of which are currently being formulated. The broad elements of the plant's Phase II program will focus on

- overall productivity
- greater employee involvement
- employee recognition
- improved teamwork.

The president felt that although employees had become more involved and loyal, the program had not yet achieved all its goals. Efficiencies had increased and waste had decreased over the 18-month period, but he felt more improvement was needed and that the plant needed to assess what steps were still necessary to reach goals in these areas.

Alston felt that combining a continuous improvement mentality with this program would contribute to significant improvements in the design, implementation, and results of similar programs in other plants throughout the decade.

## Quantitative Results

Changes in key performance indices for the plant's operations are summarized in Table 1. As indicated in the table, at the end of Phase I, improvements were obtained in each performance index. Whereas yearly production variances were $17,800 above standard costs prior to the OD program, annual production costs were $88,300 below standard costs at the end of Phase I. Overall, this improvement resulted in a net annual savings of $106,100. Production efficiencies increased in all three production areas, and material waste decreased in both indices.

**Table 1. Changes in key performance indices for plant operation.**

| Index | Prior to Phase I | End of Phase I |
|---|---|---|
| Variance from standard ($) | 17,800 above standard | 88,300 below standard |
| Efficiency (%) | | |
| Flexo-Printer/Cutter | 88.0 | 92.0 |
| Press I | 87.0 | 91.0 |
| Press II | 90.5 | 93.0 |
| Waste (%) | | |
| Printer/Cutter: cluster-pak | 6.0 | 3.5 |
| Printer/Cutter: glued cartons | 7.0 | 5.0 |
| Absenteeism (days/month) | 5.1 | 3.3 |
| Safety (violations from checklist) | 8.5 | 6.0 |
| Housekeeping (violations from checklist) | 7.0 | 5.0 |

Improvements also occurred in absenteeism, safety violations, and housekeeping. Absenteeism decreased from an average of 5.1 to 3.3 days per month, a 35 percent improvement. There were an average of 2.5 fewer safety violations per month, a 29 percent improvement; and housekeeping violations decreased from an average of 7.0 per month to 5.0 per month, a 29 percent improvement.

Alston looked at his watch, realizing he would make his presentation in a few minutes, and he began to feel comfortable about his evaluation approach. Although he was sure to get some tough questions from Jamisson, Alston looked at this as an opportunity to educate senior management about the limitations of evaluating programs such as this one in the same way as financial or product development programs.

## Questions for Discussion

1. On what basis do you agree or disagree with Alston's view that using an ROI analysis was not appropriate for this type of program?
2. What factors or issues do you think Alston might have been referring to?
3. In what ways could the focus of some human resource development (HRD) programs place limits on the evaluation model used?
4. Based on the information provided in the case, use an HRD evaluation model to assess the costs and benefits of the OD program.
5. What steps could be taken to determine if all of the quantitative results were actually caused by the OD program?

## The Author

Michael Albert is a professor of management at San Francisco State University, teaching courses in advanced management, organizational behavior, and organization development. He is the author of *Effective Management: Readings, Cases and Experiences* and a coauthor of *Management: Individual and Organizational Effectiveness*. Both books were published into third editions (1988) by Harper & Row. He also has written numerous articles in the area of human resource development and corporate culture and has provided consulting services to numerous organizations in these areas. Albert can be contacted at the following address: San Francisco State University, 15 Sotelo Avenue, San Francisco, CA 94116.

# Total Quality Management Training for White-Collar Workers

## Causeway Corporation

By Robert O. Brinkerhoff, Lorrie Formella, and Karolyn Smalley

*Although total quality management programs may work well in manufacturing settings, their results may be questionable in white-collar situations. The following case describes training that supports a TQM program for employees in a financial services division. This case shows how results can be obtained by designing evaluation into the training process. Only preliminary assessments are available now, but the process and procedures are in place to calculate the program's future return.*

## Overview

This case study describes the evaluation of total quality management (TQM) training provided to financial services professionals in the Financial Services Division (FSD) of the Causeway Corporation, a worldwide direct-sales company. The evaluation approach used in this case was to embed ongoing measurement into the training design so that trainers could demonstrate continuous improvement methods, the training managers could make midstream revisions, and impact data could eventually be reported.

Causeway Corporation is one of the largest companies in the direct-sales industry, with 10,000 employees and several million distributors around the world. The evaluation in this case took place at Causeway's world headquarters offices, a complex housing 5,000 employees in 11 divisions. The company's strategic plan calls for increasing growth, while maintaining labor and other costs as close as possible to present levels. Like its competitors, Causeway must continuously seek ways to gain operating efficiencies so that prices can remain competitive and profits can continue to grow. In this context, efforts such as TQM are critical strategic initiatives, because the pressure to operate ever more efficiently is unrelenting.

## Background

The Financial Services Division comprises accountants, financial analysts, computer analysts, clerks, secretaries, supervisors, managers, a controller, and a vice-president, who is also the company's chief financial officer. The mission of FSD is to provide accurate and meaningful financial analyses and reports that help Causeway owners and management make effective decisions. Given the size and complexity of Causeway, and the continuing cost and pricing fluctuations in the direct-sales industry, the financial function must not only work quickly and accurately, but must also serve a diverse group of customers whose needs change rapidly and frequently.

As in many businesses, Causeway executives and managers were concerned with quality and effectiveness. They decided to implement a variety of improvement efforts that could be defined as TQM initiatives. In FSD the general goals of quality improvement would be to increase the timeliness and accuracy of reports and to improve continuously the consistency of formats and the user-friendliness of report structures and systems. An accurate and timely report is of little business value if the recipient must ask questions to understand it or, worse, is confused and misunderstands the report.

FSD was one of several divisions at Causeway that had participated in a pilot TQM training program provided by an external vendor. The pilot TQM program had provided training only to managers, from a variety of Causeway divisions. Three FSD managers attended the pilot, after which they decided it would be a good idea to provide similar training in TQM concepts and methods to all employees in FSD. At this point, the FSD director and the director of human resource development (HRD) met to discuss options for such training. It was clear to them that successful implementation of quality improvement efforts would hinge on involving all employees.

### About the Training Request

When the FSD director and two top managers from her division contacted the director of HRD to inquire about extending TQM training to all FSD employees, they expressed some concerns about whether the HRD division could meet their needs. They were worried about the relative youth of some of HRD's new trainers, and they noted that HRD had no prior experience in providing any customized training services to FSD. Also, the FSD management group had some very specific notions about the content of the training they wanted and had even thought about particular learning activities they thought would be useful. Finally, the FSD group liked the vendor-supplied program.

These issues (and a fundamental difference in training philosophy between the FSD group and the HRD division) were sources of potential conflict that the HRD director realized had to be managed. She has extensive formal education in industrial/organizational psychology, with a particular focus on behaviorally based concepts of performance systems analysis and performance improvement strategies. Her approach to training would lead to a performance-based design. In contrast, the vendor-supplied program that the FSD group liked had a more traditional instructional design not rooted in performance systems analysis.

The difference in approaches was not a direct bone of contention. But, like many line managers, the FSD group was familiar with the typical training model: large group sessions, with virtually no follow-up, and rarely a direct connection to job behavior and business results. Although such managers will say that they want "results," they usually have low expectations and often are not aware of, nor ready to support, the sort of careful design and lengthy training process that is necessary to have a truly significant and sustained effect on performance. It was clear that some "selling" would be required in order to get FSD to agree to have the HRD division design and implement TQM training for all FSD employees.

### Coming to Agreement

The use of evaluation methods played a key role in the HRD and FSD leaders agreeing to an approach. HRD wanted to provide a training program that would lead to real, demonstrable changes in employees' behavior and FSD performance. This goal suggested the need for an intensive training program with considerable follow-up and support from FSD supervision. Of course, such a comprehensive intervention is more complex and lengthy and, therefore, more expensive than the more common training-only approach of a brief, high-energy, and action-packed workshop.

The FSD group was rightly concerned with having a positive experience for employees, and was wary of the risks involved in launching a lengthier, more complex intervention. FSD was also concerned about keeping the costs and disruption of training to a minimum. Thus, FSD was looking for a brief, less obtrusive intervention that would make the employees feel good about TQM and certainly not scare them off.

The HRD director suggested a segmented rollout of training that would incorporate a series of brief learning interventions with specific and targeted application assignments between learning sessions. The training interventions would be combined with ongoing meetings and briefings with the FSD management group so that they could keep close tabs on progress and continuously influence training content and application efforts. The HRD director promised to provide a steady stream of evaluation results so that everyone would be kept informed in a timely manner. This design and management process, with considerable ongoing evaluation built in, accomplished two key objectives. First, it demonstrated that the HRD group had thought through the training design carefully and understood the TQM process thoroughly. Second, it was clear, though never explicitly stated, that the FSD group could "blow the whistle" on the training if at any point they became uncomfortable with the direction it was taking.

The value of evaluative feedback was increased by a delivery schedule that would begin training delivery to one major group of employees before a second major group of employees would commence their training. In this way, the reactions and experiences of trainees who had progressed further in the process could be captured and used, if indicated, to revise training designs before the subsequent group of trainees reached that point in their training process.

## The Training Design

The training design included a half-day orientation session to overview TQM and the training design and four 2½-hour sessions spread out over 60 days. Each training session held 20 participants. To achieve these numbers, the two major groups of employees in the finance division, Groups 1 and 2, were subdivided into four subgroups and six subgroups, respectively. Subgroups in Group 1 all started their training in November and attended sessions every two weeks until they had completed the sequence. The subgroups in Group 2 started in February and proceeded through the same biweekly schedule.

Each session concluded with a specific assignment to be completed prior to the next training session. For example, after Session 1, participants were to complete a vision statement and identify several potential "critical business issues" that, in their estimation, could become the focuses of improvement efforts. Session 2 had participants design and conduct a customer survey. Session 3 included a business process simulation to enable participants to pinpoint failure points; they then further refined their understanding of customer issues through interviews with customers and analyses of results. In the fourth and final session, trainees used what they had learned to finalize changes they wanted to make in one or more key business processes.

The training sessions were followed by a 150-day period of three application phases. Phase 1 saw teams (or individuals) complete their analyses of process improvement needs, Phase 2 had them design specific process improvement plans with measurable objectives, and Phase 3 had them implement these plans and track results. In the final 30 days of the training cycle, teams were to write up and present their results.

## Key Roles and Responsibilities

The following individuals and teams were part of the training design:

- *The FSD vice-president* sponsored the training, attended some sessions, and, through visible participation, supported the entire effort.
- *HRD division staff* included the HRD director, who sold and coached the design, and a training department professional staff member, who designed and implemented the training.
- *Participants* were all other FSD management and employees.
- *The steering committee* consisted of the controller, senior managers, two midlevel managers, and the HRD training advisor, who reviewed evaluation results and approved all training plans and midstream revisions.
- *TQM coaches* came from a cross section of identified employees who received training in how to coach other trainees. Coaches were selected after the first training session and represented all levels in the FSD organization, including clerks, secretaries, and managers. (Several coaches worked with "clients" senior to themselves.) Coaches helped trainees assess and refine their efforts.

A number of checkpoints and specific reports were included in the training process. For every work step, trainees received a worksheet that usually required review and approval. The Individual Improvement Plan, for example, was completed by each individual proposing a specific process improvement. Often, the trainee's coach assisted in writing the plan. This form was reviewed in the training session and then provided both in hard copy and via computer to all trainees. A trainee and his or her coach would then use a checklist to assess the plan and make further refinements. Finally, the steering committee reviewed and approved (by signature) the plan. Similar procedures were employed at other key steps.

## The Evaluation Design

To a great extent, it is not possible to isolate and describe the evaluation design as separate from the training plan. For example, evaluation was built into the process by which trainees learned about and completed the Individual Improvement Plan form. The criteria for completing the worksheet and assuring it defined an adequate improvement plan were distributed during training as a self-implementing checklist. The trainees learned about the checklist by reviewing examples and applying the checklist to hypothetical improvement plans. Then, after the training session, they completed (as "homework") the improvement plan worksheet for their own, real projects, using the checklist to assess and revise their draft plans. Next, the steering committee (who had also received training in the plan worksheet and use of the checklist) reviewed the plans that trainees submitted, using the checklist to provide feedback and, eventually, to approve the plans.

As this example shows, trainees were learning how to evaluate their own progress and give themselves feedback to improve their work. The evaluation tools were part of the training content and helped trainees see what was important. When it came time for the HRD staff to report on the progress of the overall project, they were able to do so readily by simply checking to see when, if, and how many trainees had completed the work steps. Evaluation of the quality of the trainees' progress could be conducted by assessing the plans themselves and by simply talking with the trainees and the steering committee members to see how they felt about their progress.

Because this monitoring helped maintain focus and gave feedback, it was, in itself, a learning intervention. In this respect, the HRD staff accomplished their goal of embedding evaluation into the training, so that evaluation, learning, and training became one integrated process. Further, this integration is precisely what TQM is all about, so the HRD staff was modeling and implementing TQM at the same time they were teaching about it. And finally, because quality improvement is a part of the job of FSD employees (as it is with other jobs at Causeway), trainees were not really "getting training"—they were doing their jobs while they were learning how to do their jobs better. As it turned out (and as the evaluation data summarized in the next section show), they did, in fact, do their jobs better, because the training led directly to measurable process improvements that appear to be returning value greater than the costs of the training.

Evaluation instruments and tools included the following:
• *End-of-session feedback forms* completed by trainees assessed their learn-

ing, collected their suggestions, and asked them to report any problems they experienced in completing their preassigned tasks.

- *The Individual Improvement Plan Checklist* enabled trainees, coaches, and the steering committee to assess and revise improvement plans.
- *The Improvement Plan Update* was a continuous record that reported the date of each coaching session, summarized project status, and defined further support needed to complete the plan.
- *The Individual Improvement Plan Report (IIPR)* summarized the effect of each individual process improvement effort in each of several categories. The trainee reported data on dimensions such as timeliness, accuracy, and customer satisfaction both before (baseline) and after the improvement intervention. The form also required an estimate of the economic effects (e.g., savings). In addition, this form summarized reactions about what worked well in the plan and what did not.

## Evaluation of Impact and Return on Investment

Evaluation of impact and the return on investment (ROI) of this training project was a relatively simple and straightforward matter once the training design was completed and implemented. The more complex, difficult, and time-consuming work had come earlier—in designing the training, getting the buy-in and support needed to earn approval for the plan, and then implementing and making ongoing improvements to the training as it was conducted.

### Impact Evaluation

Impact of the training was defined as the results achieved by each team that implemented a process improvement plan. A team might, for example, have studied and then revised the process by which they completed and returned financial analyses to their internal customers. If they revised their work such that financial reports were delivered more quickly and with fewer errors or questions from recipients, then these results were reported by the team as the impact of the training. Each process improvement project was tracked carefully (this was a part of the process that trainees learned), and progress was reported. Furthermore, the system of progress reports helped ensure a positive result; if progress were thwarted or disrupted, the report process provided substantial early warning, and the project was steered and resteered until results were achieved.

The results of each project were summarized in an overall report, and these summary results were provided to upper management as evidence of the impact of the TQM training project. Although results were of varying importance and magnitude, most individuals were successful in achieving at least some improvements. In this respect, the HRD group felt comfortable in concluding that the project resulted in high impact.

Customer impact was given special consideration, given the critical importance of the customer in total quality thinking. All impact report formats gathered and highlighted reactions from customers of the financial services group. By singling out customer reactions for special attention, the training designers were reminding the trainees of the paramount importance of the customer. In many cases, data about customer reaction consisted of verbatim and aggregated comments from customers. In some cases, it was expected that customer benefits (such as receiving a more accurate and timely report) could be readily translated into dollar values, but this analysis had not been completed at the time this case study was written.

The IIPR asked improvement teams to define, describe, and estimate the benefits, including cost savings, of specific improvements they achieved. If a team, for example, improved accuracy and timeliness of reporting, they might provide data about the number of hours that such improvements saved for different employees or customers. As noted, the IIPR also asked for nonsavings benefits, such as improvements in customer reactions and satisfaction. Team members were encouraged to report such estimates, but were also directed not to "stretch" these, so as to avoid overestimating results. Figure 1 shows an excerpt from the IIPR to illustrate how savings of impovement solutions were reported.

Table 1 includes a small sampling from the dozens of impact statements included on IIPR forms submitted thus far. These are excerpted verbatim to provide a picture of the nature of results achieved, and also

**Figure 1. Excerpt from the Individual Improvement Plan Report form showing the format for reporting savings.**

| Category | Before implementation (What was it like before the plan?) | After implementation (What is it like now?) | Savings (hours, etc. saved) |
|---|---|---|---|
| Timeliness and accuracy | | | |
| Material savings | | | |

to show that when trainees are shown how to focus and refine their improvement projects, ROI calculations can be readily made from the trainees' own evaluation efforts.

## Table 1. Excerpts from the impact statements of trainees.

- "reduced processing time"
- "reduced processing time three days per month"
- "reduced research time two hours per report"
- "issue reports earlier each month"
- "saved five hours per month per analyst"

- "reduced disk storage"
- "saved 700 pages per month"
- "reduced phone charges per report"
- "no copies required"
- "saved 6,600 pages of copying per year"

## Assessing ROI

The ROI assessment process is ongoing at the Causeway Corporation because the project was still under way at the time of this writing. Nonetheless, it is possible to explain the ROI assessment procedure in detail and even to include some preliminary (and positive) results.

In general, the method for assessing ROI is a two-step process. First, the HRD team defined and calculated the costs of the training. Currently, they are reviewing the results achieved by each team. When a team reports results in dollar savings, these amounts will be verified, then recorded. When a team reports results in nondollar terms, the HRD staff will discuss the results with the team and FSD managers to agree on a cost-conversion procedure. The ROI calculation is a matter of comparing the dollar amounts of savings and other benefits achieved with the total costs of the training. This section explains this procedure in some detail and contains some preliminary data.

TQM PROGRAM COSTS. Training costs were analyzed and calculated carefully. In this case, costs of trainees' time in training (typically the largest, but often unaccounted for, cost factor) were included in the total costs for the TQM effort. Table 2 shows these cost factors and amounts.

As can be seen from the calculations in Table 2, sending trainees to training and then providing ongoing coaching through the application period cost Causeway about $280,000. This figure was considered relatively accurate, though it should be pointed out that trainees' time costs were underestimated. In many cost-calculation approaches, the salary paid to trainees is at least doubled, to include their lost productivity. In reality, if the company is profitable (i.e., people earn more for the company than the company pays them), even this doubled amount is too low an estimate.

## Table 2. TQM program costs.

| Cost factors and equations | Costs ($) |
|---|---|
| • Cost of each trainee's time, based on average hourly salary rate and 35 percent fringe benefits: $22.42 per hour x (20 hours of training + 28 plan preparation hours) | 1,076.16 |
| • Facilitator cost per trainee: (salary + fringe benefits + expenses + etc.) x hours in delivery and preparation ÷ number of trainees | |
| • Administrative costs of delivery and planning per trainee: clerical + set-up time + coordination + management + steering committee wages + etc. | + 11.64 |
| | + 19.29 |
| • Total training costs per trainee | 1,107.09 |
| • Total number of trainees | x 196 |
| • Total training costs | 216,989.64 |
| • Coaching costs: cost of facilitator of coaching training + direct costs of training + (number of hours coaching and planning coaching meetings x hourly salary of coaches) | + 57,228.60 |
| • Total TQM program costs | 274,218.24 |

At Causeway, however, the HRD leaders decided to calculate only the direct costs of training, thus limiting trainees' time costs to their salaries paid during training. From this total cost, the HRD division could establish comparison figures for other sorts of training, as well as proceed to estimate cost-return ratios. They could, for instance, compare their TQM program costs with the costs of other programs, such as the vendor's original program. These comparisons showed a considerable savings: The HRD-designed program cost nearly 12 times less than the vendor program. Savings are not worth anything, of course, unless a program also produces significant results that address real needs, and Causeway moved ahead to look at cost-return comparisons.

CALCULATING ROI. The TQM program leaders developed an impact-reporting format to summarize savings in each of the FSD departments. The data in this format are aggregated, after they are verified, from the IIPRs submitted by teams and individuals during and after coaching and implementation. For each department, total savings are calculated by comparing costs before and after the improvement plans.

Causeway was still in the process of implementing and monitoring this TQM effort at the time of this writing, so overall data are not available. It is possible to see, however, that some very positive results are forthcoming. To date, 55 of the first 60 people who attended training have completed process improvements and submitted reports. Dollar amounts of savings achieved are not yet available, but are expected to total about $50,000 for this first group. A second group of 136 trainees will be submitting reports in a few weeks, and these savings are expected to total just over $100,000. (Estimates are made from draft reports and interim data reported by coaches.) There are, of course, considerable variations in achievements. One employee, for example, was able to reduce her work process by half, while another reduced time by only 5 percent.

The FSD departments involved have been so pleased with their success that almost all individuals are planning a second round of improvement projects, many more ambitious than the first, now that they feel comfortable with the process. Additionally, some individuals are planning to work as teams to tackle more complex cross-functional improvements that will yield much greater savings. In summary, the training division expects that about one-half of the total $280,000 investment will be earned back after the first round of training and improvement projects is completed. At this rate, the entire amount should be regained within a year after training began.

## Conclusion

Because of the intensive follow-up support built into the design of Causeway's TQM training project, the rate of implementation is high. In turn, because more than 95 percent of people completing training are applying their learning and implementing successful cost-saving and quality-improvement projects, the pressure on individuals to produce large savings is reduced. The overall results are even greater than the ROI calculations indicate; the project is having strong effects on customer satisfaction, yet no effort has been made to include these results in the calculations.

The HRD department expects equally positive, if not greater, results when the training is provided to other departments because this first effort enabled them to refine their design. The formula and formats used to calculate ROI are simple and easily understood by all evaluation data recipients, and they have helped the HRD department strengthen its image as a results-oriented business partner.

## Questions for Discussion

1. How critical is the role of training in the TQM process? Please explain.
2. Critique the evaluation design. What is the advantage of incorporating evaluation in the training design?

3. Assess the effectiveness of the data collection methods, including the improvement planning process.

4. Do you agree with the assumptions made in calculating costs? How do these costs compare with those that would be calculated using other cost-tracking systems?

5. Would the eventual level of savings be expected to be higher or lower than reported in the initial results?

6. How could this process be improved?

7. Should the nonmonetary savings be reported? If so, in what format?

8. What are the strengths of this process?

## The Authors

Robert O. Brinkerhoff has been a training and development professional since 1965, when he began his career as a training officer in the U.S. Navy, and earned his doctorate in program evaluation from the University of Virginia in 1974. An internationally recognized expert, Brinkerhoff has provided consultation to dozens of companies and agencies in the United States, Europe, Russia, Singapore, Australia, and South Africa; recent clients include the U.S. Postal Service, The World Bank, Electronic Data Systems, IDS Inc., Apple Computers, Upjohn, SteelCase, and AT&T. Brinkerhoff can be contacted at the following address: Western Michigan University, Ed Leadership, Kalamazoo, MI 49008.

Lorrie Formella works as an internal human resource development consultant designing performance-based instruction, managing process improvement projects, and building performance management systems. She has consulted with other HRD professionals in analyzing, designing, implementing, and evaluating their training. She is a graduate of the University of Wisconsin and is in the final stages of completing her M.A. degree in industrial/organizational psychology at Western Michigan University.

Karolyn Smalley is manager of HRD for an organization having annual sales of more than $4 billion. The HRD department specializes in internal process consulting and performance-based training. Recent successes provided the opportunity to design an integrated HRD strategy that could be implemented worldwide. Smalley is a graduate of Michigan State University, the programmed learning workshop of the University of Michigan, and the M.A. program in industrial/organizational psychology at Western Michigan University.

# Built-in Evaluation

## U.S. Government

By Mary L. Broad, Lisa Szymanski, and Alex Douds

*A government setting offers a challenge for return-on-investment calculations. The following case describes a comprehensive and unique way to assess the ROI of a basic introduction-to-supervision course. Evaluation was built into the program by the design team, and the method for determining the course's payoff is innovative. This case should provide encouragement for professionals in the government sector as they approach evaluation projects. And the approach should be useful with other programs designed to build competencies.*

## Background

The federal government is one of the world's major employers, with close to 3.5 million civilian employees worldwide. They are organized in well over 100 departments, agencies, commissions, and other offices of all sizes, locations, and missions. The structures, cultures, and histories of these organizations vary widely.

The Government Employees Training Act (GETA, 1958) provides the legal basis for human resource development (HRD) for federal civilian employees in the executive branch, which comprises more than 98 percent of all federal civilian employees. GETA makes the management of each agency responsible for the necessary development of its workforce and sets some specific limitations on allowable types of training. Within these boundaries, the HRD approaches of the various agencies differ considerably. HRD investments government-wide are significant; in Fiscal Year 1991, both direct and indirect costs (including salaries of instructors and support personnel, travel, per diem, and tuition) amounted to $1.4 billion for more than 2 million instances (that is, individual employees participating in training events of all types), for an average cost of $643 per instance (Office of Personnel Management, 1993).

The Office of Personnel Management (OPM) has centralized authority for human resource management (i.e., hiring, promotion, development, and retirement) for civilian employees. Primarily, it has served in a leadership role, conducting research and providing policy formulation and guidance, technical assistance, information, and coordination among agencies. In addition, OPM has provided some direct reimbursable services to agencies. (Under the National Performance Review, directed by the vice-president in 1993, these responsibilities may change in some respects.)

OPM has one of the largest training delivery systems in the world, operated largely on a fee-for-service basis. It conducts training throughout the continental United States, with additional delivery points overseas, and it operates the National Independent Study Center, which specializes in development and delivery of correspondence courses and computer-based instruction. Agencies use OPM's training services, as well as other public- and private-sector sources, colleges, and universities, to develop employees' job-related skills. Because of this competition from other training sources, OPM has placed a high priority on improving the quality of its products and services.

Since there are approximately 35,000 new civilian supervisors appointed each year throughout the government (including team and group leaders and wage-grade supervisors), basic supervisory training has long been a staple of the OPM Human Resource Development Group (HRDG) training programs. An Introduction to Supervision course had been designed some years ago and delivered throughout OPM's regions. Over time, course content and delivery became inconsistent.

In 1991, several factors converged to lead to a systemwide revision of this course (informally referred to as "Intro"). First, for some years, OPM's regional and central office managers had been moving toward greater collaboration, sharing information and best practices. As this collaboration strengthened, they proposed a systemwide commitment to develop a national core curriculum to enhance consistency and upgrade the quality of major programs. Both regional and central office managers were concerned with Intro's lack of consistency across regions. For example, agencies with personnel in more than one region wanted a consistent course for all their employees in all locations.

Second, OPM had begun the design of an executive-management-supervisor (EMS) career path as a "second career" for employees in all positions across the government. Clearly, the shift from individual technical, administrative, or professional responsibilities to the supervisory role is a critical transition point for new supervisors. If they could receive high-quality skills training in effective supervisory methods, many of the common difficulties associated with less skilled supervision could be avoided.

Third, in 1978 OPM had begun a comprehensive research study that culminated several years later in a competency-based model of effective performance for federal managers (OPM, 1986). Called the Management Excellence Framework (MEF), the model focused on common tasks and actions that executives, managers, and supervisors must be able to do to be effective. These became the basis for an assessment and diagnostic tool, the Management Excellence Inventory (MEI), developed and first implemented by OPM in 1984. The MEI helps organizations identify managerial job requirements and skills, and helps individuals and organizations assess the individuals' management strengths and development needs (Flanders and Utterback, 1985). In 1991, OPM began a rigorous research process to update the MEF. Results of this research reinforce the importance of the basic supervisory competencies addressed in Intro. A systemwide revision of Intro would allow MEF- and MEI-based supervisory competencies to be incorporated into the course design.

Finally, OPM HRDG leadership had mandated use of the Instructional Systems Design (ISD) process as the standard for course design and redesign throughout OPM. ISD, which has its earliest roots in the military during World War II, is widely accepted in both the public and the private sectors as a highly effective process for developing instructional programs that produce desired behavioral changes among learners. To support ISD use, OPM sponsored a nationwide series of workshops in 1990 to train OPM central office and regional employees in ISD principles. The workshops were designed and presented by Sharon Fisher, an ISD expert with one of OPM's contractors, Human Technology Inc. (HT).

These four factors combined to make the redesign of Intro an opportunity for OPM to break new ground worldwide. The redesign would be the first step in the development of OPM's national curriculum. The revised Intro course, incorporating competencies based on the MEF research, would provide the gateway to the managerial second career for federal employees moving toward roles as supervisors, team and group leaders, and wage-grade supervisors. And, finally, in redesigning the course, regional and central office contributors could model collaboration and use of the ISD process to ensure instructional quality.

## The Design-Team Approach and ISD

To gain both consistency and the infusion of creative best practices, course development at the national level clearly would require full involvement, commitment, and support from each region. Under the leadership of Judy Jaffe, OPM's assistant director for executive and management policy, a team of experienced OPM trainers from the regions, the National Independent Study Center, and the Washington Area Service Center was brought together to form the Executive Management Supervisor (EMS) Design Team. The mission of the design team was to provide guidance and oversight for the design, development, implementation, and evaluation of OPM's national curriculum of supervisory training. With the redesign of Intro as its first target, the team engaged HT to

**Figure 1. The EMS Design Team.**

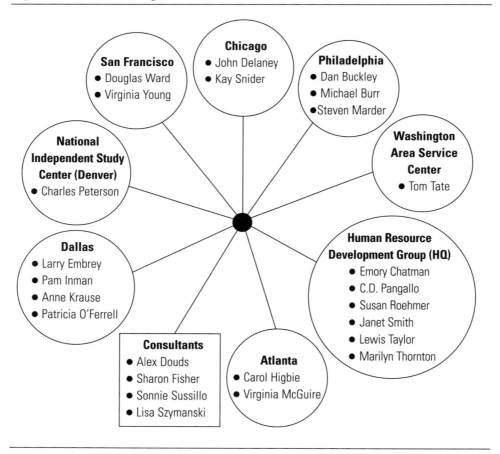

facilitate team meetings, provide additional expertise in ISD, and produce the course materials. Team members involved throughout the project are shown in Figure 1; at any given time, about 12 OPM people from this group were actively involved, supported by HT consultants.

Each EMS Design Team member had extensive experience in supervisor training and provided a view of what supervisors in each region needed in an introductory course. Several HRDG members from OPM headquarters also served on the team, but they deliberately limited their role to observing the process, not managing it; answering administrative questions (about budgets, production requirements, etc.); and coordinating meeting logistics. "Headquarters played a project management role, keeping things moving," observed OPM's project manager, Janet Smith. "Headquarters people basically said to the team, 'You are the experts and we trust you'."

To redesign Intro, the team followed the five steps of the ISD process: analysis, design, development, implementation, and evaluation. Team members worked toward consensus during the process. Although trying to reach consensus seemed "excruciating and time-consuming" to some team members, it ensured that everyone's views and ideas were heard and discussed, and that every team member could buy into and support the decisions made.

## Analysis and Design

Analysis of existing regional curricula for the course revealed it was delivered differently in each region and that its content needed significant updating. The team turned to HT consultant Sonnie Sussillo, an experienced instructional designer and instructor in supervisory-managerial content areas, as the expert who could create the blueprints for design and development. Working with her ideas, the team came to agreement on the course objectives, content, teaching strategy, and evaluation strategy, resulting in a master design for the revised course.

The new Intro course is targeted toward new government supervisors who have been in that role for less than one year. Intro covers the breadth of supervisory responsibilities; its major objective is to help participants gain the knowledge, skills, and tools needed to move successfully into a supervisory role. The five-day course addresses eight key competencies (as shown in Table 1), which the MEF research found to be important to a supervisor's job success. The revised course is highly experiential and skill based. It maximizes participants' involvement through use of in-class exercises, small-group discussions, role plays, and case studies.

**Table 1. Important supervisory competencies.**

- **Role and responsibilities of a supervisor.** Making the transition to supervision; understanding the role and responsibilities of a supervisor; identifying resources available in the areas of personnel management, labor relations, and equal opportunity
- **Communications.** Listening; giving praise and constructive criticism
- **Planning, assigning, controlling, and evaluating work (PACE system).** Planning the work unit's objectives, productivity, goals, and work schedules; assigning work to employees and delegating responsibility and authority; tracking productivity; monitoring quality and employee performance; assessing the effectiveness of work and evaluating employee performance

- **Leadership and motivation.** Using different leadership styles, such as directing, coaching, supporting, and delegating; using a variety of ways to motivate and reward employees
- **Analyzing performance problems.** Analyzing and handling performance problems, both formally and informally
- **Customer service.** Identifying work-unit customers and providing good customer service
- **Ethics.** Demonstrating ethical conduct and ensuring the ethical conduct of employees
- **Managing diversity.** Communicating and interacting with a diverse workforce; understanding and following equal employment opportunity and affirmative action guidelines

## Development

With the go-ahead from the design team, Sussillo next prepared a detailed set of instructional materials to ensure standardized and consistent delivery by any staff or contract instructor. The Instructor Guide gives a step-by-step "script" describing each module's objectives, content, exercises, key points, and logistics. The Participant Manual includes objectives, key points, and exercise materials for each module. The Development Guide helps participants assess themselves on all knowledge and skill areas covered in the course and helps them identify specific applications to their job situations. The Supervisor's Guide, developed by the OPM Central Office, is a job aid to help supervisors perform administrative and personnel tasks (e.g., equal employment opportunity requirements and performance management).

The team critiqued each guide and the course package as a whole, and HT incorporated the revisions. The next step was to teach a pilot session in one region, with Sussillo as the instructor and several team members as observers. A special module-by-module participant evaluation form was used, and observers met daily with Sussillo to compare notes and review the evaluations. Their revision recommendations were discussed with the entire EMS Design Team and incorporated. Now, the course was ready for a trial period of nationwide implementation.

The revised course was tested in the field for nine months across all regions. The design team conducted an exhaustive review of more than 1,100 end-of-course, module-by-module evaluations from participants and nearly 30 instructors. The team came to consensus on the adjustments needed, for example, in sequencing, content, exercises, and videos. Working collaboratively, OPM and HT instructional designers prepared the final instructional materials.

## Implementation

The team established standards for consistent nationwide delivery: precise delivery of all sessions according to the Instructor Guide, training for all instructors, standardized packaging of all materials, centralized ordering and distribution of videos, and centralized printing and distribution of participant materials. The design team continued to play a major coordination and collaboration role in ensuring the smooth and consistent implementation of the course.

## Evaluation Strategy

HT designed an extensive evaluation plan, based on four levels of evaluation: learners' reactions at the end of the course (Level 1), learning attained by the end of the course (Level 2), behavioral changes on the job (Level 3), and business results or return on investment (Level 4). There was some consideration of using a control-group design, but the idea was abandoned because of the difficulty of the process in a complex, multiagency situation.

"The buck stops at Level 4" could well have been the motto for the evaluation effort. For OPM to be a successful player in the training game, competing against a full field of private contractors, OPM's products had to have clear and measurable benefits and results. The team knew that Intro had to demonstrate a payoff for their customers and took this project seriously. They wanted to go beyond the "smiley face" level of evaluation, toward determining cost-effectiveness. Introduction to Supervision was their prototype for excellence in course design, development, and evaluation, and it could become a model not only across OPM, but across all federal agencies.

OPM and HT agreed that a sound Level 4 evaluation had to be built on evaluation at previous levels. As explained by Shelton and Alliger (1993), "Levels 2 and 3 are used to evaluate the quality of training, and they provide additional support for conclusions about the training's effects on business results. In particular, Level 3 evaluation provides evidence of the transfer of knowledge, skills, and attitudes back to the job. If transfer of training didn't occur, a Level 4 evaluation can't show any results" (p. 44). The OPM evaluation strategy is summarized in Table 2.

**Table 2. Evaluation strategy for the Introduction to Supervision course.**

| Evaluation level | Measurement | Methodology |
|---|---|---|
| Reaction (Level 1) | Participants' reaction to and satisfaction with course | Participants' end-of-course questionnaire |
| Learning (Level 2) | Participants' perceived learning gains | Participants' end-of-course questionnaire (self-assessment) |
| Behavior (Level 3) | Changes in on-the-job behavior | Posttraining interviews with participants and their managers |
| | | Pre- and postcourse questionnaire of participants and their managers |
| Results (Level 4) | Return on investment to participants' agencies for their employees' improved skills | Pre- and postcourse questionnaire of participants and their managers (same as above) |
| | | Calculation of dollar value of behavioral change |

Level 1 evaluations during the field-test period were unusually detailed. In addition to rating overall course effectiveness, participants rated the effectiveness of 10 key activities from the modules, the instructor, other course components (e.g., handbook, role plays, and videos), and the training facilities. They were also asked for their suggestions for improving the course.

For Level 2 evaluations, participants rated their perceived knowledge and skill levels in the course content before and after the course.

The Level 3 and Level 4 evaluations used information from a pre- and postcourse questionnaire derived from the MEI. The instrument presented a subset of 42 supervisory behaviors that, taken together, made up the eight major competency areas on which the new Intro course was based. The questionnaire and its complex administration process were piloted and validated in the Philadelphia region by Mike

Burr and in the San Francisco region by Virginia Young, before being used nationwide for 10 sessions during the field-test period.

Course participants (new supervisors) and their managers completed the questionnaire one week before the course and six weeks afterwards. For each item, they rated the skill level the supervisor's job required and the supervisor's current level of skill. From these data, the evaluators could derive a skill gap, the difference between required skill and current skill.

For the Level 3 evaluation of changed behavior on the job, the skill gap that existed before the course was compared with the skill gap after the course. The Level 4 evaluations put a salary-based dollar value on behavioral improvements resulting from reducing the skill gap and calculated ROI based on the costs of training to the agency (including tuition, travel, and participants' salaries and benefits while in training).

A critical aspect of computing ROI was to determine the degree of job success attributable to the set of behaviors addressed by the course. This information was provided by the responding managers (to whom the new supervisors reported), who answered the question

> Think for a moment about the full range of competencies (e.g., technical, administrative, and supervisory) that are required for your subordinate to be successful in his or her job. Then indicate what percent of your subordinate's job success is accounted for by being effective in the eight competency areas covered in the course.

## Evaluation Results

Results from all four levels of evaluation were quite encouraging. Participants had positive reactions and confidence in new skills at the end of the course. On-the-job behavior changes were significant, and the ROI was positive.

### Levels 1, 2, and 3: Highlights

End-of-course evaluations were collected from 1,113 participants nationwide, representing 55 sessions taught during a nine-month period. Level 1 ratings of course effectiveness were extremely high, averaging 4.32 on a 5-point scale, and the course met the expectations of nearly all respondents. For Level 2, participants reported a net gain in their level of skill from an average of 2.15 before the course (on a 5-point scale) to 4.15 after the course.

For Level 3 data, several key players on the EMS Design Team handled telephone interviews with a random sample of 53 course graduates, their managers, and 24 training officers across the country. It was a labor-intensive process to identify and contact interviewees, but well worth the effort. They described more than 200 specific examples of changes in graduates' on-the-job behavior—instances of improved listening skills, better understanding of roles and responsibilities, use of appropriate leadership styles, increased self-confidence and maturity, and greater sensitivity toward other people. Hearing course graduates describe their newfound skills and confidence gave the team a morale boost. The course had provided participants with transferable skills and tools, although some participants reported roadblocks in transferring the skills to the job, chiefly lack of time and lack of support and encouragement from management.

Also for Level 3 evaluation, 169 new supervisors and 162 of their managers completed the precourse questionnaire, and 128 supervisors and 120 managers completed the postcourse questionnaire. Statistical analysis ($t$ tests of significance) revealed very few significant changes (at $\leq .05$) in scores for job requirements, meaning that supervisors' and their managers' perceptions of job requirements remained essentially constant before and after the course. What did change, however, were their perceptions of current skill before and after the course. Both supervisors and their managers perceived statistically significant improvements (at $\leq .05$) in skill. (For example, supervisors' scores in the 42 items ranged from 3.90 to 6.17 on a 9-point scale before the course; after the course, scores ranged from 4.90 to 6.63.) With job requirements constant and with current skill levels improved following the course, there were significant reductions in skill gaps.

## Level 4: The Bottom Line

The final step in the evaluation process was measuring business results. Calculation of a return on agency investment was based on a methodology used in research conducted at the U.S. Naval Ordnance Station in 1989 through 1990 (Schneider and Wright, 1990; Wright, 1990). The steps included assessing the overall degree of job success attributable to a given set of skills or behaviors and then assigning a salary-based dollar value to those competencies. This information was then used—with job requirements ratings and pre- and postcourse skill ratings—to translate course benefits into dollars.

OPM used five steps to determine ROI to the agency.

STEP 1: ASSESS THE OVERALL DEGREE OF JOB SUCCESS. As described earlier, managers indicated the percentage of job success accounted for by the new supervisors' effectiveness in the eight major competencies covered in the course. On average, the managers indicated the eight competencies accounted for 81 percent of the first-level supervisors' success on the job.

STEP 2: DETERMINE THE COMPETENCIES' DOLLAR VALUE. What was the value to an agency of an employee performing successfully in these eight competencies? If a person received $40,000 a year in salary and benefits, and these competencies accounted for 81 percent of success on the job, then the competencies would be worth 81 percent of $40,000, or $32,400. The worth of the competencies was computed by multiplying the average salary and benefits of course participants by the percentage obtained in Step 1.

Participants' annual salaries were determined using the grade information they provided in the questionnaire and the 1992 federal pay schedules. Benefits were computed as 22 percent of an individual's annual salary, the figure OPM uses for congressional budget purposes. Based on these calculations, the average annual salary plus benefits per course participant was $42,202.

Multiplying this figure by the degree of job success accounted for by the competencies (81 percent) yielded a dollar value of $34,184 per participant. That is, if a person were performing successfully in these competencies for one year, the value to the agency would be $34,184.

STEP 3: COMPUTE THE WORTH OF PRE- AND POSTCOURSE SKILL LEVELS. This step determined the degree to which participants were performing at or near the required competence level prior to and following the course, and it assigned a dollar value to each level of performance. The managers' skill ratings (on a scale from 0 to 9) were averaged across the 42 items to derive composite ratings:

- The average level of skill required to be successful in the job was 6.44.
- Graduates' average level of skill prior to the course was 4.96.
- Graduates' average level of skill following the course was 5.59.
- Therefore, prior to the course, participants were performing at 77 percent (4.96 divided by 6.44) of the job requirements. After the course, they were performing at 87 percent (5.59 divided by 6.44).

Dollar values were assigned as follows:

- Performance at the required level was worth $34,184, as determined in Step 2.
- Precourse performance was worth 77 percent of required performance, or $26,322 (77 percent times $34,184).

- Postcourse performance was worth 87 percent of required performance, or $29,740 (87 percent times $34,184).

The difference between pre- and postcourse performance was $3,418 ($29,740 minus $26,322). This amount represents the average gain, or benefit, per person, attributable to the training.

Table 3 summarizes these composite ratings and dollar values.

**Table 3. Composite skill ratings and dollar values, per participant.**

| Variable | Required skill | Precourse skill | Postcourse skill | Gain in skill |
|---|---|---|---|---|
| Composite mean rating (manager) | 6.44 | 4.96 (77% of job requirements) | 5.59 (87% of job requirements) | 0.63 (10% increase) |
| Dollar value (rounded to the nearest dollar) | 34,184 | 26,322 | 29,740 | 3,418 |

STEP 4: DETERMINE COURSE PARTICIPATION COSTS. After determining the dollar value of course benefits, the next step was to determine the cost to the agency for each person who attended a course session during the study. Costs included tuition (which OPM charges to cover course development and delivery costs), travel and per diem, and participants' salary and benefits while in class. The average tuition for course participants during the study was $322.

Travel and per diem costs were determined from responses to two survey questions: "When you attend the course, will it be an overnight, out-of-town trip for you?" and "If yes, please provide an estimate of your travel costs for the training, including transportation, meals, and lodging." The average travel and per diem per participant during the time frame of the study was $234. Finally, participants' salaries and benefits for the week they were in class were determined using the grade information they provided in the questionnaire, the 1992 federal pay schedules, and an estimate of benefits as 22 percent of annual salary. The average salary and benefits for course participants for one week was $812.

Adding all costs yielded a total cost of $1,368 per participant ($322 plus $234 plus $812).

STEP 5: COMPUTE ROI. From two sets of figures—costs and benefits—the ROI was calculated, as shown in Table 4. The ratio of benefit to cost was 2.5 to 1 per participant ($3,418 divided by $1,368). The ROI formula yields the following:

$$\text{ROI} = \frac{\text{net benefits}}{\text{costs}} = \frac{\$3,418 - \$1,368}{\$1,368} = \frac{\$2,050}{\$1,368} = 1.5, \text{ or } 150\%$$

Over the nine-month period, 1,113 participants completed the course, representing a net benefit of $2,281,650, a significant improvement for any program to produce.

**Table 4. Return-on-investment calculations, per participant.**

| Component | Value |
|---|---|
| Costs | $1,368 |
| Benefits | $3,418 |
| Benefits-to-cost ratio | 2.50/1 |
| **Return on investment** | **150%** |

## Conclusion

The high quality of the development and evaluation for the Introduction to Supervision course resulted in the EMS Design Team receiving the OPM Director's Award for Superior Accomplishment and the Outstanding Instructional Product of the Year Award from the Federal Training Officers Conference. OPM is using the combined ISD and design-team approach to develop additional new courses for the EMS curriculum.

What made this project such a success? The design-team approach and commitment to ISD were primarily responsible. First, the design-team approach fostered ownership and commitment to the product and the process, feelings critical for bringing the regions and central office together. Working toward consensus ensured that each team member participated fully, and that each region could live with the decisions the group made. The team approach created a synergy that drew on each person's unique talents and contributions and led to the creative resolution of problems and issues. Given their strong commitment, the design-team members served as champions for the product.

Second, using an ISD approach to course development provided a framework that continually served to anchor the team and the process. ISD helped the team see the big picture—performance requirements, course objectives, training approach, evaluation—as well as the details that can make or break the grand plan. ISD encouraged evaluation every step of the way, not just when the final product was delivered. Clearly, taking the time to carefully assess the quality of each course component allowed the design team to fine-tune the course so that it would meet users' needs.

Finally, the ROI calculations clearly showed agencies that they would get a significant return on their investment in this training for their supervisors.

## Questions for Discussion

1. What are the strengths of the evaluation methodology used in this project? What are the weaknesses and limitations?
2. What are the advantages of using a nationwide design team? What are the potential disadvantages?
3. Given its goals and the overall context, OPM clearly needed to pull together a national team to redesign the Intro course. What are some factors that should be considered in deciding whether instructional design should be a centralized or decentralized process? What are the pros and cons of each approach?
4. As an HRD professional, what are your reactions to the ROI methodology and results? If you were presenting these results to senior management in your organization in support of your training and development efforts, what reactions would you anticipate?
5. Some people might argue that the changes in on-the-job behavior from "soft skills" training (e.g., supervisory training) are too nebulous to measure for the dollar values of benefits for ROI calculations. What is your response?
6. What if the Level 4 results had not been so favorable or had even been negative? As a decision maker, what would your next steps be? How would mediocre or unfavorable results influence your willingness to do Level 4 evaluations in the future?
7. Would a control-group design be appropriate for this evaluation? What are some difficulties in using a control group in this multiagency, multioffering situation? Please explain.

## The Authors

Mary L. Broad, Ed.D., of Performance Excellence helps public- and private-sector organizations achieve lasting performance improvement. She focuses on action learning, instructional systems design, transfer of learning to the workplace, and strategic planning. Before retiring from the federal government, she directed the Human Resource Development

(HRD) Division at the Defense Information Systems Agency. An adjunct faculty member for George Washington University's HRD graduate program, she was recently elected to the board of directors of the American Society for Training and Development. She coauthored *Transfer of Training: Action Packed Strategies to Ensure Full Payoff from Training Investments* (Addison-Wesley, 1991). Broad can be contacted at the following address: Performance Excellence, 3709 Williams Lane, Chevy Chase, MD 20815-4951.

Lisa Szymanski is an instructional technologist and Alex Douds is a senior instructional technologist at Human Technology Inc. in McLean, Virginia. Through a contract with the Office of Personnel Management, Douds, serving as project manager, and Szymanski participated in the development and evaluation of the Introduction to Supervision course described in this case study. They have more than 10 years' experience in the design, development, delivery, and evaluation of training programs. They have consulted with a number of private- and public-sector organizations, including General Dynamics, H.B. Fuller, Air Products, Tenneco, Internal Revenue Service, Federal Aviation Administration, Defense Intelligence Agency, Department of the Navy, Defense Mapping Agency, and Department of Health and Human Services, among others.

## References

Flanders, L.R., and D. Utterback (1985). The Management Excellence Inventory: A tool for management development. *Public Management Forum*, May/June, pp. 403-410.

Office of Personnel Management, Human Resources Development Group, Office of Executive and Management Policy. (1986). *The Management Excellence Framework: A competency-based model of effective performance for federal managers.* Washington, DC: U.S. Government Printing Office.

Office of Personnel Management, Human Resource Development Group, Office of Research and Information. (1993). *Human resource development in the federal sector, Fiscal Year 1991* (Report No. HRI-93-14). Washington, DC: Office of Personnel Management, Human Resources Development Group.

Schneider, H., and C.C. Wright (1990). Return on training invest-ment: Hard measures for soft subjects. *Performance & Instruction, 29*(2), 28-35.

Shelton, S., and G. Alliger (1993). Who's afraid of Level 4 evaluation? *Training & Development, 47*(6), 43-46.

Wright, C.C. (1990). *Research report: Return on investment and learning transfer.* Unpublished report prepared for U.S. Naval Ordnance Station, Indian Head, MD.

# ROI Opportunities in Program Revision

## Insurance Company of America

By Eric Davidove

---

*A program revision provides an excellent opportunity to implement the return-on-investment concept. The following case presents a very thorough approach to evaluation as it was applied to a redesigned underwriter training program for a large insurance firm. At the request of the organization, the results are stated in general terms, but they are still impressive. The model is very comprehensive—probably the most comprehensive in this book—and can be useful in a variety of settings.*

---

## Background

With assets of approximately $70 billion, Insurance Company of America (ICA) is a leading provider of insurance and related financial services throughout the United States and the world. It is among the largest investor-owned insurance organizations in the United States and is the second largest U.S.-based insurer active in international markets.

Andersen Consulting was engaged by ICA to efficiently produce a competitive workforce of underwriters who would maximize the company's earnings. Toward this end, Andersen worked with ICA to modify an Underwriter Training Program to accomplish several goals: provide training on demand, quickly train proficient underwriters, support both fast and slow learners, reduce instructors' preparation time, assure consistent quality and accurate subject matter, and allow underwriters the freedom to learn at their own pace.

The revised 23-week program breaks down into approximately eight

*All names, dates, places, and organizations have been disguised at the request of the case author or organization.*

weeks of self-study reading, five weeks of classroom lecture and demonstration, four weeks of individual case practice, and six weeks of on-the-job practice. Trainees are asked to complete both written and practical mastery tests at the conclusion of each course and major functional area. There is daily contact with the training coordinator to answer immediate questions. In addition, the advisor (an experienced underwriter) meets with the trainee on a scheduled basis to review main points, clarify misconceptions, and introduce subsequent course subject matter.

The Underwriter Training Program helps ICA reduce its operational costs, improve quality, and provide more timely service, because underwriters are trained to make fewer errors and learn best practices to achieve results-driven performance.

## Evaluation Problem

Andersen Consulting did not have to convince ICA that training evaluation is important. The challenge was to demonstrate the need to modify the existing tools and techniques for training evaluation to make them more cost-effective and comprehensive. The existing evaluation approach was labor-intensive, unreliable, and invalid. Also, it did not include behavior (Level 3) or business results (Level 4) outcomes.

ICA had already been using a case test to evaluate the instructional effectiveness of their Underwriter Training Program (i.e., Level 2 evaluation). At the conclusion of each major topic, trainees were asked to complete a case and defend the answers to a panel of experts.

Experienced underwriters (or graders) spent about four hours scoring each case. There were no standard forms for capturing and organizing case answers. Graders often had no answer keys or scoring guides. Case material was loosely stored in folders, unbound and without page numbers. Case reports and case facts were often outdated and inaccurate. Content covered in case tests was not always covered in training. Graders had to spend a considerable amount of time reviewing case tests before scoring answers, because the case content was frequently updated or replaced.

## Marketing the Evaluation

An evaluation marketing strategy was developed around four key messages: improve customer service, measure only mission-critical skills, continuously improve training, and evaluate beyond learning.

### Improve Customer Service

An analysis of the situation demonstrated that underwriters might deliver poor customer service when evaluation procedures are time-consuming. That is, when underwriters spend time grading tests, they have less time to reduce their backlogs, catch errors, or help other underwriters. These conditions usually lead to high turnover rates. In the end, customers end up waiting longer for service, and the quality of service they receive is irregular.

Underwriters tend to quit when their backlog exceeds their capacity to act, or when action taken by management to reduce the backlog is too late or ineffective. Newly hired underwriters tend to quit if they do not receive guidance and support from experienced underwriters.

The underwriters who decide to stay generally assume the backlog responsibility of those who quit, resulting in more overtime for underwriters and more pressure to meet deadlines. The experienced underwriters usually become too busy trying to reduce the backlog to help newly hired underwriters. With little support, newly hired underwriters tend to make too many errors and spend too much time doing rework.

As turnover rates continue to rise, the backlog continues to increase, and supporting newly hired underwriters becomes a low priority. Before long, more underwriters quit and the situation worsens.

Andersen Consulting suggested reducing the time needed to score tests by developing answer keys, scoring guides, structured answer sheets, and multiple-choice and true/false questions, and by organizing the case test materials in a workbook format. These changes to evaluating the training program were expected to reduce scoring time for one underwriter by 75 percent (or from four hours to one hour). What was found, however, was that experienced underwriters saved even more time (three and a half hours), because newly hired underwriters were able to help with test-scoring tasks.

## Measure Mission-Critical Skills

ICA became convinced that trainees would be more likely to apply newly learned skills on the job and positively influence the bottom line if they were tested on mission-critical skills. Some skills and knowledge were not worth testing, whereas others warranted more attention. The intent was to communicate clearly to trainees what it takes to be a successful underwriter.

The tests for the program did not emphasize memorization of information that is well documented in reference materials and job aids. Tests were developed to determine if trainees could use tools, work fast, make few errors, and convince customers and salespeople that the trainees' "answers" were correct.

To reduce the number of test questions, only higher order skills of critical importance were addressed. For example, one test question was developed to measure the extent to which the trainee was able to select and apply a procedure most appropriate for a given situation. ICA's original test used one question to test the trainee's ability to state the procedure, a second test question to determine if the trainee was able to select the most appropriate procedure, and a third test question to test how well the trainee applied the procedure.

### Continuously Improve Training

ICA's original approach to training evaluation focused only on final test scores. There were no intermittent checkpoints, nor any way of knowing what went wrong. One marketing message communicated to ICA was that if timely and specific feedback about the success of the training program were received, the training program would be more current, accurate, complete, and effective.

Among the suggestions were frequent testing of how well trainees performed during training and tracking test scores for each enabling objective (see Figure 1). Andersen Consulting demonstrated how this periodic and detailed performance information could help trainers and training coordinators continuously adjust the training or provide immediate support to ensure trainees mastered prerequisite learning.

Andersen Consulting also suggested using surveys to capture information on activities, transactions, and effects occurring within the training program. For example, training coordinators were asked to judge the behavior of trainers and trainees, trainers were asked to judge the performance of trainees, and trainees were asked to judge the performance of trainers.

### Evaluate beyond Learning

The director of training, chief underwriter officer, and chief financial officer intuitively saw the value of Level 3 and Level 4 evaluation data. Consequently, relatively little time was spent marketing this type of evaluation to the underwriting department.

The biggest challenge was getting consensus on which information to collect. Andersen Consulting did not want to waste time collecting information that was not influenced by training, did not facilitate decision making, or was relatively insignificant. Different kinds of information were classified into priority categories according to whether they measured factors influencing high-priority business objectives or factors affected in large part by skill and knowledge deficiencies (see Figure 2).

# Figure 1. Forms used to analyze test scores by enabling objectives.

The student survey is used to see where an individual student might need help; the class survey summarizes results from an entire class. These forms can be used to analyze results for any of the tests used in this training program.

**Student Test Survey: analyzing test scores for one student before (Test A) and after (Test B) he or she completes one module.**

Module_____

| Test A | Test B | Percentage correct | Enabling objectives |
|---|---|---|---|
| Circle each test question the student answers incorrectly. | Circle each test question the student answers incorrectly. | (Total number of correct answers ÷ total number of questions) × 100. | |
| 1 ②  ③  ④ | 1 ②  3  4 | Test A $(1 \div 4) \times 100 = 25\%$ Test B $(3 \div 4) \times 100 = 75\%$ | The enabling performance objective is written here. |

**Class Test Survey: analyzing test scores for one class before (Test A) and after (Test B) the class completes one module.**

Module_____

| Test A | Test B | Percentage correct | Enabling objectives |
|---|---|---|---|
| Write the total number of students who correctly answer each item. | Write the total number of students who correctly answer each item. | Total number of correct answers ÷ total class size × total number of questions × 100. | |
| 1  10 2  5 3  8 4  4 | 1  10 2  10 3  8 4  7 | Test A $27 \div (10 \times 4) \times 100 =$ 67.5% Test B $35 \div (10 \times 4) \times 100 =$ 87.5% | The enabling performance objective is written here. |
| 5  2 6  5 7  4 | 5  3 6  1 7  6 | $21 \div (10 \times 3) \times 100 =$ 70% | The enabling performance objective is written here. |

Knowing what information to collect is only half the battle. Another challenge was trying to collect information from employees working in other functional areas (e.g., sales, claims, and audit). Generally, information "owners" were either unwilling to share information or were not then collecting it. In the end, ICA failed to get the information needed to evaluate the effect of training on key performance indicators.

**Figure 2. System for prioritizing information requirements.**

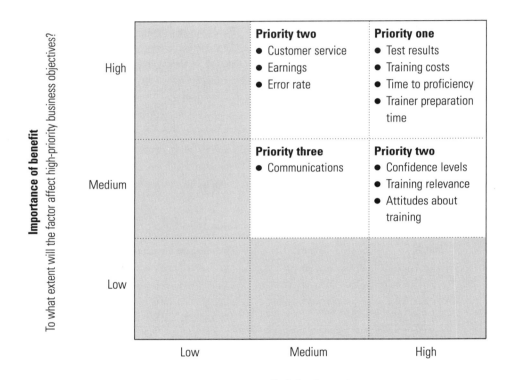

## Evaluation Plan

The primary purpose of the evaluation plan was to find out if predetermined training objectives were achieved, inform decision makers, ensure accountability, and understand how to improve training further. The evaluation results were used to portray ICA's training department as a bottom-line contributor.

Five critical success factors (CSFs) were developed, with input from ICA, to measure success and guide the evaluation process. The reliability CSF concerned use of data collection instruments and techniques that were objective and consistent. The validity CSF was created to ensure that data were defensible and believable. A usefulness CSF was established to provide data that aided in decision making. A feasibility CSF was developed to ensure that the evaluation model and technique were easy to implement. The generalizability CSF addressed the extent to which the data collected from one group of individuals represented the performance and opinions of another group of individuals. Collectively, these CSFs guided the development of this program.

The evaluation model required the use of 12 instruments and collected data in 10 domains from four sources (see Table 1). The surveys measured attitudes, perceptions, confidence, and training costs. The tests measured how well people recalled names and facts, classified ideas and actions, applied rules, and innovated solutions to novel situations (see Table 2). ICA generally collected data before, during, and after training, as outlined in Table 3. Subject matter experts and learning specialists suggested revisions that were incorporated into the training materials.

## Data Analysis

ICA analyzed a variety of data to judge the training's effectiveness and to determine ways of improving it further. The effort was also concerned with determining the reliability and validity of the data collection instruments and techniques. ICA stressed the importance of presenting believable and defensible conclusions. See Table 4 for a summary of the six evaluation questions and their associated data analysis techniques.

The effectiveness of the revised training program was determined by making three comparisons of trainees' test, survey, and performance appraisal scores. ICA's data analysis approach examined differences between trainees within a class, between trainees in one regional class and trainees in another regional class, and between trainees who complete the revised training program and trainees who completed the original training program.

The return on investment was defined as the rate of recovery and time to proficiency (see Table 4). ICA assessed the rate at which training development costs were recovered through reduced costs for trainer preparation, training delivery, and test administration. Additional cost savings were calculated by tracking how quickly trainees became productive.

Six months after training, trainees were asked to complete a compre-

## Table 1. Evaluation model and techniques.

| Evaluation domain | Data sources | | | |
|---|---|---|---|---|
| | **Trainers** | **Trainees** | **Training coordinators** | **Line managers** |
| **Characteristics** that affect learning and performance | | Survey 1 | | |
| **Attitudes** toward the training materials and training strategy | Survey 2 | Survey 3 | Survey 4 | |
| **Confidence** in ability to perform after training | | Survey 5 Survey 6 | | |
| **Relevancy** of content and practice | Survey 2 | Survey 5 Survey 6 | | |
| **Feasibility** of implementing the training program | Survey 2 | | Survey 4 | |
| **Cost** of training | | | Survey 7 | |
| **Entry-level ability** before studying one module | | Test A (written and practical) | | |
| **Learning** immediately after one module | Survey 2 | Test B (written and practical) | Survey 4 | |
| **Learning** immediately after one functional area | | Test C (written and practical) | | |
| **Transfer** of learning to the job | | Test D (written and practical) | | Performance Appraisal |

hensive test (i.e., Test D). The same test was administered to newly hired underwriters six months after they completed the original training program and to experienced underwriters (i.e., with three or more years of experience). Test scores were compared to determine if the graduates of the revised training program approached the performance of experienced underwriters faster than graduates of the original training program.

Several factors, in addition to training, can influence performance. For example, some trainees may perform better than others because they have better instructors, different experiences, or more confidence. To gain insight necessary to improve the training's effectiveness further, moderating variables such as content sequence, content completeness, and training conditions were analyzed.

Because trainees and training conditions differ, measurement controls were necessary to ensure all training classes whose results were compared were equal. ICA used a one-shot case study and a separate-sample pretest-posttest research design to control for differences in group structure and training conditions (Davidove, 1993). This approach made it possible to isolate the effects of training on training objectives that were aimed directly at accomplishing important business objectives.

## Results

At the request of ICA, specific results about the training program's effectiveness are not reported in this case study. In general, however, ICA believes the revised training program is significantly better than the original program. Test scores suggested that trainees who completed the revised training program learned more and became productive sooner than trainees who completed the original training program. The return on investment for the revised training program was relatively high, because delivery costs were considerably less than those of the original program: The revised training program required less trainer preparation time, learning time, and administration time. Also, the revised training program received high marks from trainers and trainees. They believed the training materials were easy to use; the training content was relevant, accurate, and complete; and the training strategies were effective.

## Limitations

Training evaluation is a diversified activity, and no one set of principles will suffice for all situations. The challenge is knowing what to change in order to provide the best evidence to answer questions about the training program (within the limitations of your budget and time commitments). The evaluation model used in this case has three major limitations.

**Table 2. Data collection instrument.**

| Instrument | Information collected |
|---|---|
| Survey 1 | The **trainee's characteristics** that might affect learning and performance, such as work location, education level, and relevant job experience |
| Survey 2 | The **trainer's attitude** about the materials' usability, content, instructional strategies, and trainees' performance immediately after one module |
| Survey 3 | The **trainee's attitude** about the materials, trainer, content, and instructional strategies for one module |
| Survey 4 | The **training coordinator's perception** of how well the trainer presented the content for one module and how well the trainees performed during training |
| Survey 5 | The **trainee's confidence level and perceived relevance** of the training immediately after completing one functional area |
| Survey 6 | The **trainee's confidence level and perceived relevance** of the training six months after completing the training program |
| Survey 7 | **Training cost factors,** including training development and support, training delivery, use of external vendors, training overhead (direct and indirect), and training days and student days |

One major limitation of the training evaluation is that it did not consider factors outside the classroom that affect job performance. Monitoring barriers to and facilitators of high-quality performance back on the job would have helped Andersen Consulting better understand which aspects of the training program were responsible for the successes and failures. For example, one approach would be to evaluate the contribution of transfer enablers such as feedback, guidance, rewards, and the organizational attitude toward risk taking.

Another criticism of this evaluation approach is that the training objectives were accepted at face value. The underwriting community asked Andersen Consulting to assume that the training objectives were worthwhile and appropriate, thus circumscribing efforts to judge the merit or worth of the training program. Andersen knew the training program had succeeded in meeting its objectives, but had no idea if the objectives themselves were ill-conceived or trivial. Gathering Level 4 evaluation information would have helped judge if trainees were learn-

**Table 2 (continued). Data collection instrument.**

| Instrument | Information collected |
|---|---|
| Test A (written) | Multiple choice and true/false questions that measure the **trainee's knowledge of facts, concepts, and procedures before** completing one module |
| Test A (case) | A timed activity measuring **how well the trainee applies facts, concepts, and procedures before** completing one module |
| Test B (written) | Multiple choice and true/false questions that measure the **trainee's knowledge of facts, concepts, and procedures after** completing one module |
| Test B (case) | A timed activity measuring **how well the trainee applies facts, concepts, and procedures after** completing one module |
| Test C (written) | Multiple choice and true/false questions that measure the **trainee's knowledge of facts, concepts, and procedures after** completing one functional area |
| Test C (case) | A timed activity measuring **how well the trainee applies facts, concepts, and procedures after** completing one functional area |
| Test D (written) | Multiple choice and true/false questions that measure the **trainee's knowledge of facts, concepts, and procedures six months after** completing the training program |
| Test D (case) | A timed activity measuring **how well the trainee applies facts, concepts, and procedures six months after** completing the training program |

ing how to do the right things right.

A third way to improve the evaluation approach would be to consider unintended positive and negative outcomes. For example, although trainees may have mastered rate projection, they may have come to hate or fear the task of negotiating rates with a salesperson. This lack of information about side effects made it impossible to assess the true cost savings associated with the training program and to form valid judgments about the value of the program.

## Evaluation Truisms

Some organizations discourage risk taking and do not reward productive failures. Especially in these settings, the evaluator must deter-

**Table 3. Data collection schedule.**

| Immediately before training | Immediately after completing one module | Immediately after completing one functional area | Six months after completing the training program |
|---|---|---|---|
| Trainee's characteristics | Trainer's attitude | Trainee's confidence level | Trainee's confidence level |
| Test A (written and practical) | Trainee's attitude | Trainee's perceived relevance | Trainee's perceived relevance |
| Training cost factors | Training coordinator's perception | Training cost factors | Training cost factors |
| | Training cost factors | Test C (written and practical) | Test D (written and practical) |
| | Test B (written and practical) | | Trainee performance appraisal |

mine who will win or lose when training results are known (i.e., who the stakeholders are). A "winner" is someone whose views are supported by the training results. For example, if the head of underwriting lobbied against using computer-based training (CBT), he or she would be a winner if the training evaluation suggested that the CBT was a poor investment. If the advocate of the CBT in this example was the director of training, he or she would probably lose some influence over future decisions regarding training technology.

Regardless of who wins and loses from evaluations, evaluators should not withhold or tamper with results. They should use their knowledge of stakeholders to justify an evaluation approach. Higher stakes require more rigorous, valid, and reliable evaluations.

Some training should never be evaluated. The conditions under which evaluation is warranted are situational (see Table 5), and their relative importance will vary.

## Conclusion

Evaluation is a complex and powerful tool. As is illustrated in this case, it is a highly political activity, is difficult to conduct, and requires participation from all stakeholders. There is no single right approach to

**Table 4. Data analysis.**

| Evaluation question | Data analysis technique |
|---|---|
| How much did the trainees learn, and how well did they transfer what they've learned to the job? | Gain score—the difference between pre- and posttest measures for individual trainees, compared against a criterion or normative standard |
| Is the training content sequenced properly, and does training cover all prerequisite skills? | Most difficult objectives—those objectives with which individual trainees or a class of trainees have the most difficulty |
| Under what conditions is training most effective? | Correlation—the relationship between training delivery, training design, perceptions, attitudes, confidence, relevancy, background characteristics, learning, and performance |
| Are the data collection techniques and instruments reliable? | Extent of agreement—the extent to which data from different sources support the same conclusions |
| Are the data collection techniques and instruments valid? | Construct and content validity—the extent to which experienced performers agree that the test questions reflect the training objectives they were written to measure and the degree to which the test questions simulate real-life conditions |
| What is the return on investment? | Recovery—the rate at which training development costs are recovered through reduced costs for trainer preparation, training delivery, and test administration<br>Time to proficiency—the cost savings realized by developing productive workers more quickly than the former training program did |

training evaluation. Every evaluation project involves choices and decisions, explicit or implicit. Yet, despite these challenges, only systematic, Level 4 evaluations will tell stakeholders, over time, the merit or worth of their training program. As does any powerful tool, evaluation comes with warnings and principles for best use, some of which are presented in this case. Undertaken thoughtfully and carefully, evaluation represents an opportunity to understand and enhance the role of training departments in accomplishing high-priority business objectives.

**Table 5. Conditions under which evaluation is warranted.**

- Physical, human, and financial resources are available
- Cost of poor training is high
- There is a 50/50 chance that the training is flawed
- Training development has been expensive
- Senior management is willing to improve training continuously

## Questions for Discussion

1. Contrast the previous and revised Underwriter Training Program. Why was there a need to change?
2. Why is it difficult to obtain consensus on which information to collect for Level 3 and Level 4 evaluation?
3. Explain the role of the critical success factors.
4. Critique the comprehensiveness of the evaluation model and techniques.
5. Is the data collection process too complicated? Please explain.
6. Critique the approach to determine the return on investment.
7. Are the limitations described in the case typical? Are there other approaches to overcome them?
8. Comment on the evaluation truisms.

## The Author

Eric Davidove, an experienced manager for Andersen Consulting's Change Management Services practice, helps his clients align their workforce with their technology, processes, and strategy to make change work. He works in the areas of organizational change, education and training, and technology assimilation. Davidove has industry experience in consumer products, financial services, and government. He received his doctoral degree in instructional systems from Florida State University and is the recipient of the 1991 Robert M. Gagne Award for outstanding student research in instructional development. Davidove can be contacted at the following address: Andersen Consulting, 101 East Kennedy Boulevard, Suite 2200, Tampa, FL 33602.

## Reference

Davidove, E.A. (1993). Evaluating the return on investment of training. *Performance and Instruction, 32,* 1-8.

# Three Rs in the Workplace

## Magnavox Electronic Systems Company

By Donald J. Ford

*As companies invest in the basic skills development of entry-level employees, literacy training is becoming a critical issue. This unique case describes the evaluation of a literacy skills training program at Magnavox. The results are dramatic, which should be encouraging for other companies that invest, or plan to invest, in this important area of human resource development.*

## Background

Workplace illiteracy is not always obvious. Many illiterate employees become skillful at hiding their problem by becoming keen observers and mimicking the behaviors they see around them. Fearful of the consequences, they are loath to admit they cannot read, write, or compute. No one wears a T-shirt proclaiming, "Illiterate...and proud of it!"

Magnavox Electronic Systems Company, West Coast Division, a high-tech manufacturer of satellite communications and navigation equipment in Torrance, California, began to observe literacy problems among its 250 hourly employees several years ago. At first, managers and supervisors misinterpreted illiteracy as a motivation problem ("they don't want to work") or a technical problem ("they don't know how to do their jobs"), when what was really preventing people from performing their jobs was a lack of literacy.

The common telltale signs of illiteracy include an influx of new immigrant and minority workers into the workforce, a drop in the quality of products or services, unsuccessful introduction of new technologies, an increase in accidents and safety problems, and changes in the characteristics or responsibilities of jobs. At Magnavox, the most obvious sign was an influx of Latin American and Asian immigrants, who gradually came to constitute about two-thirds of the hourly workforce. Many of these immigrants had poor English skills, so they conversed among themselves in their native languages. Although English is the "official" language of the company, 11 other languages—especially Spanish, Tagalog, Vietnamese, Chinese, and Korean—were also being spoken in the factory.

The polyglot work environment began to take a toll on company communications. Memos never seemed to get read, meeting announcements failed to assemble people in the right place at the right time, and misunderstandings about who was doing what became chronic. Additionally, scrap and rework costs jumped, a clear signal that employees were committing too many errors in their work. Accident rates and workers' compensation costs escalated as well.

When the company decided to implement statistical process control (SPC) to improve the quality of products and reduce inspection time, they found that many employees lacked the basic math and reading skills to understand and properly implement the concepts they had supposedly learned in class. The failed introduction of this new program got management's attention.

## Organizational Profile

Magnavox Electronic Systems Company, West Coast Division, was part of Philips Electronics North America, one of the largest companies of the European electronics giant, N.V. Philips, until 1993, when it was sold to the Carlyle Group. The West Coast Division began as a small research laboratory in the 1950s, pioneering breakthroughs in digital facsimile, antijam communications, and global positioning system (GPS) technologies. Starting in the late 1970s, the division experienced rapid growth for a period of 10 years, especially during the military buildup of the Reagan presidency, because 60 percent of the division's business is in military electronics. Since 1988, the division has shrunk from its peak employment of 1,500 to about 600, primarily because of cuts in the defense budget and increased overseas competition in its commercial markets.

In addition to military satellite communications equipment and fax machines, the division has a commercial business that consists primarily of navigation sales to ocean-going freighters and pleasure craft, in more than 100 nations around the globe. This commercial business accounts for 40 percent of the division's total sales. At its peak, the division had annual sales of about $130 million, though this total has declined to about $90 million recently.

The company was traditionally split into military and commercial divisions. Many of their functions were duplicated, though both divisions shared a common factory for production. As the company downsized, the two divisions began to merge and share administrative and financial functions to the extent possible. (Because of contractual requirements, some parts of the military business must remain separate.) The divisions are organized around product lines, with a vice-president in charge of each. A matrix organization is used to deploy engineering resources. Engineers report to both a technical and a product or program manager.

The workforce has always been led and dominated by engineers, but at its peak the company was composed of roughly one-third engineers, one-third professional support staff, and one-third factory production workers. As the company downsized, the percentage of engineers increased to about 50, because support and hourly staff were laid off in larger numbers.

## Industry Profile

The electronics industry has been volatile for the past several decades, experiencing periods of booming growth followed by recession, fierce competition, and retrenchment. Military electronics, although relatively insulated from the buffeting forces of competition blowing through the commercial sector, has been characterized by periods of boom and bust as well. Compounding market volatility is the recent trend to open up military electronics to commercial producers in an effort to control costs.

Meanwhile, commercial electronics has come to be dominated by Japanese firms, with a few notable American exceptions such as Motorola, Hewlett-Packard, Texas Instruments, IBM, Intel, and AT&T. Efforts to shore up the American electronics industry have shown mixed results. In some areas (notably, personal computers, telecommunications, and specialized components), American firms are holding their own, but in consumer electronics and basic computer chips, the Japanese reign supreme, with Philips providing virtually the only serious global challenge to Japan.

In such a competitive environment, three imperatives determine survival. First, companies must continuously develop timely new products and applications to keep pace with rapid changes in technology. Second, they must design and produce these products at the lowest possible cost. Finally, they must provide customers with a high degree of quality and value for their money.

## Character Profile

To provide guidance and oversight for the literacy program, a management steering committee was formed. It comprised the vice-president of operations, the vice-president of human resources, the director of quality assurance, and the managers of manufacturing, quality control, quality improvement, and human resource development (HRD). The HRD manager served as chair. The key decision maker was the vice-president of operations, who managed manufacturing, purchasing, and manufacturing engineering. He was a staunch supporter of training and encouraged all who worked for him to pursue further education as well. The primary catalyst for the workplace literacy program was the manager of HRD, who conducted the initial needs assessment, identified literacy as a root cause of many manufacturing problems, and tirelessly sold the merits of the program to his superiors and colleagues. The other members of the steering committee played supporting roles, either in convincing the head of the division to spend money on the program or in helping to implement it.

## Need for a Literacy Program

The historical development of the workplace literacy program is a saga lasting nearly three years. When a new manager of HRD was hired in 1989, he met with the vice-president of operations to introduce himself and learn about key training issues confronting manufacturing. The vice-president requested help from the HRD department to improve hourly employees' job performance. The mandate was broad and vague at that point, but after initial discussions and observation in the factory, a pilot program for assessing basic skills was created to determine the extent of illiteracy in the workforce. Magnavox chose to team up with El Camino College, a nearby public community college that possessed expertise in testing and assessment. Under the agreement, Magnavox purchased copies of the Test of Adult Basic Education (TABE) and administered the test to a sample of its employees. El Camino scored the tests and helped identify resources to assist employees in improving their basic skills.

The assessment involved 109 employees who volunteered to take the test. They represented a cross section of the manufacturing workforce, from entry-level, unskilled assemblers to test technicians and supervisors with college educations. The results confirmed the HRD manager's suspicions about literacy problems. Average reading ability was at the eighth-grade level, and math ability was at the seventh-grade level.

The HRD manager then took a sample of work-related materials, including manufacturing process instructions, engineering change notices, routing cards, charts, and blueprints, and analyzed these to determine their average reading and math levels. For reading, he used the Fry Readability Formula (Fry, 1977) and the Department of Defense's Readability Formula, both of which estimate the reading grade level of materials based on the complexity of vocabulary and sentence structure. Based on this analysis, he concluded that employees needed to read at an eighth-grade level to comprehend workplace documents. He used the experience of other companies in the aerospace industry to estimate that workplace documentation required a sixth-grade math level.

Comparing these workplace literacy requirements with the tested skill levels of employees in the sample, he was able to determine the extent of the skill gap. Although average test scores were at or above the minimum, further analysis by job function revealed significant areas of concern. When the HRD manager removed salaried employees from the data, for example, he found that hourly employees had, on average, seventh-grade reading levels and sixth-grade math levels. Among entry-level assemblers, average reading ability was only at a fourth-grade level, well below the level needed to read workplace documentation (see Figure 1). The HRD manager concluded that 52 percent of the hourly workers were functionally illiterate in reading and 36 percent were illiterate in basic math.

When these results were presented to management in their weekly staff meeting, it was as if cataracts had been removed from their eyes. They began to see many of their employee performance problems in a new light. These data were the turning point in convincing management to pursue a training program in workplace literacy.

## A Systematic Approach to Achieving Workplace Literacy

As companies awaken to a workplace literacy problem, they sometimes rush out and hire a consultant or adult education specialist who provides them with an off-the-shelf academic or functional literacy program. Most of these companies wind up disappointed when nothing changes at work. A functional literacy program alone will not solve work-related literacy problems, because of the specialized technical vocabulary and processes used in the workplace today.

A model for workplace literacy programs appears in Figure 2. This model, based on the extensive experience of Educational Data Systems Inc. in Dearborn, Michigan, includes six key steps. By following this model, Magnavox was able to improve employee performance quickly

**Figure 1. Reading and math levels by job group.**

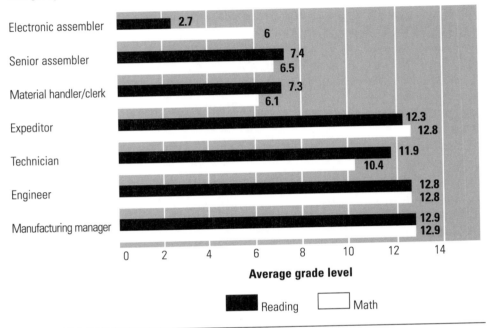

**Job group**

Electronic assembler — Reading 2.7, Math 6
Senior assembler — Reading 7.4, Math 6.5
Material handler/clerk — Reading 7.3, Math 6.1
Expeditor — Reading 12.3, Math 12.8
Technician — Reading 11.9, Math 10.4
Engineer — Reading 12.8, Math 12.8
Manufacturing manager — Reading 12.9, Math 12.9

**Average grade level**

Reading | Math

and alleviate the most pressing literacy problems in the workplace. The company therefore avoided the waste of time and money that often results from unfocused academic literacy programs, which cannot hope to address workplace literacy problems.

Magnavox decided to assess and analyze carefully the problems that workplace illiteracy was causing and to design a training program that used workplace materials and processes as the basis of the curriculum. In this way, employees learned just the language and basic skills needed to perform their jobs, resulting in an immediate payoff to the company. Once they had mastered this limited set of literacy skills, they were referred to adult schools or community colleges, where they could become functionally and academically literate.

Once the need for workplace literacy had been established, attention turned to how to implement a successful training program. A number of delivery options were considered, including private literacy firms, public schools for adults, community colleges, and even computer-based literacy training.

**Figure 2. Workplace literacy model for Magnavox's training programs.**

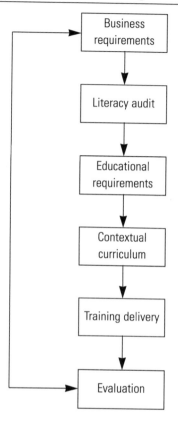

Then Magnavox learned of the availability of federal funding through the Carl D. Perkins Vocational Education Act, which provides grants to the states for adult training programs. The California State Department of Education has created a model program that teams up private industry with local public schools. The private employer pays nothing for the training, but is required to finance a literacy audit to ensure the program addresses workplace literacy issues. In return, the employer receives up to $13,000 in literacy training funds, which are channeled through the school partner.

Magnavox chose this approach for two reasons. First, it was the most attractive alternative because of its low cost. Second, it appeared to have the greatest potential to address work-related literacy problems, because it emphasized the link between literacy and job performance.

The literacy audit, conducted by Educational Data Systems, confirmed many of the literacy problems already uncovered through the initial assessment. The audit then went a step further by identifying the exact skills in reading, writing, listening, speaking, and arithmetic that were required of employees on the job in order to be able to comprehend work materials and documents. An occupational analysis identified the following seven major tasks required of production workers:

- use work instructions
- complete forms
- complete mechanical assembly
- complete electrical assembly
- solder electrical components
- perform work as a member of a team
- use SPC.

Each task was subdivided into work activities and learning goals, sorted according to their difficulty level using Bloom's taxonomy of learning objectives. For example, reading the detailed manufacturing process instructions required 12 enabling objectives, such as understanding technical terms and abbreviations and following a written sequence of events. This task analysis formed the basis for the instructional design.

## Implementing the Program

The management steering committee played a key role in the successful implementation of the program. The committee served as liaison to Torrance Adult School, the public education partner; interviewed and hired an instructor from a pool of applicants provided by the school; and assisted the instructor in developing a work-related, contextual curriculum consisting of the manuals and documents employees were expected to use to perform their jobs.

The steering committee also played an important role in marketing the program to hourly employees. The committee recognized at the outset that this training would require skillful marketing, because employees would be reluctant to come forward on their own and seek help. First, because of the negative connotations associated with illiteracy, the program was named Process Improvement and Communications (PIC), which dovetailed nicely with the company's total quality management initiative.

Next, all hourly employees received a survey, in English, Spanish, and Chinese, that briefly described the PIC classes and asked employees to choose one of four class sessions to attend. To encourage attendance, the company donated two hours a week of work time to the program, requiring employees to attend an additional two hours on their own time by coming into work an hour early or staying an hour late twice a week.

Once the initial survey results became available, the vice-president of operations scheduled a series of information meetings for all hourly employees to explain the program in more detail and solicit additional enrollments. These meetings, held on company time, helped to double the enrollment, from 30 to 60 employees.

The 18-week program was divided into three six-week terms. Although employees were encouraged to remain for the entire program, management recognized that such a long commitment might discourage participation. Shorter terms meant employees could sign up, try out the classes, and finish them without making a lengthy commitment. It turned out that half of the original enrollers completed all three terms.

The instructor was a key factor in the success of the program. He brought a unique blend of public school, private industry, and overseas experience to this assignment. This experience helped him establish rapport with the mostly immigrant population, rapidly master the complex technical documentation he was asked to teach, and infuse the class with a variety of interesting learning activities. Furthermore, his energy and enthusiasm for the assignment became contagious.

The primary target audience for the training was entry-level electrical and mechanical assemblers whose skills in English and math were the lowest. These individuals were primarily Hispanic, Asian, and African-American women with limited education. Although most had graduated from high school, their average English reading scores were around fourth grade, with some as low as second grade, and their average math scores were around sixth grade, but as low as third grade. Most of these employees had previous experience as assemblers, in either the United States or their native countries, but their knowledge was limited to the most basic operations and had been learned largely by rote.

Unfortunately, the target group proved difficult to enroll in classes for a variety of reasons. The biggest stumbling block was the decision to make attendance voluntary and to require employees to donate some of their own time, either before or after work. This latter requirement proved difficult for many of the female employees in particular because of their child-care and homemaking responsibilities. Moreover, some of these employees lacked the motivation to invest their own time in education, either because of cultural norms that discouraged women from pursuing education and career advancement or because of a distrust of the company's motives and sincerity in offering such classes at work.

As a result of these difficulties, only about half of the participants came from the primary target audience. These employees were organized into two classes of 15 employees each. The classes taught primarily English as a second language (at beginning to intermediate levels) and basic arithmetic.

The other two classes were filled with more experienced and advanced workers who wished to pursue any opportunity to improve themselves and increase their chances to maintain their jobs or win promotions. They included senior electrical and mechanical assemblers, inspectors, technicians, and even a few first-line supervisors, most foreign-born. The content of these classes more closely approximated GED (high-school equivalency) classes, with emphasis on the technical vocabulary of the workplace, basic statistics, and the advanced arithmetic needed to perform SPC and to read schematics and blueprints.

During the first week of classes, employees took the TABE. The results established a baseline for measuring progress during the course and were also used as a diagnostic tool to ensure that each student was placed at the proper class level. Although management did not get all the target population to participate, the availability of different class levels contributed to the success of the program by ensuring that the individual needs of employees were met.

## Method of Delivery

Classes were conducted in an informal lecture-discussion format most of the time. The instructor generally started class sessions by introducing a text or sample work document; asking participants to read it, either silently or aloud; and then discussing the content and vocabulary until participants understood the material thoroughly. Ample use was also made of small-group skill practice, including role plays, individual written assignments, paired exercises, and simulations. Participants were encouraged to bring sample work materials and problems into the classroom for discussion. This practice yielded some of the most meaningful learning, because participants were able to solve work-related problems on the spot. In some cases, errors in work instructions were identified and corrected. Inconsistencies in the way certain operations were being performed by different assemblers were also clarified and corrected.

Additionally, the school district provided two Apple computers that participants could use for more practice in basic reading and math skills. The computers were set up in a quiet area away from the factory and were available before and after work, at lunch, and at break times. Because the software provided was not high quality and the computers were rather old, few participants took advantage of the extra practice, but those who did found it somewhat beneficial. Unfortunately, a newer Apple Macintosh with more advanced software was ordered late by the school district and did not arrive until the program was over.

## Evaluation Design

Evaluation was designed into the project as a requirement of the state and federal funders. The specific models and techniques to be employed were at the discretion of the local site, however. The responsibility for evaluating the program rested with the HRD manager, who had the expertise and time to pursue a thorough evaluation. Other members of the steering committee agreed that an evaluation of the program was worthwhile, considering the time, money, and effort that had been expended. The school district also wanted an evaluation and assisted with administration of the posttest.

Planning for the evaluation began early in the program, at the needs assessment stage. The HRD manager had decided to collect data on all four levels of evaluation: reactions of employees, as measured by postcourse surveys; learning of employees, as measured by TABE scores before and after training; changes in behavior of employees, as measured by their daily actual efficiency ratings (measured for each employee in the factory, based on daily work output); and bottom-line results, measured in dollars saved from increased productivity and reduced scrap and rework costs.

The evaluation was conducted in stages, so that data were collected at the appropriate times. The test data needed to be collected at the very outset of the program to establish the pretest baseline and again on the last day of class, to ensure that everyone completed the posttest. Reactions of employees were also collected on the last day of class, while their memories of the experience were fresh. Data on productivity, scrap, and rework were tracked on a monthly basis by the company anyway, so it was necessary only to tap into existing data collection schedules to access this information. The only special requirement for this evaluation study was to isolate productivity data for the 60 employees enrolled in the PIC classes. A computer programmer who worked in manufacturing engineering helped with this latter analysis.

The evaluation used three basic models. First, participants' reactions were collected using a standard postcourse questionnaire that asked for reactions regarding the instructor, the written materials, the audiovisual materials, relevance to the job, and overall success. Second, the amount participants learned was measured using pre- and posttests, plus a control group consisting of all employees who were tested but did not attend PIC classes. The test that was used, TABE, is widely employed in adult education and possesses outstanding reliability. Its validity for use in a workplace setting is a matter of some debate, but at the time, it was the best instrument available to measure basic reading and math skills. Third, the behavioral and bottom-line results of the program were measured using an interrupted-time-series design, as shown in Figure 3. This longitudinal evaluation technique relies on data collected at regular intervals before, during, and after an intervention such as the PIC classes. In this case, the specific measures tracked were productivity (average daily work output efficiency), scrap costs, and rework costs. All these measures were tracked by manufacturing for its own purposes, so the HRD manager was able to simply tap into this existing data bank and use it to look for monthly changes in these key measures.

**Figure 3. Interrupted-time-series evaluation design. M = measurement (regular intervals); T = treatment (training classes).**

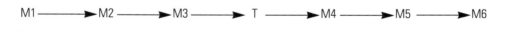

## Training Costs

The costs of providing workplace literacy training fell into two broad categories: direct and indirect. Direct costs included money spent for the assessment, the literacy audit, the instructor's salary, and the computer system. Indirect costs included participants' wages for the two hours a week they attended class on company time; the wages of the management steering committee, which devoted considerable time to the effort; the wages of the HRD manager, who administered and evaluated the project; and miscellaneous costs to duplicate and print flyers, handouts, and other course materials. The total costs are summarized in Table 1.

Of the total cost, the state provided $13,000 (34 percent). Magnavox financed the rest, although its total additional outlay beyond the salaries it would have paid anyway was only $4,000 (10 percent), a very inexpensive investment for the return received.

## Table 1. Costs of the literacy program.

| Type | Item | How calculated | Costs ($) |
|------|------|----------------|-----------|
| Direct | Initial testing | Negotiated fee with college plus test administrator's wages | 415 |
| Direct | Literacy audit | Negotiated fee with consulting firm | 3,500 |
| Direct | Instructor's salary | Hourly salary ($26) times 180 hours plus administrative time | 7,000 |
| Direct | Computer | Purchase price, including software | 6,000 |
| Indirect | Participants' wages | Average hourly wage ($11) times 36 hours times average number of participants per session | 15,840 |
| Indirect | Steering committee's wages | Average hourly wage for management ($23) times estimated number of hours spent (18) times number of committee members (7) | 2,898 |
| Indirect | HRD manager's wages (administration and evaluation) | Hourly wage ($26) times estimated number of hours spent (80) | 2,080 |
| Indirect | Printing and miscellaneous | Charge-backs from internal printing department | 500 |
| **Total costs** | | | **38,233** |

## Analysis and Results

A great deal of data was generated and analyzed in the course of this evaluation study, much of it with the help of computer software. This section describes specific techniques used and the results for each type of data.

### Participants' Reactions

Postcourse reactions of participants were captured on the Course Evaluation Form, which asked participants to rank the class as excellent, good, adequate, or poor, on 21 dimensions. The survey also included three open-ended questions. Students reported satisfaction with the course, the instructor, and the materials used. More than 94 percent felt the class was good or excellent. They especially appreciated the instructor and the on-the-job usefulness of the content.

### Participants' Learning

The amount participants learned in the course was analyzed by means of a paired $t$ test that compared pre- and posttest scores for each participant to determine if the differences between them were greater than what might be expected by chance alone. Reading skills for the 30 students who completed the entire program increased by an average of 1.1 grade levels, from 7.3 to 8.4, a 15 percent improvement. This gain was statistically significant as measured by a paired $t$ test ($t$ = 6.468, $p < .001$). Likewise, mathematical skills improved an average of 1.4 grade levels, from 6.8 to 8.2, a 21 percent gain. This gain was also statistically significant ($t = 3.824$, $p < .001$). The results are shown in Figure 4.

**Figure 4. Pretest and posttest reading and math scores for the 30 employees who completed the workplace literacy program.**

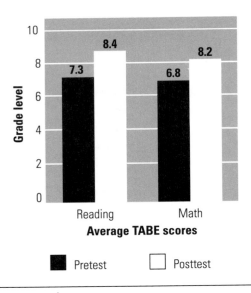

### Behavioral Change

The extent to which participants' on-the-job behavior changed as a result of the PIC classes was measured by examining their monthly average productivity before, during, and after the training. Data for the 60 employees who enrolled in the PIC program were extracted from the company's monthly efficiency reports, which measured each employee's work output efficiency against an ideal standard that had been determined by time-and-motion studies conducted by manufacturing engineers. These data, in essence, measured how long it took each employee to complete each assembly operation. Data were collected by means of scanners connected to a mainframe computer. Every time an employee completed a batch of work, he or she scanned a routing card that entered the assembly operation number, the assembler's name, and the time it took to complete the assembly before sending it on to the next assembly station.

To determine whether significant improvements in productivity had occurred, an analysis of variance (ANOVA) was performed with the help of a computer program on one year's worth of productivity data. The ANOVA compared month-to-month changes in productivity and also pre- and posttraining productivity averages for both the 30 employees who completed training and a control group consisting of the approximately 190 production employees who did not attend training. The average actual efficiency of the 30 employees who completed the program showed steady improvement. Prior to the beginning of the class in June, their average monthly efficiency was .18, or 18 percent of the ideal efficiency for their positions. In the four months after the program started (i.e., June through September), the average monthly efficiency of students rose to .26, or 26 percent of ideal efficiency (see Figure 5). This 44 percent increase, which can be directly attributable to this program, was statistically significant at the $p < .001$ level. For the factory as a whole, productivity rose a scant 5 percent during this period, further strengthening the conclusion that the workplace literacy training had a dramatic, measurable effect on the productivity of employees who attended.

## Bottom-line Results

The extent to which the workplace literacy training saved the company money was examined by tracking monthly scrap and rework costs for a one-year period before, during, and after the training occurred. Additionally, the productivity savings resulting from greater worker efficiency were translated into labor savings.

Scrap and rework data were collected monthly for the entire factory, broken down by type of product (military or commercial), and published as part of the monthly cost-of-quality report. These figures were analyzed for a one-year period beginning several months prior to the

**Figure 5. Average monthly productivity (efficiency rating) in 1991 for the 30 employees who completed the workplace literacy program. Training began in June.**

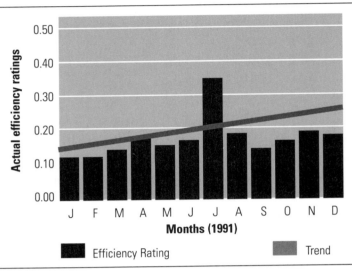

start of PIC classes and continuing three months after they ended. Average monthly scrap and rework figures from before and after the training were compared, and an average monthly savings was calculated by taking the difference. Scrap and rework rates for the company as a whole declined dramatically during the course of the workplace literacy program. As of December 1991, Magnavox had saved $262,000 on scrap costs over 1990, a 35 percent decline, and had saved $74,000 on rework costs, a 25 percent decline (see Figure 6). Although many factors contributed to these savings and it is impossible to isolate exactly how much was attributable to the workplace literacy training, Magnavox estimates that the training may have saved about $2,300 per month in reduced scrap and rework in 1991. This figure represents about 8 percent of the total scrap and rework savings achieved that year. The estimate is based on the following assumptions: About 24 percent of the production workforce attended at least one of the workplace literacy sessions, and about one-third of the scrap and rework savings was achieved through better employee performance (the rest came from better materials, methods, and machinery).

Productivity savings were calculated by multiplying the average percentage improvement in productivity attributable to the training times the average hourly factory wage times the average number of hours

**Figure 6. Monthly scrap and rework costs, 1991. Training began in June.**

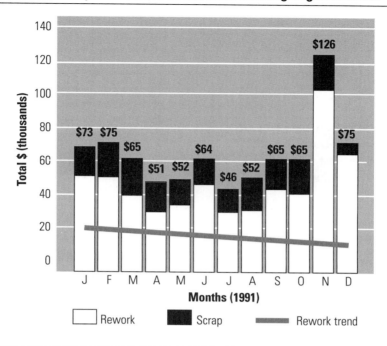

worked per month times the number of employees who completed training (30). This calculation resulted in a conservative estimate of the monthly gross savings in labor costs due to increased worker efficiency. The total monthly labor savings were estimated to be $24,500 in 1991:

| % productivity increase | × | average hourly wage | × | average hours per month | × | number of employees trained | = | monthly labor savings |
|---|---|---|---|---|---|---|---|---|
| 45% | × | $11 | × | 165 | × | 30 | = | $24,503 |

Because lower labor costs reduce the cost to build products, this monthly savings went directly to the bottom line in the form of higher profits.

### Return on Investment

The total return on investment (ROI) from this training is the net benefits of the training (as shown in Table 2), divided by the total cost.

**Table 2. Benefits achieved by training.**

| Benefit type | Total monthly value | Total yearly value |
|---|---|---|
| Reduced scrap and rework | $2,300 | $27,600 |
| Increased productivity | $24,500 | $294,000 |
| Total benefit | $26,800 | $321,600 |

The total cost of the program, including both direct and indirect costs borne by both Magnavox and the State of California, was $38,233. Thus, in the first year after the program concluded, Magnavox received the following benefit-to-cost ratio from workplace literacy training:

$$\frac{\text{total benefit}}{\text{total cost}} = \frac{\$321,600}{\$38,233} = 8.4.$$

Thus, in one year Magnavox reaped benefits more than eight times the total outlay for the training, a truly impressive result. Put another way, the training paid for itself in less than two months. The ROI formula shows a return of 741 percent:

$$\text{ROI} = \frac{\text{net benefits}}{\text{total costs}} = \frac{\$283,367}{\$38,233} = 7.41, \text{ or } 741\%.$$

When one considers that Magnavox's direct cash outlay for the training was only $4,000, the ROI becomes a staggering 7,940 percent. No other investment the company made in capital, facilities, research and development, sales and marketing, or anything else even came close to matching this performance. In fact, for 1991, the West Coast Division reported an overall ROI of about 10 percent (or 0.1), which was extremely good by industry standards.

The evaluation results were presented first to the members of the steering committee, officials from the school district, and the program participants in a public ceremony held to honor those who had completed the entire 18-week program. The results were then presented in written form to the state and federal funders. The widespread dissemination of the evaluation results established Magnavox's workplace literacy classes as a model program, and it was subsequently referenced in a document published by the California State Taskforce on Workplace Literacy (Adult Education Institute for Research and Planning, 1993).

Clearly, investments in workplace literacy, especially for employees who directly build a company's products, can result in higher returns than any other investment a firm makes. This fact should cause manufacturers throughout the United States to invest heavily in the training of their production workforce posthaste, as their foreign competitors have been doing for years.

## Conclusions and Recommendations

Overall, this was a very successful project that achieved outstanding results. Its success was a product of several factors:

- an excellent instructor
- the planning and guidance provided by the steering committee
- the superb advice and consultation provided by Educational Data Systems, the California State Department of Education, and the Torrance Unified School District.

Despite its success, the program could be improved in two ways. First, the dropout rate was higher than Magnavox would have liked (about 50 percent of the participants did not finish). This disappointing result was primarily due to the fact that employees were required to attend half of each class on their own time, by either coming in to work one hour early or staying one hour late. This requirement restricted the initial sign-up to about 24 percent of the eligible workforce and was the main factor cited by students who dropped out prior to completion. To ensure maximum participation, literacy programs should be held entirely on company time. Second, the curriculum development process was more time-consuming and difficult than originally anticipated. Instead of taking two weeks to develop a custom, work-related curriculum, as originally envisioned, the instructor and the steering committee spent the entire 18-week course working on the curriculum. Many hours went into this effort, taxing everyone's schedule. Magnavox now realizes it would be better in the future to budget more time and money for curriculum development, because this was a key element to the success of the program.

If America hopes to remain economically competitive, businesses must take responsibility for workplace literacy. No one else is going to solve this problem for them. To many business leaders this is bad news, because it is not going to be cheap or easy to raise the literacy levels of millions of workers. But what Magnavox discovered is that workplace literacy can be good news, too. By forming partnerships with public education and carefully designing literacy curricula based on the materials used in the workplace, employers can achieve dramatic improvement in literacy skills, which translate into higher quality, productivity, and profitability.

## Questions for Discussion

1. What were the primary factors that led Magnavox to pursue a workplace literacy program?
2. Which implementation strategies were most responsible for the successful results achieved?
3. How did the evaluation of the program highlight the benefits of the training?
4. What specific techniques were employed to collect data and measure the value added by this "soft skills" training?
5. What weaknesses emerged in this training program? What steps might have been taken to avoid them?
6. How could the effect of training on reducing the scrap rate be isolated?

## The Author

Donald J. Ford owns a consulting business specializing in training, vocational education, and human resource management and is training design supervisor for Southern California Gas Company. Ford also teaches graduate courses in human resource development for Antioch University, Southern California. He has 10 years of experience in HRD, having also worked for Magnavox, Texas Instruments, and Allied-Signal. He holds a B.A. and M.A. in history and a Ph.D. in education, all from the University of California, Los Angeles. He has published 30 articles and one book on topics in training, computers, and education, including two articles in *Training & Development*. Ford can be contacted at the following address: Training Education Management, 3950 Atlantic Avenue, Suite 22, Long Beach, CA 90807.

## References

Adult Education Institute for Research and Planning. (1993). *California state plan for workplace literacy.* Sacramento: California State Department of Education.

Fry, E.B. (1977). Fry's readability graph: Clarifications, validity and extension to Level 17. *Journal of Reading, 21,* 21-30.

# Self-Directed Work Teams

## Litton Guidance and Control Systems

Morris Graham, Ken Bishop, and Ron Birdsong

*Self-directed teams have been receiving increased attention recently. The following case tracks the progress of implementing teams at a high-tech manufacturer. The case evolves slowly over time, focusing on a variety of team-building and employee involvement activities. The results achieved are dramatic and show the potential power of the self-directed teams process.*

## Background

Litton's Salt Lake City (Litton SLC) manufacturing plant is one of three plants that make up the Guidance and Control Division of Litton Industries. With approximately 600 employees, the plant assembles, integrates, tests, and delivers the inertial navigation systems required to give extremely accurate guidance to military aircraft and cruise missiles. Assembling and testing gyroscopes and accelerometers is highly labor-intensive, detailed, and quality-sensitive work. It allows very little room for error in the assembly process, and "inspection" simply cannot assure quality and reliability. The product must be built right the first time.

In 1981 Litton SLC had been in operation for approximately 20 years under a traditional top-down management structure. Litton was the world leader in inertial navigation systems and had very little competition. The product line was expanding and the plant was growing in size and employment. An initiative for change came from the plant manager, Larry Frame, who envisioned a vast potential for getting employees responsibly involved in a process of continuous improvement. In early 1981, Frame started an Employee Participation Circle Program, with three circles. By 1982 Litton had 15 circles, but realized that circles were not going to produce the desired quality. This was just another "program," with very little commitment or involvement from midlevel management. These voluntary groups received minimal training and facilitation; their suggestions often received only lip service from management. Basically, members were not able to make responsible decisions about their own work or carry out their own suggestions. Results were marginal.

In late 1983, after convincing the division president to transform circles into teams, Frame started a total employee involvement process that he coined Perfect Teams. Most of the top management team expressed a total commitment to a plantwide imperative that would focus on continuous improvements and redistribute decision making to the lowest levels through teams.

During the next 18 months, more than 100 production, test, and support teams were formed. Everyone in the plant was on one or more teams, which ranged from a senior staff team to manager's teams (which included section managers and supervisors) to employee teams. Litton established weekly team meetings with production and test groups and called these Perfect Build Meetings. The basic intent of the meetings was to improve management-employee communication by discussing quality performance and by getting feedback from employees concerning problems over which they had no control. This evolution allowed for workers' greater participation in decision-making processes.

Part of management's investment was to allocate and dedicate space for teams to meet one hour per week during work time and to organize a small facilitation staff to support the effort. Two experienced facilitators were hired from outside Litton to balance the in-plant personnel. The facilitation staff's responsibility was to get the process started by providing facilitation and training during team meetings. Four rooms were built in the plant for teams to hold their weekly meetings, and each team selected a specific hour and room. A facilitator was assigned to each team to assist with tracking performance, training team members, and implementing the team process.

## The Perfect Teams Rollout

At the outset of Perfect Teams, the senior staff spent considerable time in committees, reviewing policy changes and other suggestions that would give employees the flexibility they needed to be more productive. It was not unusual to see senior staff members on the factory floor or in employee team meetings encouraging change. Questions such as "What is the dumbest thing I asked you to do this week, and how can we change that?" were commonplace.

Functional work groups were formed gradually under the direction of a newly organized team steering council, with the understanding within Litton that this concept and practice were being taken seriously. Employees were grouped into teams of eight to 15, each with a leader and a facilitator and responsible for a well-defined work segment. Each team was asked to work on improvements in its immediate area, on things that were within its control to change and improve. The focus was on quality improvement and reduction in scrap and waste.

Litton management was committed to the teams. In one instance, a supervisor was refusing to form a team in his department. Subsequently his manager called him in and stated: "Litton is teams. If you do not want to participate, then there is no place for you here."

Along with the rollout of teams, Litton's management sustained a "perfect build the first time" philosophy (similar to zero-defects) of continuous quality improvement of products and services. Many people in the organization thought the teams were just another management scheme to have employees think they were in charge of their own work, and that the teams would go the way of quality circles. However, to set the stage for teams to do what was needed to meet constantly changing customer demands, management introduced a fourfold mission statement:

- focus the full intellectual ability of the entire workforce on how to work smarter and more effectively, and harmonize the personal needs of the employees with the strategic needs of the division
- demonstrate that all employees are valued and must be treated with dignity and respect
- encourage improved communications vertically and laterally within and between all directorates and facilities
- reinforce the importance of the highest standards of ethics by building trust and personal accountability.

Employees at Litton SLC were encouraged to constantly grow, develop, and learn. Helping each team member achieve his or her potential became the main role of leadership.

## Early Gains and the Need for Continued Investment

By the end of the first year of implementing functional teams, management had completed a feasibility study on the organization, hired a consultant to assist the implementation, set up an implementation committee, studied leading-edge companies that use teams to establish benchmarks, gathered articles and data on work teams, established a mission and underlying philosophy for its own teams, analyzed the results from the pilot teams, and designed leadership training for functional work groups.

Teams that were already up and running were beginning to demonstrate innovativeness, improvements in productivity and process, lower scrap rates, enhanced communication between employees, and improved relations between departments. Improvements were to be measured objectively by weekly accounting indicators and subjectively by yearly surveys. The surveys would assess each team member's perception of communication, quality, productivity, team work, and management styles, establishing a data base for sorting out responses by teams in the plant and serving as an indicator of change. It was discovered, for instance, that one of the primary sources of employee anxiety was that middle management did not take action and provide feedback on team recommendations. Establishing teams was not enough; management had to follow through on team-established performance expectations to help overcome their own apprehension about whether teams would turn out acceptable work.

Confusion of roles was greatest among those employees not yet trained in the three-day Perfect Teams course (which outlined a vision of the transformation, clarified team roles, and trained employees in needed team skills, such as group communication, problem solving, and self-management). Supervisors and midlevel management manifested more concerns and resistance than did production employees. Team facilitators identified many of the individuals having difficulties in the change process and provided one-on-one counseling and coaching support. A part-time grief psychologist was employed to work with troubled supervisors who were being displaced.

## An Evolution into Self-Directed Work Teams

By 1987 the Salt Lake City facility had sustained 100 percent team involvement for more than two years, averaging 133 teams covering all three shifts. Part of Litton's 1987 survey was conducted by outside consultants, who interviewed 100 team members and provided a trend analysis since 1983. Overall indicators suggested that many of Litton's teams were ready to take on greater responsibility and initiative for their day-to-day activities. A closer examination revealed that the more successful teams were positioned around one or two team members perceived to possess strong leadership abilities. Resistance was considerably less at this stage than during the teams' initial involvement with participative management.

Most teams elected new leaders during this period, and many began rotating leaders as they finished improvement projects. Supervisors remained with their teams but changed roles from team leader to team member. Trust between employees and their immediate supervisors improved as they became equal partners during the team meetings.

Litton began looking at the next steps in team involvement by late 1987. The new focus was on intact, self-directed work structures—teams that would be empowered with the authority to manage their own work—to identify problems and solve them. A self-directed work team (SDWT) committee consisting of senior facilitators and management staff was organized. A primary committee function was to coordinate all SDWT training. Litton's managers and committee members visited and studied companies such as TRW, Tektronix, Motorola, Williams International, and Honeywell.

## The Evolution of Focused Factories

Although there were some periods of slowdown in the Perfect Team process, there was, for the most part, a gradual evolution in improvements. Teams realized that many of their problems were entirely within their control, and they were increasingly able to solve problems outside their own work areas through better communication and the use of hybrid teams, as well. The authority and responsibility for day-to-day decision making were being transferred to the lowest level, and both employees and managers were experiencing the benefits.

A reward system was established. As teams accumulated points for performing certain activities, they became eligible for quarterly recognition dinners and bonuses. At this stage, most teams were organized around members highly committed and accountable to producing observable results.

Members of the SDWT committee, along with key management personalities, began to define how SDWTs were to run the organization. The business became organized around SDWTs that clustered into focused factories (see Figure 1). Each factory produced a specific, independent product. Most teams worked within one factory, although some cut across factory lines.

The SDWT committee selected two pilot focused factories. One was the P-500 product line, which consisted of a stable, well-established, senior workforce that had worked together for more than 10 years. The second, the ring lazer gyro product line, consisted of younger employees who had worked together less than a year. In addition, their costs were over budget. This line was purposely selected to identify how a focused factory would compare with earlier, similar lines that had matured under a traditional management structure. Both lines had approximately 60 members involved from "stock to dock."

**Figure 1. The focused factories concept.**

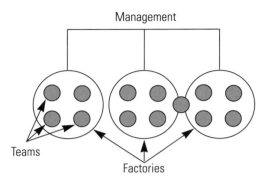

Each product line, or focused factory, had a team coordinator who was selected for possessing experience in the product line and demonstrating a participative management style agreeable to structuring highly committed, tightly formed teams. Coordinators needed the skills to work with a diverse group of associates (i.e., inventory analyst, scheduler, production control worker, stockkeeper, engineer, test technicians, and administrative clerks).

Each focused factory held a weekly "core" meeting at which representatives of the member teams shared information and worked toward solving conflicts and barriers. Core members rotated quarterly. The only permanent members were the coordinator and quality engineer. Issues included production problems as well as social difficulties. In addition, at the focused factory meetings held once a month, the teams reviewed their production standards and their vision of the future state.

The changes at Litton were dramatic, beyond what many people had ever envisioned the company doing. As one core group member said, "It's like a learning laboratory, and we are all active contributors."

## The Training Investment

By 1984 every employee had received three days of off-site training and had been integrated into a team. Supervisors attended a 24-hour workshop on conducting effective meetings, problem solving, communications, generating ideas, and group dynamics. After the completion of this leader training, supervisors formed their own teams. Each team met weekly, and for the first eight weeks the facilitation staff provided training during the meetings. The problem-solving methods the supervisors learned in leader training were then taught to the teams. As the

Perfect Teams evolved into more self-directed work groups, additional training was added.

In 1985 and 1986, leadership training was provided to all levels of management and to most of the workforce. The trainers—senior internal consultants hired at the division level—focused on effective delegation, communication and management style, conflict resolution, and team building. This type of training, along with the successes teams were experiencing, began to make managers' jobs easier. More and more managers began to realize the value of the team process, a change reflected in their visibility at team meetings and also on the factory floor. They brought many of their problems to their teams for help.

After most employees had completed the 24-hour leadership training course, Litton facilitators recognized the need for ongoing training. The results of an anonymous plantwide survey made it apparent that there was a need for interpersonal skills training at all levels. There was an admitted lack of trust in some managers who were not willing to "let go" in order to empower other employees. Most people felt that communication had improved but that there were still barriers to overcome. Some responses indicated that teams felt they were directly responsible for saving the company money, but they saw nothing in it for themselves. They did not think this was fair. Levels of participation seem to be directly related to the amount of ownership perceived by team members.

In response to this survey, the next session of training was a 12-hour team-building course developed by the facilitators with assistance from an outside consultant. The training was conducted off site during company time, and after nearly two years all employees in the plant had participated. The focus was on improving team dynamics. There were modules on communications, motivation, perception, and building trust, plus several problem-solving exercises for large and small groups. This time, upper management trained alongside other employees, rather than having their training separately. According to evaluations following each training session, one of the most meaningful parts of the training was a four-hour forum during which employees could ask questions (many controversial) and talk about their needs.

Teams responded favorably as the modules were reinforced in their team meetings. Group dynamics improved, and so did the flow of ideas. Two five-hour training modules were developed to strengthen team participation and ownership: One was on assertiveness and listening skills, the other on creative problem solving.

The next training implemented was a two-day session designed to cluster teams into focused factories. As of December 1989, more than 50 percent of Litton's employees had received the additional assertiveness and creative problem-solving training and the crosstraining needed for the focused factories. Since 1984 every employee had received more than 70 training hours. This training represented a continuous commitment and effort to improve skills in working together, gathering new ideas, and implementing changes that added value to the product and to the people.

From 1990 to 1993, the scope of skills training was broadened as employees took on more of the day-to-day responsibilities of running their own areas. Production teams spent considerable time learning Litton's business system (i.e., material procurement and control, scheduling, and cost)—knowledge of which had previously been confined to the support groups. For example, Annual Move Safe and safety classes became mandatory for every employee. Litton's training department developed an extensive library of training videos for individual and team use. In addition, the training department worked with teams to create their own videos, which were shared with the entire plant.

Team facilitators attended local and national workshops and seminars on work teams and socio-technical systems. All information gatherers met twice each week for one to three hours in a cross-functional team to share perceptions of self-directed, autonomous structures. This cross-functional team discussed, analyzed, and critiqued advantages and disadvantages of various structures in search of the next steps in the development of SDWTs.

## Total Quality Management and Q-Maps

By the beginning of 1991 Litton SLC had become an acknowledged leader in implementing high-performance work systems; however, the organization was sailing into turbulent seas. The summer of 1991 was not a good time to be involved in the defense industry. Although the country was still feeling the euphoria of the Gulf War, détente and a large government deficit were combining to create cutbacks in defense spending. In addition, the military was shifting from traditional cost-plus contracts to fixed-cost contracts. The changing environment worried firms involved in defense. Many observers felt that an industry shakeout was about to occur and would leave only the most efficient firms to compete in this arena.

One of Litton management's responses to this turbulent environment was to implement a reward system based on total quality management (TQM). Factories would be rewarded based on levels of production of good-quality parts. The change to a TQM-based reward system in the plant also served as a motivator to develop a measure of the effectiveness of support groups. Litton had approximately 20 support groups ranging from shipping and receiving to human resources. The effectiveness of these support teams was difficult to measure, because they did not produce a quantifiable output.

To date, no measures with which support teams felt comfortable in tracking their own performance had been developed. This was a critical TQM-implementation problem that facilitators faced. The solution to this problem was identified with Q-Map, a software product designed by Pacesetter Software to increase communication between support groups and customers and to measure the effectiveness of the support offered.

The Q-Map process starts by having the support group and the customer group meet separately to determine their individual mission statements. They then determine the major services currently offered by the support group, and both groups rank these services as to their importance to the customer group and the effectiveness of the support group in offering them. From these responses a "talking paper" that compares the responses of the support and customer groups is developed.

Representatives of the two groups are brought together to discuss the differences in their perceptions of the need for and quality of support-group services. In addition, the customer group presents a list of services that they feel would assist them, but that they currently do not receive. Ideally, discussion helps the support and customer groups to arrive at a consensus—of which services should be offered and what the priorities were.

The next step is to get a series of quantifiable measurements to determine the effectiveness of the service delivery system. Q-Map maintains a data base that tracks these measures over time and produces a series of graphs and charts. A cross-plant implementation was established by late 1991.

The agenda for most team meetings was to review the previous week's performance at the start of the meeting. All teams developed their own matrices to measure output, and they kept daily performance charts visible in their work areas. These charts were important, because they allowed team members to know what was expected of them from a business standpoint and whether they were performing to expectations. The charts also created an atmosphere for setting goals toward constant improvement. As teams reached their goals, a winning situation was created. Team members achieved their own personal best, and Litton's recognition system rewarded them for their efforts.

By 1993 focused factories had become the overarching framework for teams to realize improved quality and productivity. Each focused factory had developed a TQM system to measure quality, customer satisfaction, cost, schedule, and scrap. These data were shared monthly with all employees and were also reviewed each month at the division level with the vice-president of operations.

Statistical process control (SPC) was added to the training program for employees in Litton's focused factories. Litton has always looked at data on final yields and at nominal data points throughout the flow. With SPC, however, teams looked at the processes in the flow that have never been monitored before. As a result of tightening these processes, the final yields began to improve.

With a process control in use, each subassembly is built in small quantities until it has been used successfully in the next assembly. This control limits the work-in-process in the event that the subassembly has a problem that cannot be detected at its own level. Putting all the parts on the assembly floor makes the production personnel as well as the material and production control planner responsible for inventory control. This effort, developed by teams, eliminated several steps involved in staging and storeroom operations and ultimately eliminated considerable waste.

## Eliminating Waste

Of special concern from the outset was eliminating waste in all areas of the Litton SLC plant. In 1982 the scrap rate was over $1 million per month; by 1992 it was a little more than $0.5 million for the entire year. Before teams were formed, management was the total driving force behind waste or scrap elimination. Management focus was usually on tangible, "high dollar" scrap issues, not on the day-to-day issues of waste that teams began to deal with (e.g., process changes, paperwork elimination or streamlining, faster and better assembly methods, better layout of work areas for greater efficiency, and design).

Teams began making presentations to management on the changes the teams had made (or were requesting to make), and management's response was positive. The number of presentations rose from 11 in 1984 to an average of more than 45 per year from 1986 to 1993. Many of the changes were intangible and hard to measure, but others, such as the elimination of steps in a build process, were very measurable. All contributed to a better, more efficient factory.

Teams also began to implement systems that would help other teams eliminate waste. Innovative ideas on identifying and tracking waste began coming in from engineering and other support teams. Hybrid teams were formed to deal with specific problems that crossed departmental and vendor boundaries. In one instance, in an attempt to identify the cause of a particular parts problem, the quality engineering team came up with the idea of videotaping the part and sending the videotape to the vendor. Using a special microscope adapter, the engineer was able to point out the problem while narrating. This system eliminated lengthy, time-consuming correspondence and phone calls, and created a much faster response time from vendors.

## Productivity Improvements

Productivity improvements have occurred in every product line in the plant. Litton's measure of productivity is labor realization—that is, the comparison of hours spent to produce a product versus an industrial engineering standard of what it should take to produce that standard. The labor realization formula is shown in Figure 2.

### Figure 2. Labor realization formula.

Labor realization simplified is calculated as follows:

$$\frac{\text{standard cost of each assembly}}{\text{actual cost of each assembly}}$$

- The standard includes the cost of hours to assemble, as well as the cost of materials, scrap, and rework. These are estimates established by measuring actual assembly (usually done by an engineer).
- Actual costs include the total number of hours used, including hours for rework, and the actual cost of materials and scrap.
- Totals are added and averaged to arrive at the actual cost.
- Dividing actual cost into a set standard allows an ongoing evaluation of productivity.

Data from several work units are used to develop a baseline performance standard. Litton compares actual performance against the standard of performance to arrive at a percentage of improvement. The improvement can be expressed in hours, or multiplied by the cost per hour (burdened labor rate) to be translated into a dollar value. To provide a constant standard for comparison, assembly or test standards are not revised once they are established. Some product lines have a much higher labor realization than others, so in addition to calculating a total labor realization, Litton SLC tracks each product line separately. Real-time data on scrap, rework, and cost to manufacture an assembly are tracked. This system tells management when efficiency is going up, even if sales of the product are declining. If realization reaches a new high, the product is being produced with higher quality and productivity than in the past.

Between 1980 and 1984, the total plant realization averaged 77 percent. As teams started up and suggestions were implemented, the total plant realization started to increase. This improvement is shown in Figure 3. Note that after 1985, when organization into Perfect Teams became widespread, labor realization showed significant gains. Over the five-year period from 1985 through 1989, total plant realization increased from 77 percent to 96 percent. And from 1989 to 1993, the plant realization increased from 96 percent to 123 percent. This equates to a 46 percent increase in productivity since 1985, directly attributable to teams. Most of the improvement occurred from 1989 to 1993. As Litton rejuvenated its process by changing from Perfect Teams to focused factories, the plant went from a 19 percent to a 27 percent gain.

**Figure 3. Labor realization at Litton's Salt Lake City facility, plant total for 1981 through 1993.**

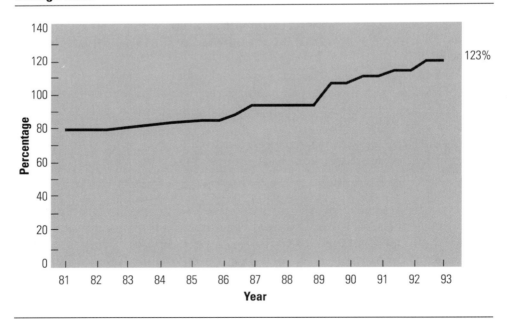

So, what really happened? Several things did: Operations in the assembly flow that were not adding value to the product were removed, tooling and test equipment was improved, methods of building and testing were made easier, inspection in areas that showed a low ratio of defects was reduced, and designs were changed for easier build.

## Quality Improvement

As previously mentioned, Litton's focus from the beginning has been on quality improvements. One good measure of quality in the manufacturing industry is reduction in scrap. Results, including scrap rates, for all product areas in the plant are measured and logged into the computer. All teams have bar-coded access to computers to get almost immediate feedback on results. Corrections are made daily. Program reviews for each focused factory come every three months. At each review, teams go over performance charts, problems, successes, and future goals.

From the middle of 1985 through 1993, Litton teams reduced waste from 16 percent to 7 percent, as shown in Figure 4. As in the case of labor realization, significant improvement occurred after the Perfect Team concept was implemented. The improvement in waste is directly attributable to improved yields at all levels of Litton's product. "Doing it right the first time" is more than just a saying in the plant; it is a philosophy Litton employees take seriously.

**Figure 4. Percentage scrap at Litton's Salt Lake City facility, plant total for 1981 through 1993.**

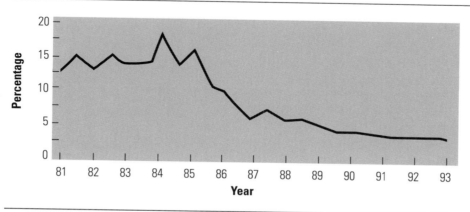

## Improved Competitive Position

As a result of these improvements, Litton has dramatically reduced its cost and, therefore, the price of products. This puts the company in a much more competitive position. The magnitude of the improvement is clear in the "dollarized" savings per year for both productivity improvement and scrap reduction. The labor realization savings increased yearly from slightly over $3 million in 1985 to more than $10 million in 1989. The total savings in productivity improvements over this five-year period was over $40 million. The total dollars saved in scrap reduction from 1984 to 1989 was over $10 million.

The clustering of SDWTs into focused factories from 1989 to 1993 demonstrated remarkable results, with labor realization climbing to 123 percent. All this happened during a period of cuts in defense spending.

## Intangible Results

The intangible results were challenging to measure. However, here are a few examples from the white-collar areas:

- Communication between the engineering groups and line personnel improved. Manufacturing and Quality Engineering spent a large amount of energy simplifying and clarifying assembly instructions, as well as showing line workers how their piece of the build fits into the whole picture. Assemblers now know their workmanship affects the end product.
- The Finance Department simplified the reporting system and trained line personnel so they know exactly how to figure their cost on a monthly basis.
- Production Control, Scheduling, and Material Control reduced their reporting system, resulting in fewer parts shortages. The assembly lines now have better visibility and understanding of the procurement system and know ahead of time what to expect.
- Many support teams created manuals of "How I Do My Job." These manuals help standardize methods and are aids for crosstraining.

The most noticeable improvement for the plant as a whole is in attitude. According to the most recent survey, there has been a significant improvement in communication both horizontally and vertically. People trust each other more, and there is a feeling of shared leadership. Employees indicate that they are happier when coming to work than they used to be. They now have ownership in and feel they have a direct influence over the destiny of the plant.

Litton's employees are more valuable than their competitors' employees. They are better trained (the average employee in 1993 received almost 100 hours of skills and interpersonal training), they understand the requirements of their jobs more thoroughly, and they are better able to respond to abnormal situations and change.

## Costs

Litton tracked the cost of the team process throughout its implementation period. Cost tracking and tabulations were comprehensive. The costs included the following:

- salaries of facilitators-trainers
- total hours for team activity, including
  —training hours
  —meeting hours
  —celebration hours (for recognition and reward)
- team room costs, including
  —cost of floor space
  —remodeling costs
  —furnishing costs
- recognition and reward costs
- miscellaneous costs.

The total cost for the program was rounded to $1 million.

## Return on Investment

Every year Litton examines the total savings in quality and productivity improvements and compares these savings with the costs of the team process. To determine the specific savings related to the team process, two steps are taken. First, when the results are tabulated, management reviews all the variables that could have influenced those results, excluding the team process. Any savings that can be accounted for by other variables, such as technology, are factored out. Second, because management wants to take a conservative approach, 40 percent of the remaining savings is removed to account for unknown factors that might have affected savings. Collectively, these two steps isolate the impact of the SDWT team process on the bottom-line results.

To calculate the return on investment (ROI), Litton took the value at one point in time after the reorganization into focused factories was well under way. The savings, after adjustments and the 60 percent factor, were $7.5 million. At that time, $1 million in costs had been invested. These figures yield a benefit-to-cost ratio of 7.5 to 1 and the following ROI:

$$\text{ROI} = \frac{\text{net benefit}}{\text{program costs}} = \frac{\$6,500,000}{\$1,000,000} = 650\%.$$

For every dollar invested, there was a net return of $6.50.

## Conclusions

Litton is extremely proud of the quality and productivity improvements that have occurred at the Salt Lake City plant over the past seven years:

- Fourteen focused factories were created, and layers of management went from seven to four.
- The benefit-to-cost ratio for the program was 7.5 to 1.
- The ROI was 650 percent.
- Productivity went up 45 percent.
- The scrap rate was reduced more than 50 percent (down from 16 percent to 7 percent).
- Total plant labor realization increased from 77 percent to 123 percent.
- Reduced costs saved the company millions of dollars.
- Quality improvements resulted in fewer rejects.
- Process innovations by employees increased.
- Communication was improved.
- Customer satisfaction was improved.
- Litton made the federal government's "Preferred List" (realizing the highest quality standards, entitling Litton SLC to go from a 100 percent inspection mode to an audit and process mode).

Litton SLC has dramatically reduced its cost and, therefore, the price of its product through dramatic increase in productivity and equally satisfying reduction in scrap. Clearly, the plant is in a much more competitive position.

Currently the Salt Lake City facility is recognized as a totally self-directed culture comprising mini-factory structures that are positioned and empowered to provide the highest quality products at competitive prices. The plant has achieved significant gains in productivity, innovations, and reductions in scrap rate and rework through the SDWT imperative. The Department of Defense has singled out Litton SLC as a showcase in participative work structures from which other defense contractors can learn. Total participation in SDWTs has become a reality. As one employee put it, "The honeymoon is over, the total responsibility of a self-managed family is before us, and we won't go back to being a bunch of kids vying for their own things."

The majority of employees in Litton's SLC plant, managers and employees alike, are open to change and improvement. No one shoots the messenger. All feedback is valuable. Teams are questioning everything they do, looking for a better way, and they are getting management support for the changes they propose. Managers are a resource to the teams, removing barriers, providing tools, accessing information for the teams, and asking, "What do you need?" and "What can I do?" By sharing leadership, teams have become responsible for leading and coordinating efforts in operations, training, safety, maintenance, scheduling, personnel, communication and information, and quality. Teams are constantly finding new ways to improve the work processes.

The strong commitment from top leadership contributed significantly to the growth of total employee involvement in the Salt Lake City plant. In the fall of 1987, Frame left the plant to become division president, and the new plant manager, John Ossowski, and his staff became even more involved in encouraging change—especially in eliminating waste. Their leadership philosophy, as stated in their staff team mission statement, was "to provide resources, leadership, and an environment in which all Salt Lake City employees can participate and develop to their full potential to achieve the highest standards of quality, productivity, and customer satisfaction."

The marketplace has changed significantly since 1981, when Litton began implementing work teams. Litton faced some tough competition. Using the Perfect Team concept as a base, Litton SLC has constantly improved the quality, productivity, and customer satisfaction in every area of the plant. Knowing the work of continuous improvement is never-ending, Litton SLC has continued to lead the industry, has realized a tremendous return on its investment in high-performance teams, and has taken giant strides toward excellence in manufacturing.

## Questions for Discussion

1. Two leaders who championed teams plantwide were plant managers, Larry Frame and John Ossowski. Why do you think most of the initial resistance came from their own management staff rather than the workers on the floor?

2. Why do you think Litton's implementation of self-directed work teams took several years before a return on investment was obvious?

3. Why would the first several years of this kind of transformation be both a very exciting and a very frustrating time for people?

4. Teams do not become high-performance teams just because we call them teams or send them through training. Explain why a plant that

manufactures inertial navigational systems for the military could realize such remarkable results through teams.

5. Team members at Litton needed training in work-team awareness, technical skills, interpersonal skills, problem solving, and administrative procedures. They continue to need training as their teams mature. Do you feel there is a point at which a team has arrived and the training investment can be significantly reduced? Explain.

6. As a consultant to Litton SLC at this date, what areas would you look into that might need strengthening? Support your reasoning.

7. The results achieved from this process developed over a long time. What other approaches would you suggest to isolate the effects of the human resource development process from other factors?

## The Authors

Morris Graham is currently a professor of organizational psychology at Brigham Young University-Hawaii. As a consultant both in the United States and abroad, he has helped organizations realize the power and potential of high-performance work systems. He worked with Litton Salt Lake City over several years to develop self-directed work teams. Graham can be contacted at the following address: Brigham Young University-Hawaii, Social Sciences, Laie, HI 96762.

Ken Bishop is currently the senior facilitator of teams and training at Litton Guidance and Control Systems, Salt Lake City. He has been with Litton for 23 years in various test, supervision, and management positions. He began employee involvement efforts as a quality circle member in 1981 and has worked in team facilitation since 1983. He has helped establish team networks in several companies in the United States and Canada.

Ron Birdsong is superintendent of production at Litton Guidance and Control Systems, Salt Lake City. He began his career at Litton 29 years ago in design engineering at the plant in Woodland Hills, California, and has since held several management positions in both manufacturing and systems test operations. He previously served as manager of employee training and development for two years.

# Unstructured versus Structured On-the-Job Training

## Midwest Automotive Plant

Ronald L. Jacobs

*On-the-job training (OJT) has grown in importance in recent years. The following case shows the comparison of a structured OJT program with an unstructured process. Intuitively, we usually conclude that structured OJT has greater efficiency and a greater influence on the quality of the work than unstructured OJT. This case reaches those two conclusions with supporting data using a forecasted financial benefits model. Although this case does not illustrate a typical return-on-investment analysis, it shows that there is a payoff for investing in structured OJT. At the request of the organization, some specific data have been withheld.*

## Background

Learning on the job has been the subject of increased interest among managers and human resource development (HRD) professionals in the past decade or so. Interest in this topic is part of the broader recognition that employees learn most of what they know and can do in the workplace while actually doing their jobs, rather than in off-site training classrooms. Unfortunately most of this learning is the result of training that is unplanned (i.e., unstructured), which more often than not leads to undesirable outcomes for the individuals and organizations involved. It is under these circumstances that structured on-the-job training (OJT) has emerged as a distinct training approach, a development that has provided the impetus for the financial forecasting case study presented in this chapter.

*All names, dates, places, and organizations have been disguised at the request of the case author or organization.*

## Structured OJT and Financial Forecasting

Increasingly, managers have sought to formalize the training that naturally occurs among employees in their work areas. The issue of most concern has been that this training has lacked the necessary planning, or structure, to produce reliable training outcomes. As a result, structured OJT has emerged as a distinct form of training in many organizations. Structured OJT is defined as the system approach of developing job expertise by having novices learn directly from experts in the workplace (Jacobs, 1992; Jacobs and Jones, 1994). When OJT is approached in this way, learning on the job ceases to be an opportunistic activity, undertaken by individuals who learn merely by watching other people or by doing tasks alone without any formal guidance. Instead, learning on the job becomes intentional and purposeful.

As do all planned training efforts, structured OJT frequently incurs substantial costs for its design and implementation. When allocating scarce resources, even managers who recognize the desirability of using structured training approaches may rightly question whether the cost of structured OJT is warranted. After all, most employees learn their jobs using informal means anyway, and this unstructured training approach does not involve any costs. Thus, the issue for many managers is basically financial. Compared with unstructured OJT, is structured OJT really a "good deal" from a financial perspective?

The case study presented here addresses this basic question by using a model for comparing the forecasted financial benefits of HRD program options (Swanson and Gradous, 1988). As shown in Figure 1, the model proposes that, to compare the financial benefits of unstructured and structured OJT, cost must be subtracted from performance value to obtain the financial benefit. Performance value is the financial worth of the work being produced using a particular HRD program option. Cost is an accounting of the expenses required to produce and deliver that HRD option, such as labor, materials, consultants, and equipment. Benefit is the extent of the financial contribution to the work produced, given the costs to achieve the performance.

In the model, unstructured and structured OJT are presented as distinct training approaches and should have different performance values and costs associated with their use. The financial forecasting model should show whether the differences in performance value and cost result in meaningful differences in financial benefits. Thus, the model can show a link between the two training approaches and the performance outcomes that result from their use.

**Figure 1. Financial forecasting model (adapted from Swanson and Gradous, 1988).**

| Unstructured on-the-job training | Structured on-the-job training |
|---|---|
| Performance value<br>− Cost<br>───────<br>Benefits | Performance value<br>− Cost<br>───────<br>Benefits |

## Case Setting

The following case presents the results of using the financial fore-casting model to address two issues important to organizations: train-ing efficiency and product quality. Both parts of the case were con-ducted in the same facility, a large truck assembly plant in the Midwest, and were undertaken to help senior management and staff determine the effects of using the current training approach (unstructured OJT) and the anticipated effects of the new training approach (structured OJT) that was about to be implemented plantwide. Where possible, completed worksheets are provided to show the calculations used to derive the results. Some of the calculations have been removed at the request of the organization.

## Training Efficiency

The purpose of this first part of the case is to compare the train-ing efficiency of unstructured and structured OJT. Portions of this part of the case have been reported earlier in the literature (Jacobs, Jones, and Neil, 1992).

Training efficiency is defined as the rate at which novice employ-ees learn new tasks to the extent that those employees can do those tasks without assistance after the training. Those employees might not be considered experts at the tasks, but they at least would possess suffi-cient mastery to handle most situations by themselves. Managers desire higher training efficiency because this capability allows employees to make more valuable contributions sooner. In a sense, training efficien-cy can be equated to the production concept of cycle time.

### Level of Analysis and Variables

The level of analysis of the case is the task level. In this organization, many distinct tasks are performed by production employees within the many assembly work areas. Given that the organization has an active total quality management program, tasks within each work area can vary from maintaining production charts, to doing the actual assembly work, to performing basic equipment maintenance and housekeeping tasks. Approximately 40 tasks were initially identified as tasks that could be considered unique to their respective work areas and that employees would likely require training in as they entered those work areas.

Three tasks were ultimately selected on the basis of the level of two variables: work-area turnover and task difficulty. A mix of these variables was considered desirable for the case study. Turnover was the total number of production employees who had entered the work area in which the task was performed, during the previous year. Task difficulty was the estimated time to master the task using unstructured and structured OJT. Time estimates were determined through a series of observations and interviews. All data were approved by senior plant officials before the case study proceeded.

Table 1 presents the turnover rates and task difficulties for the three tasks selected in the case study. Subsequent analyses have confirmed the forecasted time estimates for using structured OJT.

## Results

Table 2 presents the Performance Value Worksheet for Task 1. (The Performance Value Worksheets of the other tasks cannot be shown.) The performance goal represents the average number of times per day that the task was repeated during the period of analysis. The dollar value per repetition represents the wages and fringe benefits required to accomplish one repetition of the task. The estimated time to master the task was determined for unstructured and structured OJT. As stated, turnover is the total number of employees who had entered the work area during the period of analysis. With these figures, the total performance gain was calculated for each option.

**Table 1. Turnover rate and task difficulty for the three tasks studied.**

| | | Task difficulty (days to reach mastery) | |
| Task | Turnover rate | Unstructured on-the-job training | Structured on-the-job training |
| --- | --- | --- | --- |
| 1 | 25 | 5 | 1 |
| 2 | 5 | 10 | 2 |
| 3 | 7 | 5 | 1 |

**Table 2. Performance value worksheet for Task 1.**

| Component | Unstructured on-the-job training | Structured on-the-job training |
|---|---|---|
| a. Performance goal | 34 reps/day | 34 reps/day |
| b. Beginning performance level | 0 | 0 |
| c. Value per repetition | $8.40 | $8.40 |
| d. Time to reach mastery | 5 days | 1 day |
| e. Longest time to reach mastery | 5 days | 5 days |
| f. Turnover rate | 25 employees/year | 25 employees/year |
| g. Average learning rate during longest time to reach mastery    $(a \div 2)$ | 17 reps/days | 17 reps/days |
| h. Number of repetitions during the time to reach mastery    $(g \times d)$ | 85 | 17 |
| i. Number of repetitions during the longest time to reach mastery    $(g[d - e] + [g \times e])$ | 85 | 153 |
| j. Performance value during longest time to reach mastery    $(i \times c)$ | $714.00 | $1,285.20 |
| k. Performance value per employee    $(j - [b \times c \times e])$ | $714.00 | $1,285.20 |
| l. **Total performance value $(k \times f)$** | **$17,850.000** | **$32,130.00** |

Table 3 presents the cost breakdown for unstructured and structured OJT for Task 1. For example, structured OJT incurred costs to analyze the task, develop the training guide, prepare the experts as structured OJT trainers, hire an external consultant to deliver the trainer training, and conduct the performance follow-up. The total cost associated with the use of one structured OJT module was calculated as $976. In contrast, unstructured OJT had no costs associated with it. This may seem odd at first, but one must consider that most unstructured OJT occurs in the workplace, without any intentional commitment of organizational resources. In a sense, the costs associated with unstructured OJT are actually represented in the performance value side of the equation.

Table 4 presents the financial benefits forecasted for each of the three tasks. The results showed that structured OJT was five times more efficient than unstructured OJT. That is, trainees were predicted to learn the tasks five times faster using structured OJT. In addition, the financial benefits of structured OJT were forecasted to be approximately twice the

**Table 3. Cost analysis for Task 1.**

| Cost category | Unstructured on-the-job training ($) | Structured on-the-job training ($) |
|---|---|---|
| Task analysis | 0 | 270 |
| Training guide development | 0 | 216 |
| Train-the-trainer costs | 0 | 303 |
| Consultant costs | 0 | 118 |
| Material costs | 0 | 15 |
| Performance follow-up | 0 | 54 |
| **Total** | **0** | **976** |

benefits for unstructured OJT. Finally, the results showed that turnover rate affected the financial benefits more than task difficulty did.

It can be concluded that structured OJT provides greater training efficiency than unstructured OJT, and that the greater efficiency brings about higher forecasted financial benefits. However, the financial advantages are not at the same proportion as the training efficiency advantages.

## Product Quality

The purpose of the second part of the case is to compare unstructured and structured OJT in terms of product quality. Product quality is defined as the outcomes achieved from doing a task. Product quality is a function of several personal and environmental variables, such as having the proper tools, resources, standards, and feedback. Product quality can also be a function of the level of knowledge and skills that employees possess (Gilbert, 1978). Thus, in a relative sense, if employees have more expertise—often achieved through more effective training programs—then they can be expected to produce better results.

### Task and Product Defect

Task 2 was selected for analysis in this section of the case. The nature of this task cannot be identified in specific terms, but it can be stated that the task requires the installation of a specific part on all trucks. When the part is not installed properly, a noticeable problem will occur, and this problem can be detected only after the assembly process has been fully completed. If a problem is detected, the part must be removed and then reinstalled to meet the inspection criteria.

**Table 4. Summary of forecasted financial benefits for the three tasks studied (in dollars).**

| Financial component | Unstructured on-the-job training | Structured on-the-job training |
|---|---|---|
| **Task 1** | | |
| Performance value | 17,850.00 | 32,130.00 |
| Cost | − 0.00 | − 976.00 |
| Benefit | 17,850.00 | 31,154.00 |
| | | |
| **Task 2** | | |
| Performance value | 3,327.00 | 6,702.25 |
| Cost | − 0.00 | − 976.00 |
| Benefit | 3,327.00 | 5,726.25 |
| | | |
| **Task 3** | | |
| Performance value | 9,877.00 | 18,766.30 |
| Cost | − 0.00 | − 976.00 |
| Benefit | 9,877.00 | 17,790.30 |

Because of rework costs, reducing the number of defects is a high priority for management. The average cost of reworking this defect before it leaves the plant was determined to be $250. This figure included time for inspection, troubleshooting, and reinstallation of the part. If the defect should go undetected before customer delivery, and the truck is delivered to a dealer, then the rework cost would likely be higher. In this situation, the dealer would perform the rework and then charge back the costs to the organization at a much higher labor rate. These cost considerations are minimal compared with the frustration and additional costs that customers incur as a result of rework after delivery.

A performance analysis was conducted to identify the most probable cause of the product defect. This analysis was critical because, in order to do a true comparison between unstructured and structured OJT, a lack of knowledge and skills had to be identified as the most likely reason the defect occurs. The performance analysis confirmed that no other cause, such as lack of tools, standards, or feedback, could cause this product-defect problem.

## Results

At the request of the organization, the completed Performance Value Worksheet for this task cannot be shown; however, table 5 presents sufficient information for understanding the performance value. The task was done an average of 34 times per day for approximately 200 workdays per year, for a total of 6,800 repetitions of the task per year. The average defect rate using unstructured OJT was reported to be an average of three defects per week, or 120 per year. The use of structured OJT resulted in no more than an average of one defect per week.

The performance value for using unstructured OJT was calculated to be $30,000 in rework costs; there was no cost for the unstructured OJT. The performance value for using structured OJT was calculated to be $10,000 in rework costs; the cost of the structured OJT was calculated as the same amount shown in the first case study, $976. As shown in Table 6, the financial burden for using unstructured OJT was $30,000. The financial burden for using structured OJT was $10,976 ($10,000 for the rework plus $976 for the structured OJT). Thus, the results show that by reducing the defect rate from an average of three defects per week to one defect per week, structured OJT substantially reduced the financial burden to the organization. In fact, analyses conducted after the case study show that the defect rate has been reduced to an average of slightly below one per week. The average cost of doing the rework has also been reduced.

It can be concluded that by using structured OJT to train employees to do this task, the organization can reduce defects, thereby

## Table 5. Summary of performance value for Task 2.

| Measure | Amount |
| --- | --- |
| Present defect rate using unstructured on-the-job training | 3 defects per week (120 defects per year) |
| Desired defect rate using structured on-the-job training | 1 defect per week (40 defects per year) |
| Average cost of rework | $250 |
| Performance value of unstructured on-the-job training | $30,000 |
| Performance value of structured on-the-job training | $10,000 |

## Table 6. Financial burden in product quality for Task 2 (in dollars).

| Financial component | Unstructured on-the-job training | Structured on-the-job training |
|---|---|---|
| Performance value | 30,000 | 10,000 |
| Cost | 0 | 976 |
| Burden | 30,000 | 10,976 |

increasing product quality. The financial benefits can be calculated in terms of the amount of money the organization does not have to pay out to fix the defects.

## Implications

The results suggest that the financial desirability of using structured OJT rather than unstructured OJT for the tasks presented is unequivocal. Although unstructured OJT incurred no apparent costs to the organization, this training approach resulted in less training efficiency and lower product quality, compared with structured OJT. Structured OJT required a sizable investment up front, but carried with it the promise of future financial benefits that were substantially higher than the costs.

The ability to generalize these results to other tasks and organizations is necessarily limited. Obviously, more case studies covering a wider range of tasks and organizational settings are required. Yet the relationships shown here may exist in most other situations, as well. If unstructured and structured forms of HRD interventions are compared, then the performance value of the structured training approach will likely be greater than the value of the unstructured training approach. The question remains whether the costs to achieve the structured training option are sufficiently low to make the investment a good deal. Obviously, performance value and cost will differ across situations, requiring that the relationships be tested for each new situation.

## Questions for Discussion

1. Under what conditions might the financial analysis show that unstructured OJT is preferable to structured OJT?
2. At what point in the planning stage can generalizations begin to be made about the costs and performance values of certain HRD program options?

3. Which individuals are responsible for using forecasted financial benefits to make selection decisions in organizations?

4. How do the forecasted financial benefits of structured OJT compare with off-the-job training options, such as classroom-based training?

5. Are there ways of reducing the costs of structured OJT in order to increase the benefits of this training approach, without reducing its effectiveness? Explain.

6. Are there nonfinancial issues involved in the selection of structured versus unstructured OJT? Explain.

## The Author

Ronald L. Jacobs is associate professor of human resource development at the Ohio State University. In the past 10 years, Jacobs has helped implement structured on-the-job training in a variety of organizations, including manufacturers, service providers, and government agencies. This case study is part of a larger ongoing research effort to study the financial implications of workplace learning. Jacobs is a frequent contributor to the human resource development literature and presently serves as associate editor for *Human Resource Development Quarterly*. Jacobs can be contacted at the following address: The Ohio State University, Graduate Program in Human Resource Development, 325 Ramseyer Hall, Columbus, OH 43210.

## References

Gilbert, T.F. (1978). *Human competence: Engineering worthy performance*. New York: McGraw-Hill.

Jacobs, R. (1992). Structured on-the-job training. In H.D. Stolovitch and E.J. Keeps (eds.), *Handbook of human performance technology*. San Francisco: Jossey-Bass.

Jacobs, R., and Jones, M. (1994). *Structured OJT: Developing expertise in the workplace*. San Francisco: Berrett-Koehler.

Jacobs, R., Jones, M., and Neil, S. (1992). A case study in forecasting the financial benefits of unstructured and structured on-the-job training. *Human Resource Development Quarterly*, *3*, 133-139.

Swanson, R.A., and Gradous, D.B. (1988). *Forecasting financial benefits of human resource development*. San Francisco: Jossey-Bass.

# Training's Effects on Tax Consulting Services

## Arthur Andersen and Company

Daniel J. McLinden, Marsha J. Davis, and Dennis E. Sheriff

*It is particularly difficult to assess the effects of training programs for professional employees such as consultants. The following case describes evaluation of a comprehensive technical training program for tax consultants at one of the largest accounting and consulting firms in the world. The results were very significant. (Portions of this case were published in* Human Resource Development Quarterly, *Volume 4, Winter 1993.)*

## Background

The need for and importance of assessing program effects has become a consistent theme in the field of human resource development (HRD). Numerous authors have cited the need for HRD professionals to view their activities in terms of specific economic benefits to their organizations (Bragg, 1989; Brinkerhoff, 1987). The feasibility of assessing these economic effects has been demonstrated, as well (Urban, Ferris, Crowe, and Miller, 1985). However, a lack of sufficient attention to the economics of developing human resource still exists (Lombardo, 1989).

This study focuses on the effects of a significant training investment for individuals in a specialty area of tax consulting. At the time of the study, the practice was emerging and was planned to expand rapidly. Both the development and the implementation of the training represented paradigm shifts from models used at that time. Although formative efforts (i.e., identifying areas for improvement) might have produced both interesting and useful findings, the client had a definite bottom-line mind-set. The stakeholders clearly wanted to know the effects of training in monetary terms: Specifically, were the tax professionals who participated in the training more productive as a result of the training, and, if so, how did this increase in productivity compare with the cost involved?

Federal taxation has been simplified to some extent by the 1986 Tax Simplification Act; however, state and local taxes have become somewhat more complex (Grossman and Mindebro, 1986). Each state and many municipalities have their own unique tax laws; there is no single, overarching tax code as with federal taxes. This and other aspects of state and local taxation have created opportunities for tax consulting in this specialty area. As a result, firms have developed tax practices to meet the needs of the state and local market.

To quickly make Arthur Andersen the premier provider of state and local tax (SALT) services in the United States, the firm took several steps. First, an experienced partner was appointed as the SALT national director. Then, several external SALT experts were hired as local office practice leaders to help expand the practice and supervise staff. Finally, highly skilled federal tax practice professionals were "converted" to SALT by immersing them in a training program that forced them to think, eat, and sleep state and local taxes. In addition to developing skills, this program was intended to foster networking during and after the training event. These trained individuals would return to various local offices around the United States. The company felt that business success would require establishing connections between the individuals functioning in this new role.

## HRD Program Description

The SALT Masters Program became the training vehicle used to develop these skills. The program began with two weeks of advance, prerequisite reading that consisted of articles, cases, state laws and regulations, and textbook reading assignments. Participants then attended a three-week training session at the firm's training facility in St. Charles, Illinois. The training focused on various state and local tax laws and regulations, their interpretation, and their application. Content was presented in a variety of learning activities, including small-group application exercises and a case study that integrated all content elements. The program instructors were selected carefully for their content expertise, presentation skills, and willingness and ability to champion the new practice area. Group meals with internal and external SALT experts were integrated into the training to build a close-knit team and buffer the intensity of the classroom training. All activities were linked back to SALT, through either content or debriefing.

The time line for development and implementation was tight. To develop this training as quickly as possible without trading off quality, a group technology (GT) cell was used. (A GT cell is a cross-functional design group that includes instructional designers, content experts, and technical support.) One goal of this approach is to break down barriers between disciplines to promote more efficient communication. Additionally, members of a GT cell are expected to work together as a team to complete project tasks. Although each task is primarily completed by or supervised by the individual with the appropriate expertise, barriers between disciplines are blurred. For example, a content expert may become involved in designing an activity, or an instructional designer may make some content decisions. The approach proved time- and cost-efficient. Compared with other approaches to training development that Arthur Andersen had taken, gains in efficiency ranged from 25 percent to 50 percent.

The project manager had overall project responsibility, monitoring budget and status, making staffing and equipment decisions, and performing quality assurance reviews on all topics. The lead designer and the project coordinator were responsible for the day-to-day operation of the GT cell. They supervised the other cell members, monitored the flow of work through various stages, and assigned tasks to other cell members. The project coordinator and dedicated word processor also trained other personnel and subject experts to use equipment and software as needed.

The SALT practice committed its best, most experienced personnel to write the technical content. The subject experts wrote and reviewed the drafts of the text and activities; the designers formatted the materials, performed design reviews, and created drafts for visual materials. A graphic artist created the visuals on-line from the hand-drawn drafts.

## Evaluation Methods

The focus for the evaluation efforts was on assessing bottom-line impact. This was considered a Level 4 effort in the Kirkpatrick (1976) model, or a Level 6 effort in the Brinkerhoff (1988) model—that is, was the organization affected, and, if so, did the intervention made a worthwhile difference. Two goals drove the design of the study. First, the study had to reach a conclusion about organizational effects. To achieve this goal, data needed to be collected at the other levels of evaluation. For example, in the terms of the Kirkpatrick model, data on reaction, learning, and job performance also had to be collected. These data became a means, not an end, contributing to the overall goal of determining organizational impact. Second, the study had to provide the stakeholders with evidence regarding the program's effects. A key point here is that the consultants' role was not to prove or disprove an effect; rather, it was to gather the appropriate evidence (see Figure 1) and draw a reasonable conclusion. With these goals in mind, a three-phase study was designed (see Figure 2).

**Figure 1. Evaluation questions and data for this study.**

| Evaluation question | Data source | Type of information | Characteristics of information |
|---|---|---|---|
| How has productivity been affected? | Organizational data bases | Fees<br>Chargeable hours | Reliable economic data<br>Allows comparisons with other individuals and groups |
| What are individuals' reactions? | Survey questionnaires | Attitudes toward practice<br><br>Barriers<br>Opportunities<br>Job responsibilities | Enhanced detail of data-base information<br><br>Formative data |
| Was the training successful? | Observation<br>Interviews<br>Questionnaires | Students' reactions<br>Opinion of tax professional<br><br>Opinion of educators<br>Review by evaluators | Basis for evaluating course |

Phase One preceded the training. Information was obtained from each of the individuals designated to attend the course; about those individual's home office; and about other offices that were not sending people to the training. The goal in this phase was to establish a baseline measure of performance against which the future efforts of these students could be measured. Much of this information was economic data, such as fees and chargeable hours. Although some of this information was obtained through self-report, the most crucial information came

# Figure 2. Time line of events.

## Organizational data bases

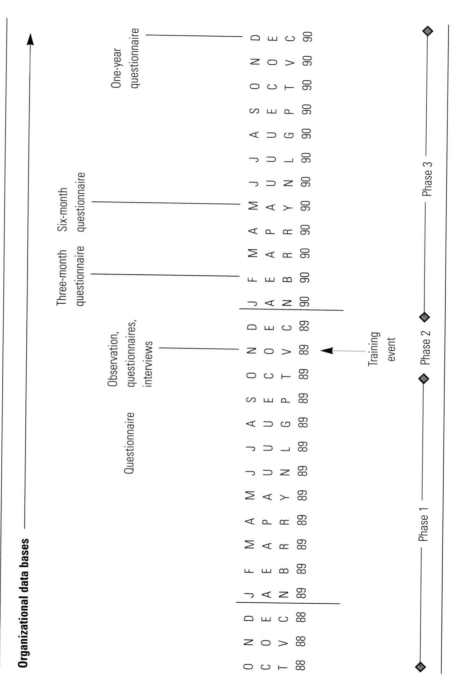

from organizational data bases. Additionally, just before the training event, each student completed a questionnaire that asked for information about various work activities and reactions to this new career direction. Although the economic data were key to reaching eventual conclusions about bottom-line impact, the study was designed to be a long-term evaluation project. Self-report information was used to identify barriers to program implementation so the organization could take action to make the program successful. Further, the self-report questionnaire provided an opportunity to solicit feedback on entrepreneurial activities, such as presentations to clients and personal selling. These efforts had not yet yielded monetary results but would do so eventually. Although important to the conduct of the study, self-report data were treated as background information; the primary focus of reporting was on the financial indicators—the same ones this case study focuses on.

The training event was evaluated in Phase Two. These evaluation efforts were summative; that is, the goal was to determine if the training event was successful or unsuccessful. If it was successful, it would be reasonable to link future productivity gains to the training intervention. Likewise, if productivity gains were not forthcoming, it would be reasonable to conclude that, although the training was done well, it did not have a substantive effect on productivity. Classroom observations, interviews, and questionnaires were used to obtain information to assess the success of this course.

In Phase Three, following the training event, the job performance of individuals and offices was monitored over the course of one year. Individuals responded to three questionnaires within this time period; they reported on their work activities, perceived barriers, and perceived opportunities, as well as reactions to issues they encountered in pursuing their work. Additionally, organizational data bases were again accessed to track economic indicators. The performance of offices that participated in the training versus offices that had not yet sent anyone to training was evaluated. A goal of the training was to develop the skills and abilities of participants. In addition, training participants were supposed to provide leadership in their local organizations. Therefore, if this goal was achieved, differences should appear between participating offices and nonparticipating offices.

Although there is literature describing methods for quantifying the effects of training, the design team needed to choose a method of analyzing and presenting the results that would be relevant to this organization (Basarab, 1990; Blomberg, 1989; Cullen, Sawzin, Sisson, and Swanson, 1978; Swanson and Gradous, 1988). There are many ways to assess the effects of an investment, but standards do not exist and any assessment must make sense within the organizational context (Davidove and Schroeder, 1992). Therefore, analyses were developed in conjunction with stakeholders. For the most part, analyses were based on descriptive statistics and accompanying graphs that illustrated these values.

Two steps in the analyses were key to the development of conclusions regarding financial results. First, the benefit of training was identified in terms of increased revenue that could reasonably be attributed to training. Second, the increased revenue was compared with costs to determine the trend and whether a complete payback could be achieved. Costs were calculated in a manner similar to that proposed by several authors (Carnevale and Schulz, 1990; Cascio, 1991). In essence, the cost of training was the sum of personnel time and expenses for development and delivery of training. Next, the payback was calculated as the amount of fees attributed to training summed over time (Phillips, 1991). When total fees equaled total cost, a 100 percent payback would be achieved.

## Financial Results and Discussion

The training event had a substantial positive influence on the success of the practice. The results showed that, individuals who participated in the training were generating more fees. A comparison of fees before and after training showed that, although this group had already been on an upward trend, the level increased beyond the trend following training (see Figure 3). Furthermore, when the cost of training was allocated at an individual level, the results showed that, on average, each participant was generating sufficient fees beyond the pretraining trend to pay for most of the cost of training (see Figure 4). The difference between the projected fees and the actual fees was calculated and totaled. Within the 12-month period for which this study was originally planned, the payback was nearly 100 percent. In fact, total payback was achieved two months later.

Comparing the results from participative and nonparticipative offices added even more weight to the evidence that training had an effect on performance. Figure 5 shows the pretraining and posttraining performance of offices in both groups. The difference in groups prior to training suggests that more than training accounts for the success of the practice. Specifically, the offices in the training group were already doing a substantial amount of work in this tax specialty. The trend line after training, however, shows an increase in level for

**Figure 3. Comparison of actual posttraining revenue with actual pretraining fees and the pretraining trend in fees.**

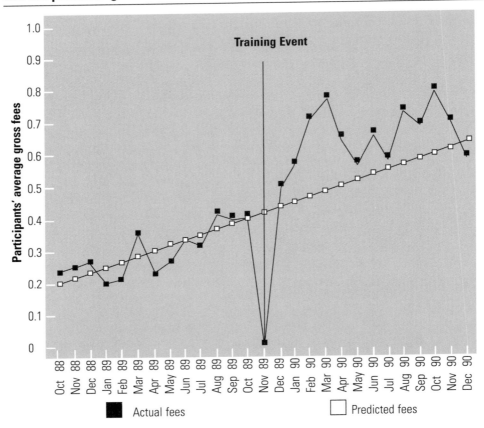

Values on the vertical axis illustrate the relative magnitude of the financial variables; the actual values for the axis are confidential.

the training group. In comparison, revenue for the nontraining group remained relatively flat throughout the same period of time. Although the positive change in trends provides further evidence for the impact of training, the pretraining trend strongly suggests that the organizational results were not achieved solely through training. Specifically, other organizational supports must have been in place for training to have an effect. It is reasonable to conclude that the training offices were poised to take advantage of the expertise that resulted from sending individuals to training. This finding supports

**Figure 4. Running total of the average revenue per participant attributed to training, compared with the average cost of training per participant.**

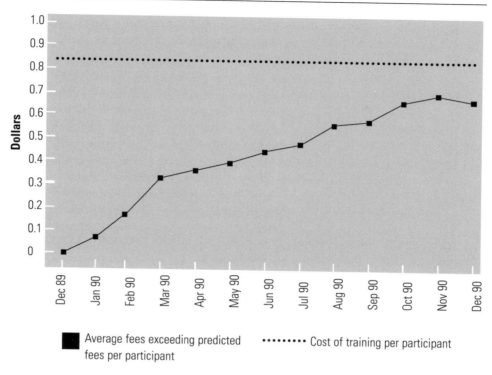

Average fees exceeding predicted fees per participant

········ Cost of training per participant

Values on the vertical axis illustrate the relative magnitude of the financial variables; the actual values for the axis are confidential.

the view that, for training to have positive effects, it requires the existence of supporting structures throughout the organizational system.

These findings showed that participants not only were actively working in the specialty in which they were trained, but also were involved in fee-generating activities. In addition, data on other activities that could not be measured in monetary terms but that were related to the success of the practice and considered an outcome of the training showed desired increases. The finding that both current and potential income-producing activities had increased was persuasive for the stakeholders.

A point worth noting here is that the pretraining trend was extrapolated linearly into the posttraining time period to test the return (see

Figure 3). It might have been more reasonable to assume a nonlinear trend in which the slope decreased over time. In other words, there may be a ceiling on the trend. Because there was no evidence to describe some nonlinear trend, however, the linear trend was used. Although this may have been a more stringent criterion, it was also more persuasive.

Another important point is that the entire cost of this training was allocated to this single group of students. At the outset of this project, this approach was reasonable; however, a later decision to train additional groups permitted the cost to be allocated to a greater number of individuals who were, in turn, generating more fees that contributed to the return on the training investment.

The economic indicators that showed a monetary return were striking, but other findings indicated that the program was not without problems. For instance, the development of this emerging practice was

**Figure 5. Comparison of revenue generated from offices that participated in the training and offices that had not yet participated.**

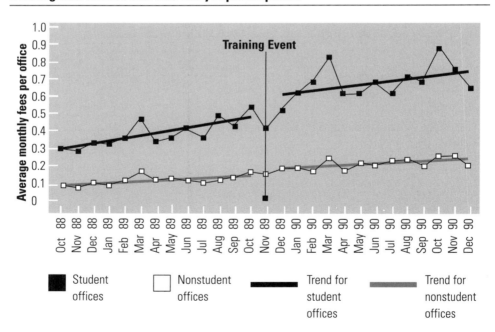

Values on the vertical axis illustrate the relative magnitude of the financial variables; the actual values for the axis are confidential.

not unlike the diffusion of a technological innovation. There were cases of resistance as well as early adoption. Full-time effort in the specialty was considered necessary to develop the practice. Some individuals quickly became full-time practitioners in the specialty, while others continued to have responsibilities outside the specialty. There were also varying degrees of support across the practice. The individuals who participated in this training had a unique skill that was in high demand. Not surprisingly, there was evidence suggesting that high demands were placed on their time, with little backup support available. Findings such as these indicated changes were needed in the program; however, the problems were, on balance, relatively minor and did not warrant any major change in policy.

This study raised an important issue with regard to evaluating results. Specifically, determining impact is not the same as trying to "prove cause and effect" in the traditional experimental sense. The consultants were challenged on this point several times by interested parties. In an applied setting, the role of evaluation is, among other things, to assist in the management of business risk. When a significant monetary or human resource investment is made, the decision makers assume a number of risks. For example, the program may fail, productivity may not increase, or productivity may not increase sufficiently to warrant further investment. Evaluation efforts ought to provide a means to minimize these and other risks instead of focusing on reaching unequivocal conclusions that an observed result is due to a specific cause (Gordon, 1991; Paquet, Kasl, Weinstein, and Waite, 1987; Robinson and Robinson, 1989). To achieve this goal, evaluation paradigms other than those that rely on control and manipulation of independent variables (i.e., experimental and quasi-experimental) become useful. An evidentiary focus proved useful in this case. That is, based on evidence about program results obtained from multiple sources, including a review of the evidence by evaluators, clients, and other stakeholders, it seemed reasonable to conclude that the training event had a substantial positive influence on financial productivity.

## Questions for Discussion

1.   The authors argue that these types of studies should focus not on establishing cause and effect (experimental focus), but on developing evidence (evidentiary focus) to support the conclusion that an effect did or did not occur. What are the benefits and limitations of an experimental versus an evidentiary focus?

2.  This study evaluated training for the development of a specific domain. If the training were more broadly focused (e.g., on management skills), how would the conduct of the study be affected?

3.  This study relied on organizational data bases to provide detailed information about revenues and costs. If the detailed information from these data bases had not been available, how would methods and conclusions have been affected?

4.  This study was concerned with training effects on professional services. How would the evaluation model have to be adapted in order to implement this type of study with different audiences such as technicians, clerical workers, or skilled labor?

## The Authors

Daniel J. McLinden is a specialist/consultant in the Evaluation Services Department of the Professional Education Division of the Arthur Andersen Worldwide Organization. His consulting work involves projects that include program evaluation and policy analysis, needs assessment, testing, statistical consulting, organizational assessment, and evaluating the investment in human resource development. He holds an Ed.D. in educational psychology from Northern Illinois University. He has authored and coauthored a number of articles that have appeared in *Performance Improvement Quarterly, Human Resource Development Quarterly, Evaluation and Program Planning*, and *Performance and Instruction*. He is currently a consulting editor for *Performance Improvement Quarterly*. McLinden can be contacted at the following address: Arthur Andersen and Company, S.C., Center for Professional Education, 1405 North Fifth Avenue, St. Charles, IL 60174-1264.

Marsha J. Davis is a manager in tax education in the Professional Education Division of the Arthur Andersen Worldwide Organization and is located at the Center for Professional Education in St. Charles, Illinois. She is responsible for developing and conducting tax schools for several U.S. tax specialty teams and service lines. She holds a B.S. and an M.S. in business education from Northern Illinois University. Davis led the project team that developed the highly successful SALT Masters Program, an intensive training program for federal tax personnel transferring to the SALT practice. In 1990, Davis and her project team were the first recipients of the Professional Education Division's Excel Award for their work on the SALT project.

Dennis E. Sheriff is a principal and director of tax international/specialty training in the Professional Education Division of the Arthur Andersen Worldwide Organization and is located at the Center for Professional Education in St. Charles, Illinois. He is responsible for the development and delivery of tax training in Canada, Latin America, the United States, East Asia, Australia, and Europe. Prior to joining the Professional Education Division, Sheriff was on the faculty at Northern Illinois University, where he taught instructional technology and also served as chair of the instructional technology program. Sheriff holds a Ph.D. in instructional technology from Texas A&M University. He has published in *Educational Communications and Technology Journal, Proceedings of Selected Research Papers and Presentations,* and the *Illinois Association for Educational Communication and Technology Journal.*

## References

Basarab, D.J. (1990). Calculating the return on training investment. *Evaluation Practice, 11,* 177-185.

Blomberg, R. (1989). Cost-benefit of employee training: A literature review. *Adult Education Quarterly, 39*(2), 89-98.

Bragg, A. (1989). Prove that you produce sales. *Sales and Marketing Management, 14*(1), 54-59.

Brinkerhoff, R.O. (1987). *Achieving results from training: How to evaluate human resource development programs and increase impact.* San Francisco: Jossey-Bass.

Brinkerhoff, R.O. (1988). An integrated evaluation model for HRD. *Training & Development Journal, 42*(2), 66-68.

Carnevale, A.P., and Schulz, E.R. (1990). Return on investment: Accounting for training. *Training & Development Journal, 44*(7), S1-S32.

Cascio, W.F. (1991). *Costing human resources: The financial impact of behavior in organizations.* Boston: PWS-KENT Publishing.

Cullen, J.G., Sawzin, S.A., Sisson, G.R., and Swanson, R.A. (1978). Cost effectiveness: A model for assessing the training investment. *Training & Development Journal, 32*(1), 24-29.

Davidove, E.A., and Schroeder, P.A. (1992). Demonstrating ROI of training. *Training & Development Journal, 46*(8), 70-71.

Gordon, J. (1991). Measuring the goodness of training. *Training, 28*(8), 19-25.

Grossman, H.A., and Mindebro, D.E. (eds.). (1986). *A complete guide to the tax reform act of 1986.* Paramus, NJ: Prentice-Hall Information Services.

Kirkpatrick, D.L. (1976). Evaluation of training. In R.L. Craig and L.R. Bittell (eds.), *Training and development handbook* (pp. 18-1 – 18-27). New York: McGraw-Hill.

Lombardo, C.A. (1989). Do the benefits of training justify the costs? *Training & Development Journal, 43*(12), 60-64.

Paquet, B., Kasl, E., Weinstein, L., and Waite, W. (1987). The bottom line. *Training & Development Journal, 41*(5), 27-33.

Phillips, J.J. (1991). Measuring the return on HRD. *Employment Relations Today, 18,* 329-342.

Robinson, D.G., and Robinson, J.C. (1989). *Training for impact: How to link training to business needs and measure the results.* San Francisco: Jossey-Bass.

Swanson, R.A., and Gradous, D.B. (1988). *Forecasting financial benefits of human resource development.* San Francisco: Jossey-Bass.

Urban, T.F., Ferris, G.R., Crowe, D.F., and Miller, R.L. (1985). Management training: Justify costs or say good-bye. *Training & Development Journal, 39*(3), 68-71.

# The ROI of Work Process Analysis

## Multi-Marques Inc.

By Denis Ouimet and Charles Boilard

*Many human resource development programs focus on the critical issue of supervisor improvement. The following case describes an inexpensive and brief training program to teach supervisors how to conduct a work process analysis to obtain improvement. Although the investment was small, the return was relatively large.*

## Background

Multi-Marques Inc. is the largest bakery in Quebec, with 3,500 employees and a volume of more than 100,000 loaves of bread produced daily by 15 bakeries across the province. The company was formed in 1985 by the merger of 15 independent bakers who wanted to keep their own brand names for marketing purposes; the French word *marques* means "brands."

This merger had a tremendous effect on production facilities. Most production centers increased specialization. Administrative services was integrated into two units, one in Montreal and the other in Quebec City. Employees from all merging bakeries brought their own personal and company backgrounds, value systems, and business practices and procedures.

The department supervisors were chosen from the office personnel of the merging companies. Some of the characteristics sought in these supervisors were the ability to adapt to the new management style, philosophy, and work procedures, plus previous leadership in helping employees change work habits.

Administrative services are divided among eight departments: accounts payable, accounts receivable, credit, payroll, sales, distribution center management, production facility management, and the

Quebec City office personnel management.

Each supervisor has a staff of two to seven people and is responsible for
- job distribution among the staff
- job descriptions and analyses
- training of employees
- introduction of new work procedures
- scheduling of work, vacation, sick leave, and overtime
- quality control
- job performance appraisal
- announcement and follow-up of disciplinary actions
- application of the labor agreement contract.

In 1990, formal in-house training on the role of supervisor was given to the newly appointed supervisors to familiarize them with this role. The four days of training were spread over three months.

## Context

A brief needs analysis by the human resource department pointed out the importance of training in helping the administrative supervisors deal with employee problems and performance appraisal issues.

In January 1993, the administrative services of the Quebec City office integrated a large part of the administrative work of the Chicoutimi-area activities. The workload of the Chicoutimi office represented at least 10 percent of the Quebec office, but no additional employees had been hired.

The main concerns of the director, Ronald Delisle, were the ability of the office personnel to get the job done and the ability of the supervisors to conduct work performance appraisals and to coach employees.

## Training Design

The external consultant who had designed the in-house training on supervisory roles suggested a series of three meetings with the supervisors. He felt that, to manage effectively, appraise work performance appropriately, and distribute the workload fairly among the employees, the supervisors needed factual information. Lacking such information, they had to rely only on impressions and feelings, a precarious situation. Supervisors were concerned that their suggestions and comments might not be accepted by the employees, and that the climate of the office would suffer.

Instead of suggesting a training program aimed at the acquisition of new knowledge, the consultant decided to focus on what the supervisors were experiencing. He suggested that the key to solving most of the difficulties would be work process analysis, a method that would yield information on what must be done, how it must be done, how long it takes to do a job, who is involved, and what resources are needed and when. With this information at hand, supervisors would be able to monitor the work flow, set performance standards, and give some challenges to their employees, while being very comfortable in pointing out deficiencies.

Each of the three meetings was held in a conference room in the company's office building and lasted from 4 p.m. to 10 p.m., with a one-hour lunch break beginning at 6 p.m. Because the training was scheduled partly during office hours and partly during personal time, it was agreed that no overtime salary would be paid but that special requests for leave for personal reasons would be received favorably by the director.

The supervisors considered this training to be like any continuing education program. There was, however, a specific advantage in this particular in-house training program, because it directly addressed difficulties related to daily activities. The knowledge the supervisors acquired would be useful in any job.

These meetings were scheduled over a three-month period, giving the supervisors time to gather factual information through the work process analysis.

The consultant insisted that the counselor from the human resource department attend every meeting and assist supervisors in their analyses, making sure that everyone completed his or her homework properly between the meetings. The consultant also asked that the director of administrative services be present at the beginning of the first meeting to explain the reasons for and objectives of these training sessions and that he attend the third meeting to express his appreciation of the work done.

The consultant's role was fourfold. He served as
- an expert in work process analysis
- a facilitator in helping the supervisors share their personal experiences
- a salesperson touting the benefits of the training program
- a motivator in keeping the pact of the training, especially when it demanded some overtime from the supervisors.

## Program Description
During the first meeting, three topics were on the agenda:
- free exchanges with the participants about their difficulties and dis-

comforts regarding job performance appraisal

- a demonstration, by the consultant, of the need to rely on factual data in performance appraisal and of the benefits resulting from such an approach
- an explanation of how to complete a work process analysis with custom-designed worksheets.

Half of the meeting was dedicated to the third topic. Sufficient time to experiment and start the analysis was provided. Because it was important for supervisors to realize the benefits of this operation and to be able to share it with their employees, this first meeting was crucial for everyone—the supervisors, the counselor, the director, and the consultant.

Before the next meeting, each supervisor had to complete the work process analysis for some major activities in his or her department, have the analysis validated by the employees, and get them personally involved in the analysis process. Employees are considered the best persons to give valid information on how the work is done and how long it takes to complete.

It is important to note that the additional work of completing these work process analyses did not delay the regular production of each department. In addition, the integration of the Chicoutimi office was under way.

During the second meeting, feedback was obtained from all supervisors on the work process analyses they had completed: what the difficulties were, how they managed to solve them, what kind of cooperation they obtained from their employees, what discoveries they made, what work process they had modified on a trial basis, and so on. The consultant expressed his appreciation for every supervisor's effort. He encouraged opinions and comments from other participants, and everyone was very enthusiastic. Some results had already been seen. For example, employees had a better perception of the work to be done in their departments and how each employee was related to fellow workers inside and outside the department. Other positive results included the willingness of everyone to cooperate in the analysis, and the fresh ideas for improved performance. This exchange lasted nearly half of the meeting.

Next, the consultant explained how to extract information from the gathered data, how to identify priorities among a list of activities, and how to modify work processes. He insisted on the importance of having not only a complete list of activities, but also reliable data regarding the duration of each activity. These data were the basic reference for setting performance standards and objectives.

Finally, because the supervisors needed to tell their employees how to do their jobs, it was decided to have the participants role-play a meeting with an employee. Each participant was then rated using a checklist of 20 managers' behaviors. For each performer, other participants noted one good behavior during the role play and one behavior that needed to be improved. The purpose of this exercise was to make the participants practice a meeting concerning performance and work processes and to have them integrate, through the rating process, appropriate managers' behaviors.

At the end, the consultant encouraged the supervisors to continue the good work and to complete the work process analyses. The objectives of this second meeting were to reinforce each participant's commitment to the program, to show some benefits of work process analysis, and to adjust the perceptions of the supervisors.

During the last meeting, three topics were on the agenda: the experience each supervisor had conducting the work process analysis and implementing modifications, how to adjust a work process, and what to do next. During approximately 60 minutes, the participants shared their own experiences. It was remarkable to see what some said: "Remember what you told us you did on such-and-such occasion? Well, it gave me an idea, and I...." In addition, the majority of the supervisors reported having discussed some problems over the telephone with colleagues. Such sharing had been rare before the previous meeting.

The focus of the meeting was the demonstration, with specific examples, of how to make a work process more efficient. The participants worked on their own work processes in a lab setting. A period of questions and answers was also provided. During the last hour, each supervisor was asked to prepare an action plan concerning work processes in his or her department. This plan was to include benefits expected in terms of efficiency, work climate, and his or her personal feelings as a supervisor. The director of administrative services attended the last hour and gave some feedback on the training process.

## Analysis and Results

Significant results were obtained, though this was only a 15-hour training program; some of the results are easily measurable, whereas others are not. In fact, as shown in Table 1, the counselor and supervisors invested much more than 15 hours in the program. Yet, according to the director, the regular work was completed as usual during this training period—including the administrative work of the Chicoutimi office being incorporated into the usual operations—and no delays were encountered because of an excessive demand on the employees and the supervisors.

**Table 1. Estimate of the time invested in the training program, by employee category.**

| Group | Preparation | Training | Between training sessions | Total |
|---|---|---|---|---|
| | | Hours invested | | |
| Director | 2 | 2 | 10 | 14 |
| Human resource counselor | 2 | 15 | 20 | 37 |
| Supervisors (8) | —— | 120* | 10 | 130 |
| Employees of all departments | —— | —— | 10 | 10 |

*Each supervisor attended three training sessions of five hours each.

To estimate the return on investment (ROI), the savings in operating costs were identified by the supervisors. Table 2 shows the savings resulting from work process modifications for the three months after the training. These estimates of savings are based on the average hourly wage of employees in the administrative services of Multi-Marques Inc. Note that work process analyses are ongoing and the savings reported here do not include all of the savings that will eventually be realized.

By the end of these three months, less than 10 percent of all the work processes had been analyzed and modified. Because the work process analysis was actually part of the supervisors' regular duties, it is difficult to obtain a long-term evaluation of the savings coming from this training.

Table 3 presents the costs of training and the ROI based on the real disbursement of funds and on the time invested in this training by all the categories of people involved. If one considers only the actual disbursement—the consultant's fee—the ROI is more than five

**Table 2. Savings resulting from modifications of work processes.**

| Activity | Time required to perform (hours) | | Time saved (hours) | Average hourly salary ($) | Number of times performed per year | Total savings ($) |
|---|---|---|---|---|---|---|
| | Before training | After training | | | | |
| **Accounts payable** | | | | | | |
| Repatriation | 1 | 0 | 1 | 15 | 52 | 780 |
| Intercompany distribution | 4 | 2 | 2 | 15 | 13 | 390 |
| **Credit** | | | | | | |
| Cashing | 8 | 4 | 4 | 15 | 13 | 780 |
| Report statements | 2 | 0 | 2 | 15 | 52 | 1,560 |
| **Payroll** | | | | | | |
| Social benefits analysis | 11 | 2 | 9 | 15 | 13 | 1,755 |
| **Production facility** | | | | | | |
| Planning and scheduling | 105 | 95 | 10 | 15 | 52 | 7,800 |
| **Total savings for administrative services** | | | | | | **13,065** |

times the money invested. The ROI significantly exceeds costs even if the employees' time investment and the supervisors' time between the training sessions is taken into account. If one uses a traditional formula, this program yields an ROI of 215 percent.

The tables show hard figures confirming the benefits resulting from this specific supervisory training on work process analysis. The figures are based on a one-year period and on the assumption that no other savings will be made afterward.

How do the results of this training design compare with the results that might have been obtained if systems-and-methods specialists from outside the organization had been involved in the improvement program? We believe that this design resulted in much more rapid improvement and greater savings, because it enabled supervisors to perform their own work process analyses; the systems-and-methods specialists would have had to convince the supervisors and employees of the benefits expected from changes imposed on them by outsiders.

**Table 3. Return on investment in training.**

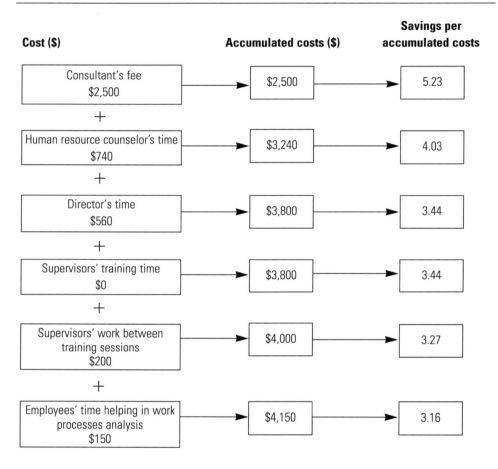

| Cost ($) | Accumulated costs ($) | Savings per accumulated costs |
|---|---|---|
| Consultant's fee $2,500 | $2,500 | 5.23 |
| + | | |
| Human resource counselor's time $740 | $3,240 | 4.03 |
| + | | |
| Director's time $560 | $3,800 | 3.44 |
| + | | |
| Supervisors' training time $0 | $3,800 | 3.44 |
| + | | |
| Supervisors' work between training sessions $200 | $4,000 | 3.27 |
| + | | |
| Employees' time helping in work processes analysis $150 | $4,150 | 3.16 |

Note. The returns shown are based on savings of $13,065.

## Conclusion

This training design was meant to help the supervisors "learn to catch their own fish." A mix of job design and people management training proved very successful and generated several benefits for Multi-Marques. The supervisors developed an ability in work process analysis that will help them in their daily activities. They learned to use factual information gathering in dealing with performance problems and to avoid letting emotional issues get in the way. Also, the training program gave supervisors an opportunity to share common concerns and develop a sense of belonging; they now communicate more openly among themselves. And they show a great deal of leadership in convincing their employees of the importance of streamlining job processes.

## Questions for Discussion

1. What were the main concerns of the director of administration? Why?
2. What was the role of a department supervisor in the administrative services?
3. What are your comments on the reasoning of the external consultant concerning how to solve the problem at hand?
4. Why did the external consultant want to minimize the time allowed for formal training?
5. What was the role of the human resource department in this project?
6. What role was expected from the director of administrative services?
7. What was the role of the external consultant during the training sessions?
8. Why was the first meeting of the training program crucial?
9. What were the main topics of the three training sessions with the supervisors?
10. What were the methods of delivery of the training program?
11. What are your comments on the method used to assess the ROI?
12. Is it possible to use this specific procedure in other training setups? What are the prerequisites and limitations?
13. What are your comments on the conclusions regarding the benefits of this training program?

## The Authors

Denis Ouimet founded in 1976 the Bureau de Recherche et de Formation en "gestion intégrée" (BUREFOR Inc.), a management training and research consulting firm. His work and research on individual satisfaction, motivation, and efficiency in the organizational context have been the subject of more than 30 publications, and he has been invited to dozens of conferences. He is the author of three books on organizational behavior. Ouimet received a bachelor's degree in pedagogy and in business administration and a master's degree in system analysis. He completed Ph.D. studies in industrial relations at Laval University. He can be contacted at the following address: 11 Nobel Street, Levis, Quebec, Canada G6V 7C6.

Charles Boilard received a bachelor's degree in industrial relations from Laval University in 1987. He worked as a training coordinator for an important naval shipyard in the Quebec City area for 2½ years. Since 1990, he has acted as a counselor in the human resource department of Multi-Marques Inc. in the field of training and industrial relations.

# Using Action Plans to Measure Return on Investment

## The Coca-Cola Bottling Company of San Antonio

By Scott B. Parry

*Supervisory training with action plans is a common approach to building skills and applying them successfully on the job. The following case illustrates the significant payoff for supervisory training and represents a classic application of action planning from a firm that has advocated the process for many years. As shown in this case, a program that is designed properly and implemented carefully, with evaluation built in, can often generate high returns.*

## Background

As part of a five-day workshop for presidents and general managers of its franchised bottlers, The Coca-Cola Bottling Company of San Antonio surveyed participants to determine the developmental needs of their employees. In every location that the workshop was conducted, results were identical: The need for supervisory training led the list.

Several reasons were cited. No such program existed. Some bottlers had hired local consultants or professors to run courses for their supervisors with little or no effect on performance. Supervisors are the primary source of training for all other employees. The legal implications and cost of poor supervisory practices were rising at a rapid rate. Finally, the era of father-to-son-to-grandson management of bottling plants was drawing to a close; future managers would come from the ranks, not from the family that owned the franchise.

In response to this need for supervisory training, The Coca-Cola Company selected Training House Inc. as the consultants who would develop a series of half-day workshops to be run by bottlers. Because most of the franchised bottlers do not have a professional trainer on staff, the workshops would be designed to be taught by members of senior management—department heads and officers. Detailed instructor guidelines and train-the-trainer workshops would be needed to make the program as user-friendly as possible.

Training House surveyed the bottlers, using a questionnaire to rank a list of 20 supervisory needs as high, moderate, or low. These data were analyzed, and the top eight topics were selected for development. A year later, the IMPACT Supervisory Series was ready for distribution. This case study outlines the procedures followed and the results obtained during the pilot test in The Coca-Cola Bottling Company of San Antonio.

## Needs of the Organization

Although the needs analysis conducted via questionnaires was useful in identifying the developmental needs of bottling plant supervisors, the San Antonio bottler also had a number of organizational needs that it hoped training could address. With a market of more than a million customers, the company had been growing rapidly and had formed several new divisions (food service, canteen vending, lunch trucks, and metered bar service). Because of this new growth, there were many newly appointed supervisors who were more comfortable handling their old jobs than supervising people. As a result, senior managers were handling problems that should have been resolved at the supervisory level.

Another organizational need sprang from major changes in the way the products reached market. In earlier times, the bottlers of Coca-Cola relied on route salesmen to take orders, deliver products, and stack the shelves in larger outlets. The proliferation of many new products and package sizes, however, had led to a reorganization of the means of distribution. Sales were now made by telephone (tel-sell representatives) and by face-to-face calls (customer service representatives). Deliveries were made by three types of trucks, depending on outlet size. And the stacking and displaying of products in the outlets were handled by a newly created position: merchandiser. This reorganization created new supervisory positions and led to the need for training.

Newly appointed supervisors often show stronger allegiance to their team of employees than to management, whose ranks they have recently joined. This factor weighed heavily on the minds of senior management. The company had managed to resist past efforts by the union to organize the employees. The prior vote had been very close, however, and management feared that the uncertainty surrounding the reorganization and the supervision that employees were receiving could give the union the edge they needed to win the next election, about six months away.

## Program Implementation

Twelve members of senior management were selected to serve as instructors. They included the executive vice-president, Bob Alford, and his division heads and officers. These 12 were participants in the first cycle of the course, taught by the president of Training House. Their focus was on content and process: what to teach and how (instructional methods, media, techniques) to teach it.

The group agreed to use team teaching, with two managers assigned to each of the eight modules of the course listed in Table 1. (Some of the managers were responsible for more than one module.) With 64 supervisors to be trained, the bottler divided them into four groups of 16 participants each.

### Table 1. The eight half-day workshops in the IMPACT Supervisory Series.

- Your Role as Supervisor
- Defining the Job and Performance Criteria
- Setting Goals and Standards
- Training and Developing the Team
- Conducting Performance Reviews
- Motivating and Managing Others
- Managing Your Time Effectively
- Personnel Policies and Procedures

Participants attended class one week and met with their managers individually the following week to agree on how to implement the actions they planned to take as a result of the workshop. Thus, every other week brought a different module, and the entire IMPACT program took 16 weeks to administer.

For each workshop, the slides and audiotape script that provided the concepts and informational input were followed by hands-on learning exercises: role plays, case studies, games, simulations, script analysis, and action plans. The selection of slides enabled each bottler to use locally shot slides, thereby customizing and personalizing the instruction.

Another benefit of the slides was that they were used interactively. After each key learning point (every six to eight slides), a "discussion slide" came on the screen and posed two or three questions. By spending three to four minutes discussing these questions, the instructors enabled the participants to apply new concepts and skills to their own jobs and employees.

Detailed instructor guidelines made it possible for the bottler's own senior managers to deliver the workshops with confidence and competence. This practice enhanced the credibility and relevance of each module. Participants knew that the program was important enough for the "top brass" to be teaching it, and senior managers drew on their own experience to illustrate the learning points.

## Action Plans: Key to High Transfer

Transfer of training refers to the degree to which participants apply in the workplace what they acquire in a workshop. Most trainers estimate the degree of transfer for "soft skills" courses such as supervisory training to be relatively low: 20 percent to 40 percent, according to a survey of more than 1,000 training managers. In short, they see little return on investment for such courses.

To overcome the tendency of supervisors to view training as a spectator sport (i.e., watching an instructor perform), Training House built action planning into each module of the IMPACT Supervisory Series. This approach views participants not as empty vessels waiting to attend class and be filled with new concepts and skills, but rather as change agents and catalysts who are being equipped with tools and techniques that they will apply back on the job. The vehicle for accomplishing this application was the action plan. At the end of each workshop session, each participant completed this form (or "transmittal document"). Participants then took the document back to their managers and subordinates for discussion and eventual agreement on how new tools and techniques acquired in class could best be transplanted and put into action on the job.

At the start of each new workshop, participants got out their action plans and discussed the results of their meetings with managers and subordinates, working in subgroups of three or four persons each. These action plan reviews served several useful purposes:
- They provided continuity to the course by reviewing the prior session's content.
- They placed emphasis on applying concepts and skills, not merely acquiring them.
- They gave instructors feedback on where participants needed help in putting skills into practice.
- They enabled instructors to follow up with managers who were not meeting with participants.
- They reinforced participants for investing the extra time needed outside class.

• They gave a meaningful way to measure the effects of the course.

Action plans were a means of putting management by objectives into operation among first-level supervisors whose typical day was activity-oriented and reactive, rather than goal-oriented and proactive. It was a way of getting supervisors to manage and to launch their own programs of continuous improvement. The 10 parts of the four-page action plan are listed in Table 2.

## Table 2. The 10 parts of the action plan.

- Subject: the specific area(s) you have picked for improvement
- Objective: what is to be accomplished, the purpose of the plan
- Goals: the specific targets by which you will measure progress
- Problems: the barriers that might hinder you in carrying out your plan
- Solutions: how you plan to avoid or deal with the problems
- Resources: what people, time, equipment, etc., you need to carry out the plan
- Activities and Time: what steps (actions), sequence, and time are needed
- Costs: what the overall cost of implementing your plan will be
- Benefits: what benefits you expect and their estimated dollar value
- Commitment: when you and your manager will next review progress

## Calculating the Return on Investment

The Coca-Cola Bottling Company of San Antonio did not make a conscious decision to calculate return on investment (ROI) following the training program. Three months after the course ended, however, the 64 supervisors gathered for a final executive briefing and graduation dinner, and this occasion enabled Training House to collect data on the program's results.

Each of the four groups of 16 supervisors came together for two hours, and each participant took five to 10 minutes to report on the results he or she had achieved by applying the concepts and skills learned in class and translated into on-the-job behavior on action plans (e.g., increased sales, reduced waste, shorter collection times, better route planning, less absenteeism). The audience for these briefings consisted of the senior managers who had taught the program and helped their subordinate supervisors to follow through on their action plans.

Using the information in Table 2, each supervisor and his or her manager calculated the cost of implementing each action plan (mostly time rather than additional expense). They also converted the benefits into estimates of dollar value (savings or additional revenues). In short, each supervisor's report on the eight action plans was actually a mini-cost-benefit analysis of the impact of the course. Here are four examples of the ROI realized by the successful implementation of the action plans:

- Marvin Rudolph reported that delinquent accounts were reduced by $100,000, resulting in a savings to the company of more than $6,000 in interest expense.
- Fernando Flores reported a reduction in over or short accounts of 72 percent in the first quarter. The reduction amounted to more than $5,800 and resulted in time and effort savings for the bookkeepers in his department and for the route salespeople.
- Zeff Hernandez noted a 2.4 percent increase in his vending routes at Snappy Snack because of better scheduling and rerouting for more efficiency. He expected that the combination of cost savings and increased income from better scheduling would amount to approximately $20,000 for the year.
- David Barnard reduced dispatching errors among the Omega truck accounts from seven per day to less than one per day. The increased accuracy resulted in savings in fuel consumption, hours lost, and trucks' wear and tear. At an estimated savings of $45 per day, this improvement would bring an annual savings of $10,000.

At the graduation dinner following the four briefing sessions, the human resource development manager and consultant tallied the total of the costs and benefits reported. The company had realized benefits of $526,000; the cost of running the training program was $34,000. In short, the benefits exceeded the cost by more than 15 to 1. Using the traditional formula yields an ROI of 1,447 percent.

Senior management considered this figure conservative, because many supervisors did not attach dollar values to the benefits realized by implementing their action plans. As Alford said, "Our supervisors are not accountants, and are wary of putting a dollar value on many of the gains reported today. They see only the immediate results in their own sections and are less aware of the 'ripple effect' that I can see throughout the organization." Moreover, no value was assigned to the results of the election in which the union's attempt to organize the bottler was defeated by a significant margin. Management attributed this victory to a greatly improved climate in the workplace, and saw this benefit alone as having a value over time in the millions of dollars.

Perhaps the most conservative aspect of the 15-to-1 ratio is the fact that most supervisors were reporting their benefits for a three-month period (i.e., time lapsed since the end of the course). Most of the savings and increased revenues are ongoing, however, and could be projected to continue for at least several years into the future. A key lesson here is that training costs occur at one point in time, whereas many training benefits are ongoing and should be projected well beyond the life of the course.

Although the reported figures are conservative, they are dramatic and impressive. Everyone at the graduation banquet felt the heady exhilaration of their achievements. Alford told the group that this was one of the most gratifying days of his life.

## Additional Nonmonetary Benefits

Throughout the action plan reports at graduation, it became clear that their successful implementation had influenced the participants personally, as well as the bottler as an organization. Three significant shifts in the perception and execution of the supervisory role were taking place.

First, the supervisors had begun a habit that was the essence of good management: goal setting as a way of life. They set goals and standards, and took time to muster up the resources—people and materials—to achieve them. When the program was launched, many of the supervisors saw themselves as "lead workers" or "section heads"—people hired to "mind the store" rather than to manage it as entrepreneurs. This thinking had changed significantly. They were well into managing by objectives. Maintaining these practices with joint goal-setting sessions and regular review meetings would provide an even greater return on investment.

Second, management had become a team sport. By mixing departments, changing the seating at each meeting, using the case method and role plays from all areas of bottler operations, and incorporating reports on participants' action plans into classes, the program had broken down isolation to form a better team. At the start of the program, supervisors did not really know each other, and sales supervisors knew less about production than the average school student after a plant tour. After completing the program, supervisors perceived themselves as members of management, and perceived management as a team sport.

Third, the participants no longer agreed with the common view of supervisors throughout the industry that employees are a commodity: "You need $x$ amount of trucks, bottles, syrup, and arms and legs to run a bottling plant." In that traditional view, if productivity is high, all is well. But when an employee's output begins to fall (or was never high enough to begin with), the average supervisor is ill-equipped to deal with the problem, other than to work twice as hard to compensate. This view had changed at the company, however. A major theme of the action plans was the commitment to job definition, performance appraisal, on-the-job training and coaching, motivation through joint goal setting and review, and better time management, so supervisors could perform as supervisors and not as star workers. Employees were being developed, not merely deployed.

## Factors Contributing to ROI

Why was this program so successful? What did the bottler and Training House learn that can be applied to other organizations that want to see their training produce tangible results?

The explanation begins by dispelling a myth. Supervisory training is not a "soft skills" course unless it is taught that way. There are hundreds of very specific behaviors that apply to anyone who supervises. These can be pinpointed, described, illustrated, and practiced in class, then shared with one's manager after class so that both parties become accountable for applying these behaviors on the job.

Moreover, supervisory training has the potential for a much greater effect on the organization than does skills training for nonsupervisory personnel. A supervisor of 10 persons has a "multiplier effect" of 10. By improving the performance of most or all of these 10 employees, the supervisor can generate a much greater return on the training investment.

A number of factors contributed to the successful ROI obtained in San Antonio. None of these factors taken alone would have had a significant effect. Taken cumulatively, however, their effects were powerful. Here are the major contributory factors.

### Top Management as Instructors

It is the responsibility of managers to develop their staff. When they serve as instructors, their message takes on more credibility, immediacy, and relevance. Also, having taught the modules, they are in an excellent position to follow up for their own direct-report supervisors. The training of supervisors is too important to be left for trainers to do on their own, although they can do it in partnership with management. Some things cannot be delegated. The raising of your children is one. The development of your supervisors is another.

### Participative Course Design

Supervisors were active throughout each workshop. New concepts and skills were presented deductively (the discovery method) rather than inductively (the lecture method). Links in the instructional chain were small and strong (stimulus-response-feedback links ran an average of six to eight minutes each). Participants worked in subgroups of three or four persons each, thereby giving maximum hands-on learning opportunity to every participant.

## Action Plans

The action plans got supervisors to commit their time and resources to transferring new concepts and skills from a workshop to the workplace. These four-page planning sheets also served to forge a partnership between each participant and his or her manager so that new behavior was recognized and reinforced (or maintained) back on the job.

## Executive Briefing

By scheduling graduation day (another session) several months after the course was over, senior management gave participants time to follow through on their action plans and begin to show results. Because managers did not want to be embarrassed by having participants with nothing to report (i.e., no ROI), there was a strong incentive for managers to follow through with their supervisors' action plans.

## Calculating Costs and Benefits

Traditionally, management has been responsible for controlling costs and maximizing benefits. Companies preach that this is "everybody's job," but they never have supervisors and workers calculate the dollar value of their efforts and their results. By going through this process for each module of the course, participants developed the skills and the habit of thinking as a manager.

## Teaching Goal Setting

Following the introductory module (Your Role as Supervisor), the next two modules taught the do's and don'ts of setting goals and standards. Without these modules, supervisors and managers would tend to describe wishes or activities when asked for goals. The quality of their action plan goals was much better, because they knew the difference and could evaluate the "measurability" of their goals and standards.

## Taking Time To Do It Right

Training House took a year to create the IMPACT Supervisory Series, and the bottler took more than eight months to implement it (one month to prepare senior management and four months to run the program, plus waiting three months before graduation day). Many supervisory training programs are run as five-day courses, with little or no opportunity to develop action plans and discuss them with managers. By scheduling one workshop every two weeks and allowing three months after the course for "germination," this program yielded a much greater "harvest."

## A Footnote

The Coca-Cola Company offered the IMPACT program to all bottlers as the course drew to an end in San Antonio, and by graduation day, 18 bottlers had installed the program. When news of the ROI realized in San Antonio reached the bottler community, many more bottlers purchased the program. To date, more than 200 franchise bottlers have run the IMPACT Supervisory Series.

## Questions for Discussion

1. Many organizations still conduct supervisory training as a five-day, Monday-through-Friday program. The bottler allowed two weeks per module, resulting in a 16-week program for the eight modules. What benefits do you see to conducting the training program extensively (i.e., over time), as was done in San Antonio?
2. What would be the benefits of conducting the training program intensively, as a week-long program?
3. What types of programs are best suited to be conducted intensively? What types are best suited to be conducted extensively? Give your reasons.
4. All 64 supervisors of the San Antonio bottler were brought together on the same day to report the results of their action plan implementation, resulting in a long day (eight hours) of 64 presentations. Would it have been better to schedule the presentations over two days of four hours each? Explain your reasons.
5. What are the major benefits of scheduling an executive briefing following the completion of a course?
6. What do you think is the ideal interval between the end of a course and the scheduling of an executive briefing and graduation day?
7. This case study ends with a list of seven factors that contributed to the success of the supervisory training program. Each is listed below. Indicate your reaction to each by noting how important (i.e., relevant and/or necessary) it is to the training programs you are responsible for, and also how likely you are to be able to sell this factor and apply

it in your organization. Enter the words high, moderate, or low in Table 3 to indicate your reaction to each factor.

**Table 3. Reaction to the author's reasons for success. Enter *High, Moderate,* or *Low* in the blanks to indicate your response.**

| Factor | Importance to transfer and ROI | Likelihood of implementing |
|---|---|---|
| Managers as instructors | | |
| Participative course design | | |
| Action plan for each topic | | |
| Executive briefing after course | | |
| Participants' calculations of costs and benefits | | |
| Teaching goal setting | | |
| Taking time to do it right | | |

## The Author

Scott B. Parry, chairman of Training House Inc., holds degrees from Princeton University (A.B., 1954), Boston University (M.S., 1960), and New York University (Ph.D., 1969). He has conducted workshops for educators and training directors in Africa, Europe, South America, Asia, and Australia and has served many organizations as a consultant. His clients include AT&T, IBM, Ford, GTE, Phillips, Mobil, Dow, Chemical Bank, Kodak, Coca-Cola, Air France, Blue Cross, and McGraw-Hill. Parry has published numerous articles in training and management development journals and addressed meetings of chapters of the American Society for Training and Development throughout the United States. He is author of four books and dozens of published training courses. Parry can be contacted at the following address: Training House Inc., 100 Bear Brook Road, Princeton, NJ 08540.

# Improving Customer Service Skills

## International Oil Company

By Rebecca Payne

*Every organization has certain stressful jobs that particularly influence the organization's performance. The following case presents an evaluation of a training program for one such job: dispatchers at an oil company. The program had several objectives, with a focus on improved customer service skills. The evaluation approach was comprehensive, using several data collection tools at four levels of evaluation. The results are very impressive.*

## Background

International Oil Company, one of the five major oil companies worldwide, has three dispatching centers. The following evaluation was conducted for the company's central dispatch, located in Los Angeles, California. The dispatch center's employees include 11 dispatchers and a delivery supervisor. The dispatchers are responsible for helping service station dealers who are unable to use the automated gasoline-ordering system for whatever reason. Dealers call central dispatch to place orders according to their gasoline needs. These dispatchers handle approximately 600 telephone calls per shift during peak times (eight to 10 telephone calls per dispatcher, per hour). Of the total calls received, 60 percent are from dealers needing information or order changes; the other 40 percent are from drivers needing advice or assistance.

Because most of the company's gas stations are open 24 hours a day, delivery times are divided into four time quadrants. A dispatcher tries to schedule delivery during the specific quad requested by the dealer. After a dispatcher calls the distribution terminal to place the order, the driver plans the delivery route to deliver the load during the requested quad. The driver loads the tank wagon to the dealer's product mix specifications and then delivers the gasoline. Safety and economic precautions mandate that the dealer take the full load ordered. If the dealer is unable to do so, the driver must "pull out" without unloading the gasoline and return to the terminal to adjust the product mix for the next station on the schedule. When this happens, dealers with high volumes or small tanks may run out of gasoline before the next scheduled delivery.

The Customer Service Design and Development Committee designed and developed the training that is the subject of this case study. The committee members were Jeanne O'Connor-Green, who at the time of this evaluation worked for the oil company and who now works for Intercom; Jim Burton, manager of the company's Retail Learning Center in Los Angeles; Bob DeGroot, developer, Sales Training America; Ashley Thornton, program designer, Intercom; and Rebecca Payne, program evaluator, ROI Evaluation Services. O'Connor-Green managed the design process.

After only a few months on the job, it had become evident to the new central dispatch manager that dispatchers were not performing to the company's expectations. He complained that dispatchers

- did not help out each other on the phone (i.e., were not working together as a team)
- had poor telephone etiquette
- had excessive absences
- would sometimes become angry with dealers
- would not double-check orders
- did not listen to each other
- did not solve problems well
- had poor rapport with the dealers.

In addition to these problems, central dispatch management was complaining that there were too many gasoline pullouts and customer complaints. Because of these performance and business problems, Burton was asked to develop training for the dispatchers. He brought in two consultants, Thornton and DeGroot.

## Program Description

Burton, Thornton, and DeGroot interviewed Greg Gaines, Operations and Delivery Support, and John Garner, dispatch manager, both with the oil company's Western Distribution Region, as part of a formal needs analysis. Gaines and Garner wanted a training program that would result in reduced pullouts (which would lower delivery costs); dispatchers who were willing and able to serve customers and handle problems in a safe, efficient, professional way; a teamwork environment to serve customers and handle problems better; and a "we make the difference" attitude displayed by all central dispatch employees.

In addition to central dispatch management, both dispatchers and dealers were interviewed. During the interviews, dispatchers said they wanted support from management in handling problems and to learn how to reduce or avoid stress on the job, to stay calm during difficult telephone calls, and to voice problems and get them solved before frustration led to "blowing up." The dealers wanted both the good and the bad news. They wanted efficient and dependable gasoline ordering and accurate information on time of delivery. They also wanted dependable, hard-working dispatchers who treated dealers with consideration and courtesy. In addition to the interviews, area dealers received a survey to measure their current satisfaction. As a result of these interviews and the survey, Thornton and DeGroot designed and developed a customer service training program.

## Objectives

Three types of program objectives were developed for all of the oil company's training programs:

- *Business objectives* indicate what the return to the oil company will be once students apply the knowledge and skills acquired in training.
- *Application objectives* indicate what the student will do on the job as a result of instruction.
- *Learning objectives* specify what students must do to show that learning has taken place.

From the training needs identified by Gaines and Garner, two business objectives were identified:

- a reduction in the number of pullouts to lower delivery costs
- a reduction in customer complaints.

The course was designed in seven modules, with an application objective for each module:

- *Telephone etiquette*—Participant will use central dispatch's telephone etiquette standards.
- *Rapport building*—Participant will use rapport-building techniques to improve communications and reduce customer complaints.
- *Listening to customers*—Participant will listen to customers in order to identify problems and focus conversations toward solutions.

- *Problem solving*—Participant will demonstrate trying to meet the customers' needs by either solving the problem while the customer is on the telephone, calling the customer back to explain what is being done, or explaining why the problem cannot be solved and offering alternatives.
- *Defusing anger*—Participant will defuse dealers' anger and frustration during difficult telephone calls and will refocus conversations toward solving problems.
- *Working as a team*—Participants will view the total job of central dispatch as their responsibility and work together as a team to solve problems and meet the customers' needs.
- *Dealing with stress*—Participant will identify personal responses to business-related stress and then take positive action to dissipate that stress before it results in negative consequences.

Several learning objectives were developed for each of the seven modules, and those objectives are shown in Table 1.

## Program Participants and Delivery

The program's trainees were dispatchers with varying levels of experience and education. For example, one dispatcher had been working for the oil company for 30 years, while another was new to the job. Some dispatchers had high-school diplomas, whereas others had attended several years of college. Central dispatch must be staffed 24 hours a day, 365 days a year; all dispatchers worked in rotating eight-hour shifts, unless working overtime.

The training was facilitated by Burton at the Retail Learning Center in Los Angeles (at no cost to participants) and was presented over a three-week period in four-hour-long blocks. This format allowed dispatchers a chance to practice newly learned skills and then respond to any problems or issues that needed to be discussed. A variety of delivery methods were used in the training, including lecture, discussion, case studies, role plays, and games.

## Models and Techniques

Most of the oil company's products training is evaluated for reaction, learning, application, and business results. The few exceptions are awareness programs and programs that are taught only once, both of which are evaluated only for reaction and learning. In the company's training department, evaluation is part of the design process, and an evaluation plan is presented before development starts. Evaluation plans are similar to proposals. They describe which objectives are to be evaluated, when they are to be evaluated, and which evaluation design will be used. They also describe where the evaluation will take place, which methods will be used (tests, surveys, observations, company records, etc.), and who will be involved in the evaluation.

The effectiveness of this particular training was measured on four levels:

- *Business results*—What are the bottom-line results for the oil company, for example, in terms of money, time, and goodwill?
- *Performance results*—Are the participants applying what they have learned?
- *Learning results*—Did participants learn what they were supposed to learn?
- *Reaction results*—What do the participants think about the training?

The evaluation plan proposed that business results would be determined by comparing company records of the numbers of pullouts and customer complaints, before and after training. A survey would also be sent to dealers to measure their satisfaction with the service they received from dispatchers, before and after training.

To determine if application objectives were being met, the participants would be observed on the job, six months after training. The application objective that dealt with stress was to be measured by comparing absenteeism records before training and six months later.

To determine the learning results of training, three methods would be used: case studies, games, and exercises. Case studies are a way to evaluate immediately whether specific learning objectives are being met. Games recreate an event, so that participants can manipulate a situation without risk, then analyze what happened. Exercises direct participants toward specific objectives and encourage high participant involvement (Abella, 1986).

A generic reaction questionnaire, developed by the oil company's training department, would be used to assess reaction results. This questionnaire is used to measure all participants' reactions to training for any course designed by the department. The advantage of having one questionnaire is that all courses may be compared with one another. In addition to the generic questionnaire, dispatchers and managers were to be interviewed to determine their reaction to the training six months after it was completed.

## Costs

The training program cost central dispatch management $60,000. This figure included the costs of situational and needs analysis, program

# Table 1. Learning objectives for the training.

## Telephone-etiquette Module

- After watching sample phone interactions, dispatchers will correctly indicate whether the sample demonstrated standard central dispatch telephone etiquette.
- Given practice phone calls to make, dispatchers will correctly demonstrate central dispatch telephone etiquette for
  —answering the phone and beginning the conversation
  —addressing the caller
  —putting the caller on hold
  —closing the conversation.

## Working-as-a-team Module

- Dispatchers will define the mission of Central Dispatch Customer Service.
- Dispatchers will identify and describe the characteristics of the ideal dispatch team.
- Dispatchers will identify differences between the real dispatch team and the ideal dispatch team.
- Dispatchers will identify and practice steps to becoming the ideal dispatch team.

## Problem-solving Module

- Dispatchers will differentiate between problems that can be solved while the customer is on the phone and problems that will need to be solved later.
- Given a real problem that might develop with a customer, dispatchers will walk through the steps in the problem-solving process.
- Given a real problem that might develop with a customer, dispatchers will demonstrate talking the customer through the process of problem solving.

## Listening-to-customers Module

- Dispatchers will identify beliefs that facilitate the use of active listening skills and will give examples of how those beliefs could affect their job at central dispatch.
- Given a sample situation, dispatchers will demonstrate the active listening skills of repeating, paraphrasing, giving acceptance responses, and asking clarifying questions to ascertain what problem needs to be solved.
- Given a sample situation in which a customer lists several problems, dispatchers will differentiate between those that they can help solve and those they cannot.
- Given a sample situation in which a customer keeps bringing up solvable problems, dispatchers will demonstrate skills in politely refocusing the customer on the solution.

## Defusing-anger Module

- Dispatchers will list signals that indicate a customer is getting angry and frustrated and will demonstrate responses that will refocus the conversation on problem solving.
- Dispatchers will list signals that indicate they themselves are getting angry and will develop a list of possible responses that will enable them to stay calm and focused on the problem.
- Dispatchers will describe common situations that lead to conflicts and will develop plans for handling them.
- Given a sample conversation, dispatchers will identify words and phrases that upset customers and will demonstrate alternative conversational techniques.
- Given a sample conversation, dispatchers will demonstrate techniques for handling abusive customers.

**Table 1 (continued). Learning objectives for the training.**

**Rapport-building Module**
- Given a sample interaction between a dispatcher and a customer, dispatchers will identify when rapport is blocked.
- Given a sample interaction in which rapport is clearly blocked, dispatchers will demonstrate techniques for overcoming blocked rapport.
- Given a sample interaction in which rapport is clearly blocked, dispatchers will learn to develop and maintain rapport with the customers.
- Dispatchers will identify cultural nuances and personality characteristics that might block rapport.

- Dispatchers will explain a customer's situation and list stresses, concerns, and attitudes on the customer's side that might block rapport.

**Dealing-with-stress Module**
- Each dispatcher will develop a stress-relief plan of action based on his or her sources of stress and support resources.
- Dispatchers will identify their personal sources of work-related stress.
- Dispatchers will identify personal support resources for reducing stress on the job.
- Dispatchers will demonstrate appropriate coping mechanisms for relief of stress.

design, program development (materials, manuals, etc.), and evaluation of the program. In fact, $60,000 may not be the complete cost of training, because the trainer's salary and other costs (e.g., training facility) were not included. This figure was the amount used to calculate the return on investment (ROI), however, because no other costs were available.

## Data Analysis and Results

At the company's request, this evaluation used only measures of central tendency and frequency distributions to show results. The participant population (11) was so small that no sampling was required.

### Business Results

As outlined in the evaluation plan, business results were obtained by comparing pullout records, dealer complaints, and the results of dealer surveys, before and after training. The evaluation of these business objectives took place 11 months after training, a month earlier than was planned.

PULLOUT RECORDS. Each pullout cost the oil company $250. Table 2 shows both the number of monthly pullouts and their cost. A reduction in the number of pullouts resulted in a savings of $354,750 during the first 11 months following training. Although the number of pullouts had shown a decreasing trend since July 1990 (see Figure 1), that

## Table 2. Pullout costs before and after training.

| Before training | | | | After training | | |
|---|---|---|---|---|---|---|
| Month | Number of pullouts | Costs ($) | | Month | Number of pullouts | Costs ($) |
| 1990 | | | | 1991 | | |
| September | 482 | 120,500 | | August | 366 | 91,500 |
| October | 503 | 125,750 | | September | 359 | 89,750 |
| November | 382 | 95,500 | | October | 367 | 91,750 |
| December | 409 | 102,250 | | November | 351 | 87,750 |
| | | | | December | 398 | 99,500 |
| 1991 | | | | | | |
| January | 555 | 138,750 | | 1992 | | |
| February | 367 | 91,750 | | January | 287 | 71,750 |
| March | 430 | 107,500 | | February | 228 | 57,000 |
| April | 352 | 88,000 | | March | 194 | 48,500 |
| May | 387 | 96,750 | | April | 208 | 52,000 |
| June | 326 | 81,500 | | May | 211 | 52,750 |
| July | 369 | 92,250 | | June | 174 | 43,500 |
| **Total** | **4,562** | **1,140,500** | | **Total** | **3,143** | **785,750** |

Difference before training and after training: 354,750.

decrease became even more dramatic after the training intervention in August 1991. The rise in the number of pullouts in December 1991 happened when several dispatchers went on vacation and untrained temporary employees filled in for them.

DEALER COMPLAINTS. Before training, concern about the potential effects of frequent dealer complaints prompted the dispatch manager to keep a log of these complaints. The log indicated that there were approximately three to five complaints each month before training, although in the month immediately before training (July 1991), there were seven complaints. For six months after training (August 1991 to January 1992), the log indicated a total of only six complaints; there have been no complaints since January 1992.

Based on an average salary for management, each dealer complaint cost the oil company approximately $50 worth of time. During the 11 months immediately before training, those complaints cost the

**Figure 1. Number of pullouts, by month. Training took place in August 1991.**

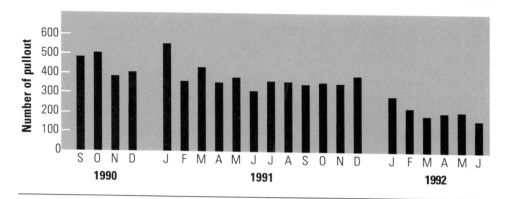

company approximately $2,200. In the 11 months immediately after training, complaints cost the oil company $300. That represents a savings of $1,900. These figures do not take into consideration the cost of the drivers' or the dealers' time.

Not only were complaints reduced significantly (85 percent) since the training intervention in August 1991, but Garner received several letters and telephone calls from dealers complimenting dispatchers on a job well done. Other benefits of decreased customer complaints included reduced dispatcher stress, improved customer relations, and an improved level of customer service.

DEALER SURVEY. A survey was sent to the 50 members of the company's Dealer Council, and 38 dealers responded. Table 3 shows responses for each question on this survey. In addition to indicating that dealers were satisfied overall with the performance of the dispatchers, the survey showed that dealers' requirements were being met by dispatchers, dispatchers displayed proper telephone etiquette, and the overall performance of dispatchers was very good.

The results of the survey suggested the following opportunities for improvement:

- Dealers wanted more help from dispatchers in identifying and solving problems.
- Dealers wanted more notification of gallon changes when load mix would be changed by more than 300 gallons.
- Dealers wanted more notification if delivery would not arrive in the quad for which it was ordered.

## Table 3. Responses to the dealer survey.

| Question | Response categories | Percentage |
|---|---|---|
| Dispatchers are cooperative. | 1 (Agree) | 58 |
| | 2 | 32 |
| | 3 | 10 |
| | 4 | 0 |
| | 5 (Disagree) | 0 |
| Dispatchers demonstrate proper telephone etiquette and courteous responses. | 1 (Always) | 73 |
| | 2 (Sometimes) | 24 |
| | 3 (Never) | 3 |
| In helping to identify and solve your problems, the dispatchers are... | 1 (Very helpful) | 50 |
| | 2 (Moderately helpful) | 50 |
| | 3 (Never helpful) | 0 |
| Dispatchers call back if they are unable to assist you when you first called. | 1 (Agree) | 24 |
| | 2 | 39 |
| | 3 | 9 |
| | 4 | 14 |
| | 5 (Disagree) | 11 |

## Application Results

When a training program is implemented, it is expected that all learned skills will be used on the job; however, skills are used only as they are needed, and some skills are used more than others. Observation of dispatchers and a comparison of absentee records before and after training indicated that the dispatchers were meeting all the application objectives.

OBSERVATION. The dispatchers were observed on two consecutive days for two hours each day. Figure 2, a frequency distribution graph, shows the results of those observations. The dispatchers applied the knowledge and skills they were taught on the job. There was only one incident when a dispatcher did not use "proper telephone etiquette." The phones were extremely busy, two callers were on hold, and the dispatcher answered, "Good morning, Central Dispatch," instead of "Good morning, Central Dispatch. How may I help you?"

## Table 3 (continued). Responses to the dealer survey.

| Question | Response categories | Percentage |
|---|---|---|
| Are you notified of gallon changes when your load mix is changed by more than 300 gallons? | 1 (Yes)<br>2 (No)<br>(Not applicable) | 42<br>37<br>21 |
| If your gasoline delivery is not going to arrive in the quadrant for which it is ordered, you received notification... | 1 (Always)<br>2 (Sometimes)<br>3 (Never) | 21<br>37<br>42 |
| Are your requirements being met by the dispatchers? | 1 (Yes)<br>2 (No)<br>Did not respond | 95<br>4<br>1 |
| The overall performance of dispatchers is... | 1 (Excellent)<br>2 (Good)<br>3 (Average)<br>4 (Fair)<br>5 (Poor) | 32<br>50<br>18<br>0<br>0 |

Note. Dealers were also asked to write down any recommendations for improvement.

ABSENTEEISM RECORDS. The performance objective for dealing with stress could not be measured by observing dispatchers on the job. Instead, the absentee rate was used to determine if the objective was met. If training reduced stress, the absentee rate would be expected to decline after training. Figure 3 shows that although a decline in absenteeism began in February 1991, that decline increased dramatically after training in August 1991. Each day of work missed by a dispatcher cost the oil company $200. During the 11 months immediately before training, absences cost the oil company $5,200. The cost of absences for the 11 months immediately after training dropped to $1,200, a cost savings of $4,000.

## Learning Results

Each time a learning objective was mastered, the objective was checked off a list by both the participant and the instructor. Learning results were assessed by using case studies, games, and role-playing exercises. All participants mastered 100 percent of the learning objectives.

**Figure 2. Results of two 2-hour observations to determine how often dispatchers applied knowledge and skills taught in the training.**

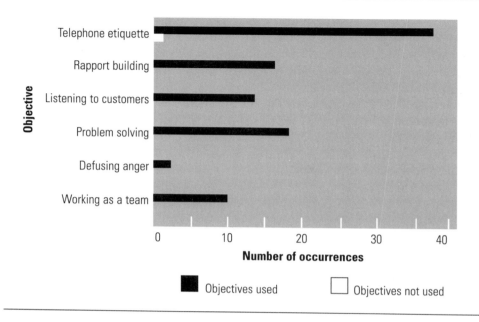

## Reaction Results

Reaction to training is usually assessed only by administering the Products Training Generic Reaction Questionnaire immediately after a training program. In this instance, however, an additional method, the interview, was used. Interviews with management and dispatchers were conducted six months after training to find out if they believed the training had met the needs they had originally identified.

REACTION QUESTIONNAIRE. The reaction questionnaire is divided into five sections. The design section contains questions addressing length of the course, amount of information, content, pace, and course timing in relation to job assignment. For example, questions in the section on method of delivery request information about job aids, case studies, role plays, pre- and postcourse assignments, lectures, and practice time. Questions about location, the training room, and equipment appear in the learning environment section. The instructor section asks the respondent to rate the instructor on knowledge of subject matter, presentation skills, classroom management, and other issues under his or her control. The questionnaire ends with an overall training section. Participants answer questions on a 5-point scale, ranging from 1 (needs improvement) to 5 (excellent). The results for each section of the Products Training Generic Reaction Questionnaire are shown in Table 4.

MANAGEMENT REACTION INTERVIEW. In interviews, central dispatch managers were asked to rate how well dispatchers met expectations after training. The questions were based on problem areas identified in the original needs analysis. Ratings were on a scale of 1 to 10, with 10 being the best possible score. Figure 4 shows both the mean ratings obtained for these problem areas during the needs analysis and the mean results for the posttraining interviews.

DISPATCHER REACTION INTERVIEW. Before training and six months after training, dispatchers were asked to rate their overall job satisfaction and how well their needs were being met. Ratings were on a scale from 1 to 10, with 10 being the best possible score. Figure 5 shows the results of these interviews.

### Return on Investment

The oil company's western region central dispatch saved $360,650 during the first 11 months after training. With $60,000 as the cost of training, a net value of $300,650 was generated. The ROI was calculated as follows:

$$\frac{\text{net benefits}}{\text{program costs}} = \frac{\$300,650}{\$60,000} = 501\%.$$

Because of this good result, the course was taught to the other two central dispatch locations, with similar outcomes.

**Figure 3. Dispatchers' absentee rate for nonoccupational disability, by month. Training took place in August 1991.**

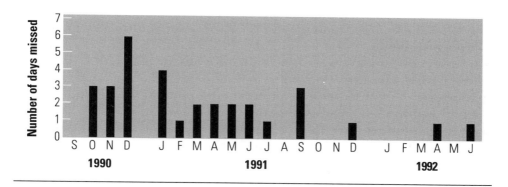

**Table 4. Results of the products training generic reaction questionnaire.**

| Section | Mean score |
|---|---|
| Design | 4.9 |
| Delivery | 4.6 |
| Learning environment | 4.7 |
| Instructor | 4.9 |
| Overall | 4.7 |

Note. Ratings were on a scale from 1 (needs improvements) to 5 (excellent).

## Conclusions and Recommendations

Several barriers had some effect on both the business and the application results of training. For example, dispatchers can schedule deliveries but have no control over the drivers. During the observation period, a dealer called to ask about the status of his gasoline delivery. After several telephone calls, the dispatcher found that the driver did not want to get involved with rush-hour traffic and had decided (without notifying central dispatch) to change his delivery schedule. The dispatchers claim that type of incident happens frequently.

Also, each plant has a different delivery procedure. The oil company has no control over the common carriers, and, therefore, there is no standardization for deliveries. Finally, some dealers do not "stick" the tanks (i.e., measure how much gasoline is left) and therefore do not order correctly. If a dealer misreads or fails to read the stick and orders 300 gallons when his tank will hold only 200, then the arriving truck will have to pull out. Thus, both the oil company and the dealer lose time and money.

In summary, customer service training for central dispatch had the following results:
- a net benefit of approximately $300,000 during the first 11 months after training
- a reduction in pullouts, saving the oil company $354,750 during the first 11 months after training
- a reduction in absenteeism, saving the oil company $4,000 during the first 11 months after training
- an 85 percent reduction in customer complaints, saving the oil company $1,900 during the first 11 months after training
- decreased dealer complaints, resulting in
  — reduced dispatcher stress

## Figure 4. Results of the interviews with management.

Before and after training, managers were asked to rate how well dispatchers were meeting expectations. Ratings were made on a scale from 1 to 10, with 10 being the best possible score.

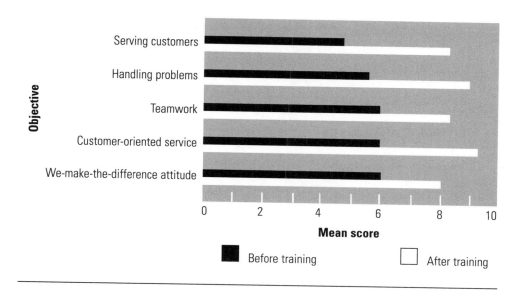

— improved customer relations
— improved customer service
• several letters and phone calls from dealers to management complimenting dispatchers on a job well done
• knowledge and skills taught in the classroom being applied on the job
• dispatchers accomplishing all learning objectives
• an overall increase in dispatchers' job satisfaction.

Management believed the training had resulted in positive changes; dispatchers felt that training had made their jobs easier and that they had more management support than before. In short, all training needs of dealers, management, and dispatchers had been met. Based on these results, additional programs were recommended, including follow-up training for dispatchers and a basic training program for all carriers (even the common carriers not directly employed by the oil company, if possible) to teach them the company's expectations and requirements. In addition, management requested that all new dispatch employees participate in the training program. Another recommendation was for a training program to let dealers know what to

## Figure 5. Results of the interviews with training participants.

Before and after training, participants were asked to rate their overall job satisfaction and how well they felt their needs were being met. Ratings were made on a scale from 1 to 10, with 10 being the best possible score.

expect from central dispatch. This training could be in the form of a booklet, job aid, or module in the Dealer Management Development Program, which is provided to all new dealers.

## Questions for Discussion

1. Is it necessary to develop program objectives at different levels? Explain. Review the objectives for this program at each level. Are they all measurable?
2. Critique the methods used to evaluate the program at each level.
3. Do you think the cost estimate for the program is adequate? Explain.
4. What is your reaction to the application results? Explain.
5. How credible are the business results? Explain.
6. Is it possible to isolate the effect of the training program on business results? How?

## The Author

Rebecca Payne is an evaluation consultant, the owner and founder of ROI Evaluation Services, and an associate with Pinebrook Holub and Associates, an organizational training and development consulting company. Payne holds a master's degree from the

University of Houston in training and development, with a specialty in program evaluation. She has conducted other evaluation research for both the government and private business, has facilitated evaluation workshops and seminars for the American Society for Training and Development, and is past research director for the Houston Chapter. Payne can be contacted at the following address: ROI Evaluation Services, 22210 Coriander, Katy, TX 77450.

## Reference

Abella, K.T. (1986). *Building successful training programs.* Reading, MA: Addison-Wesley.

# Measuring ROI in an Established Program

## Midwest Banking Company

By Jack J. Phillips

---

*Implementing the return-on-investment concept for the first time can bring anxious moments. The following case highlights the difficulties encountered when an organization places tremendous pressure on an individual to produce results with a program. Although some of the tactics may be questionable, some of the methods are instructive.*

---

## Background

The banking industry has become extremely competitive in the 1990s, and one market in which banks are striving to gain a competitive edge is consumer loans. A bank's loan officers are now sales representatives, as they seek potential loan customers and persuade them that the bank offers superior products, competitive prices, and excellent service. For years, banks have taught loan officers how to document and process loans. In recent years, more emphasis has been placed on sales techniques. This case describes the evaluation of a consumer loan seminar with a focus on teaching new consumer loan officers how to use sales techniques to increase consumer loan volume.

## Organizational Profile

Midwest Banking Company (MBC) had been chartered for more than 40 years. Having grown primarily through acquisitions, MBC had more than 100 offices in three states. Its recent acquisition strategy had been steady, adding approximately $1 billion in assets each year for the

*All names, dates, places, and organizations have been disguised at the request of the case author or organization.*

past five years. Future growth was planned at about the same pace. Assets were at $10.4 billion, with deposits of $8.5 billion.

In addition to acquisitions, the bank had grown through increased loan volume, particularly in consumer lending. With an aggressive consumer lending department, MBC had increased consumer loan volume by more than $200 million per year in the past four years. MBC's rates were competitive, the salesforce was very aggressive, advertising support was effective, and branch locations were excellent.

To survive in the current competitive environment, MBC had to continue to grow while maintaining a profitable, efficient, innovative, and cautious strategy. The bank's conservative philosophy helped it avoid the high-risk loans that destroyed some commercial banks in the late 1980s. In consumer lending, MBC had concentrated on traditional types of lending, such as automobile loans (both direct and indirect), home equity lines, and home improvement loans. All three product lines had been very profitable. MBC avoided risky consumer lending programs, such as programs for mobile homes, lake lots, and airplanes.

In the future, MBC needed to add loan officers and train them to be aggressive, effective sales representatives. At the same time, additional volume had to be booked at lower cost so that the bank could remain profitable.

## Harry Johnson

Harry Johnson's training programs at MBC had always received excellent feedback. Loan volumes increased after participants attended the Consumer Lending Seminar (CLS), and testimonials about the effectiveness of the program's techniques were occasionally offered. When Johnson received the assignment to calculate a return on investment (ROI) for his CLS, he was a little frustrated. Why was management interested in a cost-benefit analysis? Was there some skepticism about the effectiveness of the program? Or was management requiring justifications of all training programs? He accepted the assignment with a cautious, yet positive attitude, determined to show management the program's return.

An outstanding loan officer with an unusual ability to coach and teach other people, Johnson had joined the training staff five years earlier, when the human resource development (HRD) manager persuaded him to manage the sales training effort. It was a move that had brought much satisfaction. He enjoyed the challenge and never regretted moving to the HRD staff. Although responsible for all sales training, Johnson was confident with his own training ability and insisted that he have a direct role in each consumer lending course conducted.

## Pressure To Change

In a conversation with Johnson, the HRD manager, Jane McCluskey, explained the rationale for the assignment: "We have more pressure for us to show the value added by our programs. For selected programs, we have promised top management that we will show an ROI analysis. It's part of our shift toward increased accountability." She added with some emphasis, "Management can no longer accept on face value that our programs are effective and that they produce results. We must show them with convincing evidence, including an ROI."

McCluskey had selected the CLS as one of the targeted programs for analysis. It had a good reputation, and she thought that Johnson had the ability to develop the ROI and present it to management.

## The Consumer Lending Seminar

The CLS was a three-day program designed for new consumer loan officers or other employees who planned to assume consumer lending responsibilities in the future. The seminar was a standard in the industry and focused on topics such as prospecting, customer needs analysis, presenting products' features and benefits, handling objections, sales closing techniques, and cross-selling. Unique to the program were 10 strategies to attract new consumer loan customers. Developed by Johnson and his staff, these strategies were quite effective, as evidenced by increases in participants' loan volumes after attending the program.

At the end of each program, the HRD staff always collected feedback questionnaires that provided detailed information about the content of the program, the relevance of the material to the job, and what participants planned to accomplish after attending the program. At times, loan volumes would be monitored in specific regions, often revealing dramatic improvements. Occasionally, follow-ups were conducted with participants to determine what they had accomplished. The results were summarized in a memo to the file, with a copy to McCluskey or Vic Andrews, senior vice-president for consumer lending.

## Jane McCluskey

An experienced HRD professional, Jane McCluskey had logged some 15 years in HRD, with the last 10 in banking. Her initial assignment at MBC had been in conducting a program for new supervisors.

After a variety of projects in management training, she had been promoted to manager, management and supervisory training. The previous year, she had been named head of HRD and, as part of that move,
inherited the sales training function, which had previously been under
the marketing function. In her new role, she assumed responsibility for
all HRD programs, including technical training.

McCluskey had earned a reputation as a true professional who was
focused on the needs of the bank. She had the respect of management.
In recent meetings with top management, she had noticed an occa-
sional concern about the effectiveness of training. Some managers
questioned the bank's investment in training, particularly as MBC was
trying to become more cost-efficient.

McCluskey accepted the executive concerns as a challenge and
agreed to develop an ROI analysis of a few selected programs. In addition, she would require that all programs be evaluated in more detail
than a typical end-of-program reaction questionnaire. As a part of this
emphasis, each HRD staff member would now be required to develop a
strategy for evaluation, which must include follow-up activities.
Although this requirement had met with some resistance from the staff,
they understood the rationale and were prepared to give it their best
efforts.

## The Assignment

The assignment for Johnson was clear. He had to show the monetary value of the benefit derived from conducting a session of the CLS.
The benefits would have to be calculated for a specific time frame and
annualized for comparisons with the cost of the program. Costs needed
to include the prorated cost of the initial development of the seminar.
With this approach, management would have an accurate comparison
of benefits versus costs. Johnson was told to use the term ROI with cau-
tion, however, because it might be confused with the typical ROI calculations from the bank's investment division.

A few questions began to surface. Which group should be selected for analysis? What monetary value should be placed on increased
loan production? How much of the improvement in loan volume
could be attributed to the program? What costs should be included in
the analysis? How much of the original development costs should be
prorated? How should the results be presented to top management?
What assumptions would have to be made when developing the ROI?
Would Johnson leave himself open to criticism if the project failed?
These questions, with no immediate answers, left him confused and

facing a bit of anxiety about this project. He decided to seek direction from McCluskey.

As Johnson began to ask these questions, McCluskey quickly interrupted, "The details are left up to you, Harry, although I would like to review the methodology and reach an agreement as to how specific issues are to be addressed." Then she added, "I have confidence in your ability to complete this project. I'm here to help if you need me. But first, you should tackle each issue."

Johnson responded a little wearily, "Thanks for the vote of confidence. I'll get back with you later."

It was made quite clear that this report, along with the reports of other programs, would go to top management. Johnson assumed that he would be presenting the results to top management at an HRD review meeting, and he viewed this as both an opportunity and a frustrating challenge. It was an opportunity to demonstrate the effectiveness of his programs. He could convince top management that his efforts were contributing directly to the bank's bottom line. The challenge was created by the presence of so many unknowns. This was new territory, and, if not completed properly, the project could be criticized or even fail.

## Program Formulation and Delivery

Johnson decided to use the next CLS, which was to begin in three weeks, for the detailed analysis. Although he was told to ensure that the target group was typical, he picked the next group so that he could get the project moving forward. As the planning for the seminar began, other questions began to surface. Should he do anything different with the group? Should they be told that they were expected to produce? Should he disclose the plans to monitor actual production? Would this action bias the results? Although in previous programs he usually communicated expectations, results were not monitored and reported to top management. Johnson decided it was imperative that the program achieve results, so he planned several discussions during the program to place emphasis on producing, monitoring, and reporting results so that the improvement of each participant could be tracked.

Because of his concern that the program show good results, Johnson was determined to assemble an outstanding group. As a routine procedure when planning a program, he sent all regional managers a course announcement requesting the names of participants. For this particular program, new requirements were added. Previously, participants were allowed to attend the course even if they were not engaged in consumer lending activity on a full-time basis. In some cases, branch employees, who worked in traditional teller and customer service representative functions, were being trained to assume limited consumer lending activities. These future loan officers were allowed to attend the program to begin developing consumer lending skills. This time, such individuals were excluded because their results might not materialize soon. In addition to making this change, Johnson phoned all the regional managers, explained the planned evaluation, and asked them to send the best prospects for this particular course. In some situations, there was no choice of participants because all new consumer loan officers had to attend the first available program following their arrival at the bank.

After all potential participants were identified, they received a memo with course details. In addition to including routine information, this memo explained that participants' consumer loan volume would be monitored for six months following the program. Johnson insisted that participants "come to the program with the determination to build skills and apply the training material to achieve results." In a similar memo to guest discussion leaders, Johnson asked for their best performance, suggesting that they teach with impressive end results in mind.

## Costs

The following costs were included in the analysis:
- Johnson's time for conducting and coordinating the program
- the time of other people directly involved in conducting and supporting the program
- direct expenses for using the training facility
- salaries of participants
- prorated development costs
- costs of training materials
- travel, lodging, and meals
- other direct expenses charged to the program.

The development costs were spread over the number of programs that had already been conducted plus the expected number in the future. A five-year time frame was used. Table 1 shows the breakdown of the costs for the program.

## Isolating the Effects of Training

After the program was completed, Johnson developed a plan for collecting data on increased loan volume. Before-and-after comparisons

**Table 1. Program costs for the consumer lending seminar per three-day session.**

| Item | Cost ($) |
|---|---|
| Instructors and coordinators (salaries) | 1,570 |
| Administrative support | 500 |
| Facilities (food, refreshments) | 1,800 |
| Participants' salaries (based on 20 participants) | 7,200 |
| Development costs (prorated) | 300 |
| Training materials | 400 |
| Travel, lodging, meals (for out-of-town participants) | 5,250 |
| Other costs | 490 |
| **Total** | **17,510** |

of consumer loan volume were used to measure improvement. For some participants, this was a simple process: An individual's record for the previous six months was averaged and compared with the corresponding figure for the six months after the program. For other participants, however, measuring improvement was more difficult. New consumer loan officers had no previous lending record at MBC; neither did participants who had just taken on additional responsibilities. Johnson selected a conservative strategy. For new recruits, consumer loan volume was obtained from the previous employer if this information was available. When it was not, volume was estimated with input from the participant. For participants in new job assignments, estimates were made based on an average consumer loan volume of employees without CLS training. As much information as possible was collected, although Johnson realized that it was not always accurate.

Three important factors that had an impact on increased volume had surfaced and had to be addressed. The first factor concerned the extent to which changes in interest rates influenced the increase in consumer loan volume. For example, four months after the program was conducted, interest rates fell by 1 percentage point. When rates fall, volume goes up, regardless of training. The marketing department provided an estimate of how much consumer loan volume increases with every quarter of a percent of rate decrease. The MBC data, combined with national data from a banking trade group, showed that consumer loan volume increased 2 percent for every quarter of a percent decrease in interest rates. This adjustment was used in the analysis.

The second factor concerned whether special promotions initiated after the seminar was conducted increased expenditures. Promotions in the six-month period following the seminar were compared with promotions for similar periods. If the magnitude of the expenditures were found to be greater following the seminar, a proportionate amount of loan volume would have to be factored out of the results using estimates from the marketing department. In this case, however, the difference in promotional expenditures was negligible.

The third factor was the fact that some improvement would be realized without training. Employees new to the job learn on their own, develop techniques, and receive coaching and counseling from superiors. Initial success generates additional confidence and subsequently more volume. Johnson desired to isolate this effect because he thought it might surface in the discussions with top management. Also, McCluskey had mentioned the issue in earlier discussions. After discussing the problem with several key executives, Johnson decided to use a 10 percent increase in consumer loans for this factor. With these issues covered, he was confident that whatever improvement remained would be directly attributable to the training program.

## Calculating the Value of the Improvement

To calculate the return, Johnson needed to know the total value of an additional loan. He examined the benefits of additional loan volume by calculating the average margin for a loan. The margin is the interest rate charged for the loan, minus the cost of funds and the expenses associated with the loan. As shown in Table 2, several components went into this calculation. The first step was to determine the yield, which was available from bank records. Next, the average spread between the cost of funds and the yield received on the loan was calculated. For

**Table 2. Loan profitability analysis.**

| Profit component | Unit value |
|---|---|
| Average loan size | $15,500 |
| Average loan yield | 9.75% |
| Average cost of funds (including branch costs) | 5.50% |
| Direct costs for consumer lending | 0.82% |
| Corporate overhead | 1.61% |
| **Net profit per loan** | **1.82%** |

example, the bank could get funds from depositors at 5.5 percent on average, including the costs of the branch. From this difference had to be subtracted the direct costs of making the loan, such as the salaries of the employees in the consumer lending area and the direct costs of advertising and supplies. Historically, direct costs at MBC amounted to 0.82 percent of the loan value. In addition, overhead costs for all the other corporate functions, 1.61 percent for MBC, had to be subtracted.

The appropriate value for the cost of funds usually stirs some disagreement. The investment department suggested that the average cost for generating deposits in a branch be used, although in some cases MBC could attract funds at a lower rate by borrowing from the Federal Reserve. Johnson took the conservative route, using the average cost of funds generated from the branch. The 1.82 percent profit on the average loan would be a reasonable figure, he believed.

## The Results

After six months, Johnson used bank records to calculate an average monthly volume increase for each loan officer who had attended the program. The volume increases were adjusted, with the factors - described earlier, to isolate the effects of training. In a follow-up questionnaire, Johnson asked loan officers to provide estimates of increased consumer loan production generated as a result of the course. Some participants actually compared their before and after values. This process provided a check of the data retrieved from bank records.

Table 3 shows the summary of the overall results from this class of 20 loan officers. (Note that data from only 18 were included; two loan officers had been reassigned to other functions and were omitted.)

**Table 3. Overall results of the training program.**

| Component | Value |
|---|---|
| Average monthly increase in loans per participant after adjustments (18 participants) | 6 |
| Total monthly amount of increased loans ($15,500 x 6 x 18) | $ 1,674,000 |
| Annual improvement in loan values ($1,674,000 x 12 months) | $ 20,088,000 |
| Profit from improvement (1.82%) | $ 365,601 |

Although Johnson planned to base the benefit analysis on changes in loan production, he wanted to list other potential benefits of training as intangible benefits. Therefore, a part of the questionnaire asked participants about other benefits of the program, such as additional cross-sell activity (i.e., selling a customer other products during the process of closing a consumer loan); number of new account relationships developed per month (new accounts are perceived to be valuable because they provide the bank additional opportunities to sell other products in the future); and improvements in personal effectiveness. It was important to find out if former participants were working smarter and more efficiently, so the questionnaire asked for ratios of loans closed per initial contact and the time to close a loan. Finally, to uncover problems and make future adjustments, information about barriers that hindered the application of the training material was requested.

## Calculating Return

With the values from the tables, the ROI could be developed. The ROI formula used divides the net annual benefits by the costs of the program. The calculations showed the following value for the return:

$$\text{ROI} = \frac{\text{net benefits}}{\text{costs}} = \frac{\$365,601 - \$17,510}{\$17,510} = \frac{\$348,091}{\$17,510} = 19.88, \text{ or } 1,988\%.$$

Armed with excellent results, Johnson was ready to present them to management. He was completely satisfied not only that his program was very successful, but also that he could convince anyone that there was a significant return on training, particularly his training.

## Questions for Discussion

1. Critique Johnson's approach to the assignment.
2. Were all the costs included in the analysis? Explain.
3. What approach was used to isolate the effects of training? Was it effective?
4. Critique the method used to convert increased consumer loan volume to a dollar value.
5. How credible was the ROI calculation?
6. What cautions would you suggest to use when communicating the results to management?
7. Critique McCluskey's role in the process.
8. Where should Johnson have gone for help?

9. What do you think will be management's reaction to the evaluation report?

10. What were the critical issues in this case?

## The Author

With more than 25 years of professional experience in the management field, Jack Phillips serves on the management faculty of Middle Tennessee State University and, through Performance Resources Organization, consults with manufacturing, service, and government organizations in the United States and abroad. Previously, Phillips was president of a large regional savings bank with offices in three states and served as senior human resource officer for three firms and training manager for two Fortune 500 firms. Phillips holds undergraduate degrees in electrical engineering, physics, and mathematics; a master's degree in decision sciences from Georgia State University; and a Ph.D. in human resource management from the University of Alabama. Phillips has authored four books and 75 articles, including the *Handbook of Training Evaluation and Measurement Methods* (2d ed., Gulf Publishing, 1991), *Improving Supervisors' Effectiveness* (Jossey-Bass, 1985), and *Recruiting, Training and Retaining New Employees* (Jossey-Bass, 1987). Phillips can be contacted at the following address: Performance Resources Organization, P.O. Box 1967, Murfreesboro, TN 37133-1969.

# Getting Results with Interpersonal Skills Training

## Information Services Inc.

By Darlene Russ-Eft, Srinivas Krishnamurthi, and
Lilanthi Ravishankar

*Because of the soft nature of the programs, interpersonal skills training is a particular challenge when calculating return on investment. The following case describes a very successful, commercially available interpersonal skills training program in a large information-services organization. The results are very encouraging.*

## Background

Information Services Inc. (ISI) conducted a return-on-investment (ROI) study in December 1990. The main objective of the study, which was initiated by ISI's Information Resources Division, was to evaluate the effectiveness of an interpersonal skills training program implemented that year and to determine if there was a dollar return on the investment made in training. Presenting positive results to senior management could gain support for the program. In addition, the Information Resources Division hoped to show that measurable ROI could be demonstrated from an interpersonal skills program. A secondary objective was to determine if using line managers rather than trainers to deliver the training made a difference in its effectiveness.

The major focus of ISI for the 1990s is initiating and managing change to foster greater competitiveness and revenue growth. One way to achieve these objectives is to provide training to employees that increases their job effectiveness. Another way is to reduce the workforce, including management layers. The organization also divested some businesses that were not in line with revenue targets. In addition, the company is in the process of expanding its markets by creating new products. The organization is currently in the process of building a worldwide company culture that will position all its subsidiaries' products and services as coming from a single large organization. This will make ISI an organization with virtually no serious competition.

## Organizational Profile

ISI is one of the world's leading marketers of information, software, and other services for business decision making. The corporation comprises 11 separate divisions and has approximately 7,700 employees in North America and 56,000 employees worldwide. ISI provides information and services that help clients improve their performance in a wide range of business activities, including marketing, advertising, promotion, and sales management; research and development; strategic planning; financial and investment management; information systems management; directory advertising and promotion; and health-care information management. Such services fall under the broad categories of

- *Global information services*—business information services that contribute to organizations' strategic planning and decision making
- *Personalized services*—services that allow customers easier access to information and the capability to store and analyze such information
- *Software services*—services for computer networks that allow customers to use their information management systems in a broader range of applications.

ISI's corporate center is based in New York. The company also has offices in 60 countries worldwide.

The organization is involved in the financial information-services industry, providing financial data on commercial enterprises around the world. Competitors to ISI are organizations such as TRW. A major success factor in this industry is the quick turnaround of financial data as information in a form most useful to the customers. Finding new ways of packaging information into new products for new markets is the key to growth in this industry.

## Character Profile

Several key individuals were involved in the evaluation and ROI study. The vice-president of operations, a 20-year employee, was responsible for unit training and development. Her major concern related to human resource development (HRD) was that the dollars spent on training should affect the bottom line. She was a participative yet demanding manager. Before this training evaluation, she believed that "how to" training (training that taught specific technical skills, such as data processing skills) was most beneficial, but she was open to evaluating interpersonal skills training to determine if there would be return on investment.

The executive director of organization and professional development had an extensive background in HRD and had been at ISI for two years. His charge was to provide the vice-president of operations with the data needed to justify HRD programs such as the interpersonal skills program. The management style of this individual was directive and strong-willed. He believed the program would show return on investment, but needed the data to prove it.

The chief financial officer was a participative manager who viewed all programs relative to their impact on the bottom line. He wanted to see a formal ROI study done on the interpersonal skills program.

The director of management development had three years of HRD experience and 21 years of related experience. He was also interested in obtaining proof that the training program had an effect. The director employed a demanding but persuasive style of management.

## Issues and Events

ISI had several issues to confront during the implementation of the training program. The organization had more than 100 locations spread out geographically within the United States. In addition, the organization wanted to bring about a cultural change to move to a more supportive and cooperative climate and to foster improved performance throughout the organization—but this change had to be inexpensive. Finding a program that could show a real impact was critical, because the budget review focused on the dollar value of all HRD programs at ISI.

The ROI and evaluation study was designed to identify two solutions to these cost-related issues. First, the organization wanted to determine if the interpersonal skills program was beneficial to them and if it had bottom-line results. Second, the organization wanted to know if the training could be delivered by line managers rather than trainers, thereby reducing the costs of implementing training.

# Program Description

The participants completed training in an interpersonal skills program developed by a California-based company specializing in interventions for effecting organizational change. The program provides basic human interaction skills, using behavior modeling to develop and reinforce recognition and practice of key actions. Skills taught are designed to

- build effective communication, judgment, and initiative
- support an ongoing quality, service, or productivity effort by complementing technical systems and processes
- help employees capitalize on the many changes taking place in organizations today
- develop employees' self-management capacity so they can use their supervisors' time and their own time more cost-effectively
- help employees become more responsive to the reality of "doing more with less"
- build personal self-worth and job skills.

The 12 key skills in the program are built into separate units, such as keeping one's boss informed, resolving issues, and being a team player. Table 1 lists the titles of all the units.

## Table 1. Titles of units in the Working program.

| | |
|---|---|
| • Introduction | • Participating in Group Meetings |
| • The Basic Principles | • Being a Team Player |
| • Listening To Understand Clearly | • Keeping Your Boss Informed |
| • Giving Feedback To Help Others | • Resolving Issues with Others |
| • Taking on a New Assignment | • Positive Responses to Negative Situations |
| • Requesting Help | • Dealing with Changes |
| • Getting Your Point Across | • Working Smarter |

Each unit represents $2^{1/2}$ hours of training, and each can stand alone or be combined with other training activities. The training is provided at the organization's locations. The frequency of training sessions depends on the organization, but ranges from once a week to once a month. The instructors attend a four-day certification seminar that covers facilitation skills, the behavior modeling process, basic program content, and implementation strategies.

There are no prerequisites for attending the training. The program focuses on all employees at the various locations, regardless of experience, prior training, or level in the organization. At the outset, the HRD group believed there was value in the program, but did not really expect to see a large ROI.

The program was delivered in three locations. In one of the facilities, a training staff member from headquarters delivered all of the units. At another location, a regional trainer delivered the units, and at a third, the local manager delivered the program. This was part of the design to identify the least expensive method of delivering training. The assumption was that it would be more cost-effective to have line managers rather than corporate-based trainers (known as "national trainers" at ISI) deliver training. The rationale for this assumption was the fact that line managers were already available to deliver training at the various locations, whereas corporate trainers had to travel to the locations and thus would incur additional expenses.

Participants in the training program were mostly professional and support personnel in the three locations. A sample of similar individuals from another location was selected for the control group. Professional-level employees were business analysts; support staff included secretaries, clerks, and data entry operators, among others. Experience levels varied from one or two months to 25 years in the job or company. The attendees were approximately 50 percent male and 50 percent female, with an estimated average age of 30. The training group included some individuals who worked primarily "on the street" (i.e., those who went out into the field and made calls on businesses) and others who worked mainly on the telephone.

The interpersonal skills training involved presentations by an instructor coupled with skills practice. Each training session started with feedback on a previous session, an introduction, and an explanation of the rationale behind each key action, followed by a brief video on behavioral cues. Participants learned to identify when to use the key actions in different situations and began to formulate action plans for both practice assignments and future on-the-job behavior. Skills practice offered participants different perspectives on how to use the key actions in work situations. In the practice situations, participants received feedback on their own use of the key actions and also had the opportunity to observe how other trainees used the key actions.

## Models and Techniques

Because of the cost-related issues identified earlier, ISI decided to use a financial approach to justify the implementation of the skills program. The parameters were defined and the evaluation was conducted using surveys designed by the training company to evaluate transfer of skills acquired.

## Evaluation Instruments

The evaluation instruments gathered ratings of subjects' on-the-job behavior, as well as ratings of organizational climate and job satisfaction (see Table 2 for sample items). Ratings were on a 7-point Likert-type rating scale.

The on-the-job behavior ratings included 44 items grouped into four categories:

- dealing with problems
- communicating with coworkers
- working with superiors
- improving work.

**Table 2. Examples of the items on the evaluation instrument, by category.**

| Category | Items |
|---|---|
| 1. Dealing with problems | To what extent does _____ let others know about needing help at work? <br> To what extent does _____ focus on solving a problem? |
| 2. Communicating with coworkers | To what extent does _____ ask questions to make sure of understanding? <br> To what extent does _____ give facts to support ideas? |
| 3. Working with superiors | To what extent does _____ know what information to provide to the boss? <br> To what extent does _____ keep the boss informed on what is going on? |
| 4. Improving work | To what extent does _____ offer to help solve work-related problems? <br> To what extent does _____ share good ideas with others? |
| 5. Job satisfaction and organizational climate | To what extent do you feel satisfied with the opportunities in the organization? <br> To what extent do you feel that decisions are made by those with the best information? |

Ratings of organizational climate and job satisfaction were obtained from seven items. In addition, members of the trained and control groups indicated the percentage of time that they spent on the job dealing with items grouped under the four behavioral categories.

## Evaluation Design

The study used pretraining and posttraining ratings of behaviors of trained and control groups, to which people had been randomly assigned. Ratings were gathered from members of both groups, as well as from their supervisors and their colleagues. These pre- and post-training ratings were matched for each respondent. Table 3 presents the number of people in each respondent group.

Pretraining ratings were gathered immediately before training. Posttraining ratings were gathered approximately one month following training.

## Data Analysis

ISI conducted a series of analyses of variance with repeated measures. These analyses compared trained participants with control participants, trained-group supervisors with control-group supervisors, and trained-group colleagues with control-group colleagues.

## Costs

Determining the costs for training was fairly straightforward. Two types of costs were recognized: variable costs and fixed costs. The variable costs consisted of the costs for running each training session. These costs were incurred if and only if a session took place. These

**Table 3. Sizes of respondent groups.**

| Respondent group | Before training | After training | Matched |
|---|---|---|---|
| Trained-group participants | 72 | 56 | 42 |
| Control-group participants | 45 | 21 | 14 |
| Trained-group supervisors | 76 | 61 | 31 |
| Control-group supervisors | 41 | 15 | 3 |
| Trained-group colleagues | 137 | 98 | 23 |
| Control-group colleagues | 85 | 37 | 18 |

costs included the following:

- trainees' time away from work (salary plus fringe benefits)
- trainers' time for preparation and training (salary plus fringe benefits)
- materials used during the sessions (workbooks, certificates, flip charts and markers, refreshments, and room rental or usage).

The fixed costs were those that had been incurred or would be incurred even if a specific session never occurred. These costs included the following:

- time for designing the sessions (salary plus fringe benefits, divided by the total number of sessions given until the time of the posttesting, and then multiplied by the number of sessions included in the present study)
- certification costs (certification fees, plus trainers' time and expenses for the certification training, divided by the total number of sessions, and then multiplied by the number of sessions in this study).

Costs incurred for the entire population of 85 trainees were estimated at approximately $70,000.

## Converting Data Values

The primary benefits from training involve changes in skill. Through the evaluation effort, ratings of trainees' skill were obtained before and after training. The major objective of this effort was to transform those skill changes into dollar benefits to the organization.

Assigning a monetary value to the behavioral improvements required several assumptions:

- that a person in a given position was paid to undertake certain activities effectively
- that the organization would get maximum return for its investment if the employee were 100 percent effective in those activities
- that the proportion of the employee's time spent in those activities could be costed as the same proportion of his or her salary (although the training effectiveness would not disappear in a year, this time period was chosen to coordinate with the annual budgeting cycle).

In order to determine the benefits for skill improvements, ISI needed to know how much time (or the percentage of time) trainees spent in the skills being rated. To simplify the data reporting for the trainees, the four behavioral categories in Table 2 were used: dealing with problems, communicating with coworkers, working with superiors, and improving work. Because these four categories might not account for an employee's total time on the job, there were four additional open-ended categories. For example, a trainee might label one of these categories as "doing work" and then specify the percentage of time he or she spent on that task.

It should be noted here that these procedures may have introduced some bias. First, combining several skills into one category assumes that they receive equal weight. Second, including only open-ended categories for activities outside the training program may have led some respondents to indicate greater than actual percentages of time devoted to the four training-related categories.

The following steps were used to determine the monetary benefits:

- An average annual salary plus fringe benefits was determined for the members of the group.
- This figure was multiplied by the percentage of time each employee undertook each activity, yielding the dollar value of the time the employee spent dealing with each specific activity. (Note that for this calculation ISI used the time percentages obtained after training. The assumption was that these percentages represented the way that the person would be working in the future.)
- Each pretraining skill rating for the employee was multiplied by the cost figure to give the return to the organization for that skill prior to training.
- Each posttraining skill rating was multiplied by the cost figure to give the return to the organization after training.
- The difference between the posttraining and the pretraining figures indicated the benefit to the organization resulting from the training.
- Total benefits for all trainees were summed to determine the total benefits for the program.

## Results

Selected results appear in Table 4. The analysis of variance showed overall improvement, comparing skill ratings before and after training and retrospectively (i.e., posttraining ratings of pretraining skill) and after training. Also, significant differences appeared between trained and control groups in these overall improvements.

### Return on Investment

The results indicated that, for a sample of 42 trainees out of the total population of 85 trainees, the total benefits were approximately $305,000. Subtracting the costs from the benefits results in a net bene-

## Table 4. Selected analysis of variance results.

| Analysis of variance | Raters | | |
| --- | --- | --- | --- |
| | Participants | Supervisors | Colleagues |
| Difference between ratings before and after training, and retrospectively and after training | $F(2, 108) = 9.02$ $p < 0.001$ | $F(1, 73) = 31.77$ $p < 0.001$ | $F(2, 80) = 8.77$ $p < 0.002$ |
| Difference between trained and control groups in overall improvements | $F(2, 108) = 3.40$ $p < 0.05$ | $F(1, 73) = 6.77$ $p < 0.05$ | $F(2, 80) = 1.92$ $p = 0.15$ |

fit of $235,000 ($305,000 - $70,000). The traditional ROI formula yields an ROI of 336 percent.

These calculations underestimate the net benefits somewhat. First, the gross benefits were determined for only about half of the population. If the gross benefits for the remaining trainees are similar to results for the first 42, then the total will be about $610,000, and the net benefits will be $540,000. Second, some indirect benefits resulted from the training in the form of changes in the percentage of time trainees spent in various activities. Table 5 summarizes these changes. After training, trainees spent more time communicating with coworkers and less time working with superiors. This can be viewed as a benefit, because trainees were handling issues and problems directly with their coworkers. None of these indirect benefits were included in the analysis, however.

## Table 5. Percentage of time spent in different categories of activities before and after training.

| Category | Before training | After training |
| --- | --- | --- |
| Communicating with coworkers | 18 | 26 |
| Working with superiors | 19 | 16 |
| Dealing with problems | 26 | 31 |
| Improving work | 22 | 22 |
| Other | 15 | 5 |

## Differences between Types of Trainers

A secondary objective of the study was to identify less expensive methods of training delivery. The HRD group was interested in determining if it made a difference in training outcomes whether the training was delivered by a training staff member from corporate headquarters, a regional trainer, or a local manager.

Results indicate that there were no discernible differences in training outcomes between the different types of trainers (see Table 6). Therefore, the organization may be able to realize a cost savings, because using a line manager to deliver training would make it unnecessary for regional and corporate trainers to incur additional travel costs.

**Table 6. Differences in ratings of overall skill improvement between participants trained by national trainers and participants trained by line managers.**

| Analysis of variance | Raters | | |
|---|---|---|---|
| | **Participants** | **Supervisors** | **Colleagues** |
| Difference between the two trained groups in overall improvements | $F_{(2, 80)} = 0.36$ $p = 0.70$, n.s. | $F_{(2, 58)} = 1.25$ $p = 0.29$, n.s. | $F_{(2, 42)} = 0.34$ $p = 0.71$, n.s. |

## Conclusion

The results of the ROI study showed that the interpersonal skills program at ISI had a positive effect on the bottom line and that the HRD expense was justified. After training, trainees were using the taught skills more often and more effectively on the job. The results from the study did not garner as much support for the program from senior management as was expected, however, partly because management was suspicious that the large ROI might be an indication of a lack of validity. Another reason was that the Finance Group at ISI contended that, although there was an ROI in terms of skill transfer on the job, a few of the skills that showed improvement were not as directly relevant to certain job functions as others. For example, a data entry operator essentially works individually. Yet one of the skills that the group as a whole showed improvement in was communicating with other people. In this sense, although skills did improve and justified the HRD expense, a few of the participants received training in skills that did not directly affect their day-to-day work.

In retrospect, it appears that organizations considering such studies should ensure at the outset that the people interested in the ROI results have a clear understanding about what is being measured. It is also important at an early stage to market the ROI adequately to senior management and gain their support for the results. It is essential that support for the ROI concept, methodology, and parameters be obtained from all interested groups prior to conducting the study. Despite some of these concerns, however, the ROI study proved beneficial to the existence of the interpersonal skills program at ISI. The organization continues to offer this training program, albeit on a more limited basis.

As for the secondary objective of the study, to determine whether training outcomes would be different if the training were delivered by corporate trainers or line managers, the results showed no differences. These results indicate that training could be conducted by line managers at the various locations of ISI, enabling the organization to reduce costs by avoiding having corporate trainers travel to various locations to conduct the training.

The results of the study indicate that an interpersonal skills program yields return on investment for the organization. Such quantitative studies that demonstrate bottom-line results can be useful in obtaining management's support for skills training and development.

## Questions for Discussion

1. What are your reactions and assessment of the climate that precipitated this program?
2. What is your reaction to the secondary objective? Should both objectives have been included in the study?
3. Critique the evaluation design and methods of data collection.
4. Evaluate the cost-tracking process.
5. Do you agree with the assumptions used to assign monetary values to behavioral improvements? Why or why not?
6. Critique the method used to convert behavioral improvements into a monetary value. What are its shortcomings? Would you recommend other approaches for this process?
7. Critique the ROI for the study.
8. How do you account for management's reactions to the study results?

## The Authors

Darlene Russ-Eft is division director of research services at Zenger-Miller Inc., an international supplier of training systems and services headquartered in California. She completed her Ph.D. conducting research on buildup and release of proactive interference in short-term memory for individual words. As senior research scientist with the American Institutes for Research and as research fellow with the Human Performance Center at the University of Michigan, she published numerous articles and books on the topic of adult learning. She has continued this research at Zenger-Miller, with an emphasis on learning through worker, supervisor, middle management, team, and total quality management training. Russ-Eft can be contacted at the following address: Zenger-Miller Inc., 1735 Technology Drive, 6th Floor, San Jose, CA 95110-1313.

Srinivas Krishnamurthi is currently the systems administrator/programmer for the Research Division at Zenger-Miller Inc. While earning his M.B.A. from Oklahoma State University in management information systems, he also supported the Office of Business and Economic Research as a systems administrator, providing programming assistance to various professors for research projects. He continues to write various analysis programs for research studies at Zenger-Miller.

Lilanthi Ravishankar is a research analyst for the Research Division of Zenger-Miller Inc. She is responsible primarily for the management of various research projects and for data analysis and reporting. Prior to joining Zenger-Miller, she attended the master's program in sociology and demography at the University of Texas at Austin.

# Turning Down Manager Turnover

## Financial Services Inc.

Cynthia Schoeppel

*Employee turnover can be very costly, particularly in key jobs, such as branch manager in a financial services firm. The following case discusses a human resource development program, involving both selection and training, that resulted in a dramatic reduction in the turnover of new branch managers. The return was extremely high, in part because of assumptions made by program designers and endorsed by management.*

## Background

From 1981 to 1990, Financial Services Inc. (FSI) experienced an annualized turnover rate of 48 percent to 63 percent for the position of branch manager trainee. Even though this was considered standard for the industry, the turnover was costly in terms of profitability, growth, and productivity. It was estimated that the turnover costs were approximately $10 million in 1989, based on the costs of screening, interviewing, training materials, and salaries and benefits for trainees. It was also estimated that there were additional profitability issues in business lost because of the branch and district managers' time spent in recruiting, hiring, and training. Moreover, newer, untrained employees produced less work and marketed fewer products than more experienced employees.

Because there were not enough employees ready to assume management positions, FSI could not expand as rapidly as it wanted. Growth was constrained by the number of experienced managers ready to assume the responsibilities of opening new offices. The high turnover reduced the number of managers available to meet expansion

*All names, dates, places, and organizations have been disguised at the request of the case author or organization.*

plans. Also, whenever an employee left, branch productivity would suffer as other employees assumed the routine duties of the vacant position. Energies were directed to meeting the pressing needs of the office, rather than providing customer service and marketing additional products and services. Turnover was identified as a key problem area, and this project was initiated in order to address these issues.

## FSI

FSI is a 90-year-old financial services company that was operated primarily by one family until 1982, when one of the nation's largest bank holding companies acquired it. FSI had an extraordinary record of consistent growth and high profitability. At the time of this project, there were approximately 5,000 employees in 800 branch office locations and a central office. These 800 branch offices were grouped into 12 geographic regions, each headed by a regional manager who had seven or eight district sales managers reporting to him or her. This company was one of the leaders in its industry, providing consumer loans, credit cards, leasing services, accounts receivable financing, and computer services for the finance industry. Each branch manager's performance was appraised on the basis of the growth and profitability of the branch. Likewise, district and regional managers were appraised on the same standards, as well as on their abilities to open new offices and streamline operations. Having a stable and well-qualified workforce was crucial to both individual and company success.

All the regional and district managers were promoted from within the company. They started as branch manager trainees and worked their way up through the ranks. Therefore, all of them thought they knew the trainee position thoroughly. It had been many years since some of them worked in a branch, however, and their knowledge of the daily job was lacking. Some of the mistakes being made in hiring were due to outdated notions about the branch manager trainee position. Trainees were often hired to fit the former service culture instead of the new sales culture.

## Industry Profile

The financial services industry as a whole was coming out of a period of steady growth but experiencing problems in regulatory compliance. The industry is highly regulated, which tends to result in a very analytical and procedure-oriented employee group. Major trends in the industry, however, pointed to a period of rapid growth in the 1990s because of deregulation in many states. Also, many small to midsize players that could not operate profitably in a high-cost-of-money environment were being bought out by larger companies. So not only was internal growth a possibility, but external growth through acquisitions was also a consideration. Traditionally, the industry had had a high turnover rate of around 50 percent in the branch manager trainee position, largely because of entry-level recruiting, ineffective training of interviewers, lack of emphasis on training and development, and a highly pressured work environment. During the 1980s, the industry moved from a service to a sales culture. This was not a planned trend, but a response to competitive conditions and customer demand.

## Program Description

The program manager was very knowledgeable about the branch manager trainee position: She had developed the programmed learning system for branch manager trainees and for almost 10 years had reviewed the file of every new branch manager trainee hired. She was well aware of what the position entailed and what mistakes were being made in the hiring process. She was also knowledgeable about the company's growth plans for opening new branches each year and the acquisition activity that was in the works. She could see it would be difficult to meet projections without correcting the turnover problem.

The major issues related to turnover were

- rapidly expanding operations, which gave little time for training and development of employees
- deregulation, which opened up new states and additional product offerings, thereby fueling rapid growth
- the need for additional employees to open branches, operate branches acquired through purchases, and fill positions opened through promotions, retirement, and terminations
- the need for continued high profitability and efficiency
- turnover's negative effects on branch and company productivity and profitability
- the need to identify more clearly the type of individual to be hired for the branch manager trainee position
- the need to train the current managers in selection methods so they could select qualified candidates to meet necessary criteria.

The program manager began by preparing cost projections of the turnover problem and then presented this information to senior management to get their attention for the project. Further discussions were held with all levels of management to develop the necessary support.

Sessions were held with senior managers to gain their input concerning the causes of turnover and to identify problems that resulted from the turnover. Through these discussions it was clearly established that salary and benefits were not the main causes of turnover, a conclusion consistent with information from a recent employee attitude survey. Information from senior management also indicated that a better method was needed to identify and select the type of candidate needed for the position. Management's support for the program was firm.

The program manager designed the project with the goal of reducing turnover by using a comprehensive approach to selection. After approval was received from senior management, each regional manager was briefed on the project and asked to identify two district sales managers to participate in the project group. Sales managers were selected with an eye toward obtaining a mix of experiences, management styles, and geographic locations.

Focus groups were held with the district sales managers to enlist their support for and ideas about the program, and to identify and discuss in detail the characteristics they thought were needed to be a successful branch manager. In these same meetings, an assessment questionnaire was introduced and reviewed with sales managers.

This assessment questionnaire was given to 24 high-performing branch managers, 24 low-performing branch managers, and 24 district sales managers who had been successful branch managers. (Levels of performance and success were determined on the basis of objective performance evaluation data collected by district sales managers.) The results were analyzed to determine the characteristics required for successful performance in the position.

Comparison of the results of these three groups reinforced the focus group's conclusions regarding behavioral characteristics desirable in a branch manager trainee. For example, the district sales managers wanted trainees who were proactive salespersons *and* detail oriented. The questionnaire results showed that the successful branch managers were analytical and detail oriented, as well as innovative, articulate, and promotion oriented.

This specific, behaviorally oriented description addressed about 30 percent of the problem. A comprehensive selection system for branch manager trainees was developed to address the other 70 percent of the issues. This system included the following elements:

- *Recruiting strategies*—This document provided the best strategies and sources for recruiting applicants, based on the established characteristics. Recruiting materials, promotional brochures, and newspaper advertisements were revised to appeal to proactive, sales-oriented candidates.

- *Interviewing guidelines*—These documents outlined possible questions to ask during the interviewing process in order to obtain information needed to determine whether a candidate had the established characteristics.
- *Evaluation guidelines*—These guidelines assisted interviewers in assessing the information to determine if an applicant's past behavior matched the behavior needed to be successful in the position. A rating scale was used to make the process as objective as possible.
- *Individualized feedback*—District sales managers received feedback on every applicant found to match the characteristics closely. This feedback indicated how the applicant needed to be trained and supervised, according to questionnaire and interview information. The manager could then decide to hire the person or investigate further, depending on the applicant's match to the characteristics.

## Method of Delivery

After the recruiting strategies, interviewing guidelines, and evaluation guidelines were developed, three two-day seminars were held with groups of eight sales managers each. They were thoroughly trained in the selection system procedures and were taught how to train their branch managers in the program's concepts. This training included interactive lecture, video case studies and exercises, workbook exercises, and role plays. The recruiting strategies, interviewing guidelines, and evaluation guidelines were key elements in the training process, as they provided the ongoing information and methods the branch managers would use in their selection efforts.

For follow-up coaching, the district sales managers visited their branches and assisted branch managers in the hiring process. The individualized feedback given to the district sales managers by the program manager was also a method of ongoing coaching and support in the skill development of field personnel.

## Action Items, Models, and Techniques

From the beginning, it was clear to the program manager that detailed information would need to be available on the rates of turnover for the one-third of the company participating in the program and the two-thirds of the company in the control group. Number of terminations, separation rates, and turnover rates were tracked on a monthly basis beginning at the six-month mark and continuing to the end of the program year. The return on investment (ROI) for the project was calculated at the one-year mark. It would be important to show that this comprehensive selection system reduced turnover in the project group and, further, that human resources had an effect on bottom-line productivity.

Each company may have a different formula for calculating separation, turnover, and ROI. The important point is to calculate these measures consistently so that comparisons can be made and results extrapolated. In this case, FSI calculated the separation rate as:

$$\frac{\text{number of terminations}}{\text{number of total hires.}}$$

The turnover rate was calculated as

$$\frac{\text{number of terminations}}{\text{number of months in period}} \div \frac{\text{average number of employees in}}{\text{the position during this period}} \times 12.$$

The ROI formula used was

$$\frac{\text{cost savings of program}}{\text{investment costs of program.}}$$

In addition to these objective data, ongoing review of new trainees' files and the individualized feedback to district sales managers provided supplemental information.

In a one-year period, 931 branch manager trainees were involved in the study. These were entry-level employees, generally in their early to mid 20s, with college degrees. Few had any practical experience in the industry, but many had degrees in business administration, marketing, and management.

## Costs

Two cost figures were tracked in this project: the investment cost of the program and the cost of turnover. Program costs included travel and lodging, questionnaire scoring, consultant fees, training meeting expenses, training materials, and seminar fees. These costs were $125,000. The time spent by the program manager was not tracked, and a percentage of her salary and benefits was not included in the costs. Neither printing costs nor computer time was tracked. These three items can be included if there is an easy and accurate way to track them in a company, and if the company decides these items should be considered. Traditionally at FSI, staff time devoted to the development process is not tracked or charged to operating groups.

Turnover costs were calculated to determine the savings of the program. This figure included salary and benefits, training materials, and screening and interviewing time. It did not include the cost of lost business due to turnover and decreased productivity in branches. The calculations were as follows:

- The turnover rate for branch manager trainees at the end of 1989 was 54 percent: Out of 847 employees, 460 left FSI.
- The average salary of a branch manager trainee in 1989 was $19,783.
- The average length of service for branch manager trainees who left FSI in 1989 was 0.872 of a year.
- Trainees who left FSI had received salaries totaling about $7,935,000 ($19,783/year x 0.872 year x 460 employees).
- These trainees received benefits worth about $1,983,980, if benefits are calculated as 25 percent of salary ($19,783/year x 0.25 benefits cost x 0.872 year x 460 employees).
- At $10 per trainee, materials cost $4,600.
- Time spent to hire a replacement was 20 hours per trainee, totaling 9,200 hours for the 460 replacements needed.
- Costs of managers' time for hiring replacements was $147,200 ($16/hour x 9,200 hours).
- The total costs for salaries, benefits, materials, and managers' time were $10,070,780 ($7,935,000 + $1,983,980 + $4,600 + $147,200).

Additional factors that might be included in similar calculations in other companies are newspaper advertising, search firms' contingency fees, applicants' travel and expenses, managers' travel and expenses, and recruiting materials fees.

## Data Analysis and Results

Table 1 presents monthly statistics beginning with the sixth month of the project. Data were tracked separately for the project group and the control group. This information was presented to senior management and district sales managers in the project group in a monthly update memo. The program manager was also able to provide subjective improvement results for districts because of the individualized feedback being given and the file reviews taking place.

By the time the research project ended, on March 31, 1992, elements of the system had begun to be used in parts of the control group, thus diluting the purity of the control group for comparison purposes and affecting overall results. The program had been so successful in the project group that managers in the rest of the company were asking for it to be implemented in their regions and districts.

**Table 1. Numerical results of the turnover reduction program.**

| Date | Number of hires | | Number of terminations | | Separation rate (%) | | Turnover rate (%) | |
|---|---|---|---|---|---|---|---|---|
| | Project group | Control group | Project group | Control group | Project group | Control group | Project group | Control group |
| 09-30-91 | 106 | 377 | 7 | 49 | 6.6 | 15.1 | 26.4 | 44.3 |
| 10-31-91 | 118 | 416 | 8 | 55 | 6.8 | 13.2 | 21.8 | 37.9 |
| 11-30-91 | 137 | 472 | 10 | 68 | 7.3 | 14.4 | 20.8 | 36.8 |
| 12-31-91 | 166 | 530 | 16 | 82 | 9.6 | 15.5 | 26.0 | 35.8 |
| 01-31-92 | 179 | 579 | 17 | 94 | 9.5 | 16.2 | 22.2 | 34.0 |
| 02-29-92 | 204 | 656 | 22 | 110 | 10.8 | 16.8 | 23.5 | 33.1 |
| 03-31-92 | 220 | 711 | 27 | 131 | 12.3 | 18.4 | 24.1 | 33.6 |

Note. The values in this table are cumulative.

Use of the selection system reduced total company turnover to 39 percent at the end of 1991. Turnover fell from 54 percent at December 31, 1989, to 39 percent at December 31, 1991, a reduction of 28 percent since the problem was first identified and FSI began working toward a solution. The company reported an annualized cost savings of $2.8 million as a direct result of the project (28 percent of $10 million). Larger savings might have been found if 1991 rather than 1989 expense figures had been used to calculate the original cost of turnover.

Using the formula for ROI yields:

$$ROI = \frac{2,800,000 - 125,000}{125,000} = 21.4, \text{ or } 2,140\%.$$

If the cost savings estimate is accurate, this result means that every dollar invested in the program yielded $21 in return, a payoff greater than most investments. Although this payoff may be exaggerated because of the assumptions made in calculating the cost savings, the important point is that management accepted the cost savings estimate.

## Conclusions

As part of the program's evaluation, responses were obtained directly from district sales managers. A sample of comments received follows:
- "The program has given me the best group of trainees I've had in my five years as a district manager. I have more than enough people ready

for promotion, and the quality of these people is outstanding. Now that turnover is so low, I can have a training session, and everyone understands what is going on; they have the background and time on the job to grasp new products and sell them effectively."

- "The individualized feedback is right on target. It has helped me avoid making hasty hiring decisions. I got information that made me go back for a second or third look to reevaluate what I thought I had."

- "I hired some people early on that weren't as good a match as what the program suggested. They didn't last. Now I look for the best possible match, and I'm getting better at identifying specifically who I want."

- "People I hired who were not close to the characteristics established proved to not have the 'get up and go' to do the job. They are average performers but not outstanding."

- "For the first time in my many years as a district manager, my branch managers are excited about hiring. Because of the program, especially the interviewing guidelines, they feel confident and professional when they interview applicants."

Several factors contributed to the success of the program. The causes of turnover were clearly identified, and the program responded specifically to those causes. The negative effects of turnover were convincingly portrayed to management. As a result, senior and middle management's support was enlisted, and their input was used in shaping the program. The program that was developed was cost-effective, easy to use, and clearly related to the business issues facing the company.

The program manager had an intimate understanding of the dynamics of the problem, the company, and the major players. Individualized feedback and her commitment were invaluable in attaining results. Ongoing reports kept the program manager informed of any problems before they became major issues. Enthusiastic support by most of the participating district sales managers made the program implementation go smoothly, so energies could be concentrated on solving the turnover problem. Involvement of the people doing the hiring was crucial in identifying the characteristics needed by a successful incumbent.

As with all programs, the potential results were inhibited in some ways. In this program, two factors limited the results:

- Not all the regional and district managers bought into the program, so implementation in their areas was less thorough than in others.

- Not all costs could be accurately identified and tracked, so costs are "ballpark" figures.

In conclusion, a comprehensive selection system can be used to reduce turnover, improve quality of hiring, increase interviewer effectiveness, and reduce costs. Proper selection sets the stage for increased productivity and profitability. Training time is decreased, management of employees becomes less arduous, and the total company becomes synchronized to one vision.

## Questions for Discussion

1. How might the components of the program and the implementation strategies have differed if the causes of turnover had been different?
2. How would the turnover rate and factors affecting performance compare in another industry?
3. What factors must a human resource department take into account when approaching this type of problem and its solution?
4. What type of person is needed in the role of program manager?
5. What stumbling blocks might arise in gaining support for an endeavor of this nature within a company?

## The Author

Cynthia Schoeppel is president of her own human resource consulting firm, The Human Resource Connection Inc. The company assists organizations in achieving higher productivity and profitability through effective human resource programs. Areas of specialization include hiring, training, and managing employees effectively to produce outstanding performance. Schoeppel has a master's degree in adult education from Drake University. With more than 20 years' practical experience in management, training, and human resource issues, she brings a down-to-earth approach to her solutions for business problems. Schoeppel can be contacted at the following address: The Human Resource Connection, P.O. Box 4106, Highlands Ranch, CO 80126.

# Measuring the Effects of an Organization Development Program

## Metropolitan Health Maintenance Organization

Catherine M. Sleezer and Richard A. Swanson

*One of the difficulties in measuring the effects of an organization development program is estimating the value of performance improvements. Although this is a subjective process, the following case presents a specific model for making these estimates, describing the financial results of an organization development program.*

## Background

This case outlines the research process used in a health maintenance organization (HMO) to compare the forecasted and actual financial benefits of a multifaceted organization development (OD) program.

## Organization Profile

Metropolitan Health Maintenance Organization (MHMO), which is located in a major metropolitan market, offered its members preventive health-care services on a prepaid basis. The organization had enjoyed the competitive advantage of being first in its metropolitan area to develop this market niche successfully. MHMO offered three types of membership: group, family, and individual. Most prepaid memberships were purchased by various organizations as part of their employee benefits packages, but a small percentage were purchased by families or individuals. At the time of the study, MHMO had grown to serve more than 215,000 members at 22 centers

*All names, dates, places, and organizations have been disguised at the request of the case author or organization.*

located throughout the metropolitan area. Although specific services varied slightly from location to location, all centers offered a general health maintenance program.

The health-care industry is both complex and competitive. Forty percent of the health-care market in this metropolitan area had been captured by HMOs, and competition among them was vigorous and escalating. MHMO's executives were concerned, because the increased competition coupled with public perceptions of insensitive treatment by MHMO health-care professionals was resulting in loss of memberships.

## The Organization Development Program

To improve customer services, MHMO's manager of human resource development (HRD) implemented a top-to-bottom OD program designed to change the way employees interacted with members. The OD program was targeted to all employees and was implemented over a two-year period. It included:

- a series of group meetings for employees to establish and facilitate a patient services team
- a program for all managers that focused on team building, sensitization to patient service, and building patient services awareness
- hiring and training 12 patient services specialists
- implementing the recommendations of the patient services working team.

The efforts of the patient services working team resulted in the following:

- job standards and accountability measures for clerical, nursing, x-ray, laboratory, and pharmacy employees
- phone standards for staff when working with patients
- a new telephone system
- a commitment that all patients who wanted same-day appointments would receive them
- a biannual award given to clinics for high performance in meeting the new standards
- remodeling of a number of clinics
- expanded clinic hours
- improved signs in the clinics
- training for all employees who were involved in direct patient services.

## Character Profiles

The HRD manager wanted to implement a project to measure HRD's financial results. His objectives were (a) to demonstrate to individuals in the organization HRD's role in contributing to the organization's financial goals, (b) to use experts from outside the organization to evaluate an HRD project, and (c) to establish working links with academia. The external evaluators selected by the HRD manager were experienced in evaluating HRD efforts and worked in academia.

The HRD manager and the evaluators selected the OD program as the project to be evaluated. They determined that the evaluation would consist of comparing MHMO decision makers' projections of the financial benefits to be gained from the OD program with the financial benefits actually realized. This program was perceived as important to the organization's strategic goals and sufficiently complex to warrant the use of external evaluators. The HRD manager also considered the politics of evaluating the program. He had originally recommended it and had coordinated its implementation, and he recognized that the program's financial contribution to the organization could have political consequences for him. He believed, however, that the political risks associated with evaluating this program were low, that the potential benefits were high, and that he would grow professionally regardless of the results. After selecting the program to be evaluated, he and the evaluators explained the evaluation project to MHMO's executives. The executives approved the project and agreed to provide the necessary information on actual performance.

## Description of the Forecasting Financial Benefits Model

The forecasting financial benefits (FFB) model (Swanson and Gradous, 1988; Swanson, 1992) is a tool for forecasting and evaluating the performance values, costs, and benefits of HRD programs. The first step in using the model is to identify reasonable program options. The next steps are to predict or assign the costs and to calculate the performance value to be gained for each option. The financial benefit for each HRD option is calculated by subtracting that option's costs from the gain in performance value. Then the financial benefits of all program options are compared to identify the one that offers the greatest financial return.

The FFB model includes worksheets for calculating the performance values, the costs, and the financial benefits. Figure 1 shows the Performance Value Worksheet, Figure 2 shows the Cost Analysis Worksheet, and Figure 3 shows the Benefit Analysis Worksheet. Readers wishing specific instruction in using the FFB should refer to *Forecasting*

## Figure 1. Performance Value Worksheet.

Note that performance units and time units for all options must remain consistent throughout the forecast.

**Program** _____  **Analyst** _____  **Date** _____

**Option name**  1 _____  2 _____

**Data required for calculations:**

(a)  What unit of work performance are you measuring?  _____  _____
                                                 unit name                  unit name

(b)  What is the performance goal per worker/work group at the end of the HRD program?
    ____  ____/____   ____  ____/____
    no.  units / time   no.  units / time

(c)  What is the performance per worker/work group at the beginning of the HRD program?
    ____  ____/____   ____  ____/____
    no.  units / time   no.  units / time

(d)  What dollar value is assigned to each performance unit?
    $_____ /unit   $_____ /unit

(e)  What is the development time required to reach the expected performance level?
    ____  _____   ____  _____
    no.   time      no.   time

(f)  What is the evaluation period? (Enter the longest time (e) of all options being considered.)
    ____  _____   ____  _____
    no.   time      no.   time

(g)  How many workers/work groups will participate in the HRD program?
    _____   _____
    no. workers/groups   no. workers/groups

*Financial Benefits of Human Resource Development* (Swanson and Gradous, 1988). A computer program (J.A. Sleezer, 1988) that supplements the book functions as a job aid in recording, calculating, and printing financial analyses.

## Evaluation Phases

The evaluation project included three major phases of activities: decision making, gathering data on actual performance, and analyzing the data. This section provides an overview of the actions involved in each phase. (For a detailed description of the implementation process, see Swanson and Sleezer, 1988, 1989).

## Figure 2. Cost Analysis Worksheet.

**Calculation to determine net performance value:**

(h) Will worker/work group produce usable units during the HRD program? If no, enter -0-. If yes, enter known performance rate or calculate average performance rate. [(b + c)/2]

_____ _____  |  _____ _____
no.     units     |    no.     units

(i) What total units per worker/work group will be produced during the development time? (h x e)

_____  |  _____
no. of units    |    no. of units

(j) How many units will be produced per worker/work group during the evaluation period? {[(f - e) x b] + i}

_____  |  _____
no. of units    |    no. of units

(k) What will be the value of the worker's/work group's performance during the evaluation period? (j x d)

$_____  |  $_____

(l) What is the performance value gain per worker/work group? [k - (c x d x f)]

$_____  |  $_____

(m) What is the total performance value gain for all workers/work groups? (l x g)

$_____  |  $_____
(Option 1)    |    (Option 2)

## Figure 3. Benefit Analysis Worksheet.

**Program** _____ **Analyst** _____ **Date** _____

**Option**  1 _____  2 _____

Performance value

$_____  |  $_____

—Cost _____

_____  |  _____

Benefit

$_____  |  $_____

Note. Circle your choice of option.

The project's first phase, decision making, focused on gathering all the data the decision makers would need to develop their predictions, choosing three people to serve as decision makers, instructing them in use of the FFB model and tools, and charging the decision makers to apply the method independently. The HRD manager chose the corporate training specialist, the manager of member services, and a clinic manager to be the three decision makers. An evaluator met with each of them to provide information about the FFB, the factors affecting MHMO at the time the OD program was implemented, and the OD program that was proposed in response to those conditions. The decision makers were asked to use the information that had been available when the OD program was implemented to forecast the financial benefits of the program. Each decision maker was asked to use the FFB tools independently to predict the performance values, costs, and benefits for two options and to choose the best option. Option 1 was to initiate the proposed OD program, and Option 2 was to continue with no OD program. Each decision maker had some misgivings about making the projections and had some difficulty in determining the unit for measuring performance, but they all completed the task. In making the projections, each decision maker relied on his or her own perspectives of the OD program and the organization.

The decision makers' projections are summarized in Table 1. The decision makers all chose Option 1, the OD program, as offering the greater financial benefit, even though they varied in their estimates of costs and performance values. The forecasted financial benefits for the OD program ranged from $127,800 to $3,900,000, and the forecasted financial benefits of having no OD program ranged from a loss of $1,773,000 to a gain of $807,500.

**Table 1. Decision makers' forecasts of performance value, costs, and benefits (in dollars).**

|  | 1 | | 2 | | 3 | |
|---|---|---|---|---|---|---|
| Forecast | OD | No OD | OD | No OD | OD | No OD |
| Performance value | 155,500 | 62,400 | 2,812,500 | − 750,000 | 22,500,000 | 812,500 |
| Costs | 27,700* | 14,000* | 211,500 | 1,023,000 | 18,600,000 | 5,000 |
| Benefits | 127,800 | 48,400 | 2,601,000 | −1,773,000 | 3,900,000 | 807,500 |

*Does not include salaries.

The second phase, gathering data on actual performance, included calculating the actual costs associated with the OD program and establishing the value that the organization placed on the performance resulting from the program. The HRD manager used the Cost Analysis Worksheet (see Figure 2) to determine the actual costs of the OD program. This amount included salaries, benefits, and training for patient services specialists and all the development activities of the OD program. The total came to $455,590.

Two MHMO executives, the manager of marketing and the vice-president of operations, had agreed earlier in the process to provide the data on actual performance, but they were reluctant to do so. They had reservations about the ability to measure the financial returns of an HRD program, were irritated about the time needed to gather and provide the information in light of more immediate time commitments, were unwilling to reveal the proprietary numbers used to calculate the performance measures, and had concerns about how the evaluation results would influence future MHMO budget allocations. To address these issues, the evaluator explained the FFB model and how to value HRD performance, agreed to meet with the executives at their convenience, provided information about the OD program and the organization, and pointed out that the total performance value could be disclosed without revealing the numerical values used in assigning performance value. The evaluator also suggested that the financial effects of the OD program should influence future MHMO budget decisions, because one assumption in funding the effort was that it would result in financial benefits for the organization. After these issues were addressed, the executives agreed to provide the data.

Both executives used MHMO memberships as the basis for their calculations. The vice-president of operations indicated that he was influenced by a recent customer survey reporting that a large percentage of members felt service and care had improved. Using this survey information, he estimated that without the OD program 14,000 members would have been lost over two years. He felt that the OD program had no effect on new memberships, so they were not included in his calculation of performance value. The manager of marketing determined the effect of the OD program on membership by estimating the percentage of change in both lapsed and new memberships. Using the most recent marketing figures, he estimated that because of the OD program, 11,984 members did not leave and 8,716 new members joined MHMO. MHMO's marginal revenue per member per year was $360. The performance values assigned by the vice-president of operations

**Table 2. Actual performance value, costs, and benefits of the OD program (in dollars).**

| Component | Vice-president of operations | Manager of marketing |
|---|---|---|
| Actual performance value* | 5,040,000 | 7,452,000 |
| Actual costs | 455,590 | 455,590 |
| Actual benefits | 4,584,410 | 6,996,410 |

*Based on marginal revenue of $360 per member per year.

and the manager of marketing for preventing lapsed memberships were $5,040,000 and $4,314,240, respectively; the manager of marketing assigned new memberships a performance value of $3,137,760.

The costs were subtracted from the total performance value of the OD program to yield the financial benefits (see Table 2). The vice-president of operations determined the actual benefits to be $4,584,410, and the manager of marketing determined them to be $6,996,410.

The third phase, data analysis, consisted of comparing the forecasts made by the decision makers with the actual performance data provided by the executives. This phase also included the external evaluators' report of the evaluation results to the HRD manager. The decision makers' projections using the FFB model led each to select the financially sound option of implementing the OD program, although the FFB model failed to lead the decision makers to estimate correctly the magnitude of the actual benefit, as determined jointly by the vice-president of operations and the manager of marketing.

## Issues and Events

Three major issues in implementing the evaluation project were the decision makers' concern about measuring financial returns of a multifaceted HRD program, their difficulty in determining the appropriate unit of measurement, and the challenge of gaining access to the actual performance data for measuring the program. Successfully completing the evaluation project hinged on addressing all these issues.

Although the HMO decision makers frequently had calculated financial returns of capital investments, they were uneasy about measuring the financial returns of an HRD investment. In any measurement activity, numerous assumptions must be made. Word problems in grade-school math teach people that every problem has a "correct" answer. In business and industry, however, there are no predetermined, correct answers—only calculations based on assumptions. The decision makers knew what assumptions were culturally acceptable within MHMO for making capital investment decisions, but because the organization had no publicly agreed upon assumptions for making HRD investment decisions, making projections in this area was riskier. Therefore, measuring the outputs of capital investments seemed easier and was more familiar than measuring the outputs resulting from HRD efforts. To address the decision makers' lack of familiarity with publicly valuing human resource programs, the evaluator explained that performance values and costs were assumed when decision makers made determinations about how many people to send to a meeting and which training sessions to endorse. These decisions were based on implicit rather than explicitly and publicly examined assumptions. The decision makers understood this explanation and agreed to use the FFB model.

The next issue to be addressed was the difficulty that decision makers had in determining the unit of measurement. They did not understand the relationships between individual behaviors, individual performance, and organizational performance. They tended to focus on the individual behavioral changes that they could see rather than on measures of organizational performance that were invisible to them. For example, one decision maker began by trying to use the number of customer complaints as the unit of performance. Only after a lengthy process did she decide that minimizing customer complaints was not financially valuable in and of itself. Instead, customer complaints had value because they influenced the performance unit, memberships. The FFB model was helpful in addressing this issue because of the inherent difficulty in determining the financial value of behavior (e.g., customer complaints) that is not closely connected to organizational performance.

The third issue to be addressed was gaining access to the HMO's bottom-line information. In this evaluation, the executives based their determinations of actual value on information that was available only to them. This information, which came from multiple sources, was "held close to the vest" by the people in power. It was viewed as a corporate secret because it portrayed the organization's competitive position. The other decision makers within the organization were not aware that this information was available. Further, they did not realize that although they had access to numerous surrogate measures of behavior, they did not have access to the corporate bottom-line measures of performance that really counted for valuing HRD programs. To resolve this issue, the executives used the bottom-line measures to value performance without giving the evaluators the actual figures and reports they used in making their determinations.

## Conclusions and Implications

Using the FFB model provided an organized method for making forecasts about the financial benefits of a human resource program and for determining the actual costs and benefits of the program. The option selected by the decision makers on the basis of their forecasts was financially sound, as determined by the actual program benefits. Implementing the FFB model and comparing the forecasts with the actual program benefits revealed three issues that had to be addressed: the decision makers' concern about measuring financial returns of a multifaceted HRD program, their difficulty in determining the appropriate unit of measurement, and the challenge of gaining access to the corporate bottom-line information needed to measure the program's benefits.

These issues have been examined here from the perspective of one organization, but can also be viewed from a more general perspective. As measuring the effectiveness of HRD programs becomes more routine, valuing programs designed to improve individual and organizational performance could become as common as valuing capital improvements. Books such as this one help make public the various assumptions that organizations and individuals use in valuing human performance and also play a useful role in describing the relationships between human resource programs, individual behaviors, individual performance, and organizational performance.

The issue of gaining access to an organization's bottom-line measures for performance presents a more difficult challenge. The paradox at MHMO was that, although top management wanted HRD to contribute to the organization's strategic position and to the bottom-line financial goals, the HRD manager did not have easy access to the information needed to value HRD. The lack of access to bottom-line measures limited the HRD manager's ability to be an effective strategic decision maker. Decision makers within an organization are responsible for determining which HRD solutions will be implemented, making choices about allocating resources to address organizational performance needs, and judging the effectiveness of the solutions (C.M. Sleezer, 1993). The HRD manager who makes such decisions without a thorough understanding of the organization's bottom-line performance measures and operating assumptions is taking a risk. Further, without this bottom-line information, it is difficult for the HRD manager to question the implicit assumptions that other people use in valuing HRD programs. Gaining access to such strategic information is a political challenge that must be overcome if HRD is to become a strategic player in an organization. Forecasting the financial benefits of HRD programs is a first step in this process, and conducting follow-up financial assessments provides important confirmation.

## Questions for Discussion

1. What is the relative strategic worth of forecasting financial benefits of proposed HRD interventions versus conducting follow-up financial analyses of the actual effects?
2. What are the strengths and weaknesses of the FFB model?
3. How do HRD professionals address the subjectiveness of performance value?
4. What can HRD professionals do to improve management's response to the evaluation process?
5. What techniques can HRD professionals use to gain access to bottom-line corporate financial measures?

## The Authors

Catherine M. Sleezer is an assistant professor at Oklahoma State University. Sleezer's research and consulting interests include needs assessment, employee training, organization development, and economic evaluation of investments in human resource development. Sleezer has authored and coauthored articles on various topics in the field, including performance analysis for training, and evaluat-ing and managing human resource programs. She is the editor of the theory-to-practice monograph titled *Improving Human Resource Development Through Measurement* (American Society for Training and Development, 1989). Sleezer can be contacted at the following address: Oklahoma State University, 413 Classroom Building, Stillwater, OK 74076.

Richard A. Swanson is professor and director of the Human Resource Development Research Center, University of Minnesota. Swanson's research interests include employee training and organization development, analysis and evaluation of work behavior, and economic evaluation of investments in human resource development. He has authored and coauthored more than 150 publications on the subject of education for work. He is the founding editor of *Human Resource*

*Development Quarterly*. With Deane Gradous, he coauthored *Performance at Work: A Systematic Program for Analyzing Work Behavior* (Wiley, 1986) and *Forecasting Financial Benefits of Human Resource Development* (Jossey-Bass, 1988). His new book is titled *Analysis for Improving Performance: Tools for Diagnosing Organizations and Documenting Workplace Expertise* (Barrett-Koehler, 1994).

## References

Sleezer, C.M. (1993). Training needs assessment at work: A dynamic process. *Human Resource Development Quarterly, 3*(4), 44-83.

Sleezer, J.A. (1988). *Forecasting financial benefits of human resource development* [computer program]. San Francisco: Jossey-Bass.

Swanson, R.A. (1992). Demonstrating financial benefits to clients. In H.D. Stolovitch and E.J. Keeps (eds.), *Handbook of human performance* (pp. 602-618). San Francisco: Jossey-Bass.

Swanson, R.A., and Gradous, D.B. (1988). *Forecasting financial benefits of human resource development*. San Francisco: Jossey-Bass.

Swanson, R.A., and Sleezer, C.M. (1988). Organization development: What's it worth? *Organization Development Journal, 6*(1), 37-42.

Swanson, R.A., and Sleezer, C.M. (1989). Determining financial benefits of an organization development program. *Performance Improvement Quarterly, 2*(1), 55-65.

# Applied Behavior Management Training

## North Country Electric & Gas

By Russ Westcott

*With the proliferation of quality and productivity improvement programs, there is continuing pressure to measure their effects on key output variables. This case involves the evaluation of a program using Applied Behavior Management training. The results, taken from the action plans of program participants, show a significant return on investment.*

## Background

This case describes the role return on quality investment (ROQI) played in selling, implementing, and sustaining an improvement program at North Country Electric & Gas (NCEG), a 2,000-person electric and gas utility. The program included training for 200 management and supervisory personnel, an organizational transformation, and improvements in customer satisfaction, quality of service, and profits.

Prior to this effort, management training programs had offered only illusions of influencing the organization's profitability. Programs were heavy with theory, short on skills practice, and devoid of any process for applying new behavior to achieve results measurable in dollars. This shortcoming was largely management's failure to demand profitability-linked results from the human resource (HR) department. But it was also due to HR's complacency and failure to identify with the mainline operations and link their efforts to the outcomes of the organization. Corporate trainers needed to get out from behind their desks and video machines and get involved with the business, or face down-

*All names, dates, places, and organizations have been disguised at the request of the case author or organization.*

sizing and possible elimination. Training had become a significant factor in the equation determining a company's competitive edge—and survival. In short, training had to count, and to do so it had to be accountable.

In this case, the HR director took the initiative to mount a major organizational transformation and quality improvement effort against nearly insurmountable obstacles. NCEG operated within a traditionally autocratic environment that was inhibited by regulations and oriented to deficit spending (in anticipation of the next rate increase). The utility (dubbed "the futility" by its employees) suffered deteriorating facilities and equipment, ever-declining service quality, a largely uninspired and angry workforce, a hugely dissatisfied customer base, and stockholder unrest.

## Organizational Profile

Serving more than 8 million consumers in 26 cities and towns, NCEG's 2,000-person organization included five departments: Operations, Customer Service, Administration, Public Relations, and Human Resources. Operations, the largest, included Engineering and Field Operations. Field Operations included five workout locations plus Emergency Services and was divided between Electric Services and Gas Services. Customer Service maintained offices in the larger communities as well as a large contingent of telephone representatives located at the headquarters. Meter Reading, part of Customer Service, operated from the five workout locations. Administration's Fleet Maintenance Section operated a repair facility at each workout location, maintaining a fleet of more than 1,000 vehicles. Vehicles ranged from small autos used by field supervisors and meter readers to giant cranes and trucks used by Field Operations to maintain both the electric lines and the underground gas distribution facilities. Electric power and gas were purchased from other utilities.

The myriad of measures of output focused on function-related quantitative standards and budgets, such as numbers of new electric and gas services installed, poles set, customer calls answered, minutes per customer call, vehicles repaired, meters read, reports produced, lost-time accidents, and grievances. Few of the measures related directly to the quality of service delivered or the bottom line.

## Character Profile

Wally Wonderlich, three years as president, formerly held positions as vice-president of construction with another utility and financial officer with a major multinational corporation. A no-nonsense boss and tough taskmaster, he had led the company's restructuring and the replacement of virtually all the principal management. On the verge of implementing improvements in work practices and needed upgrading of equipment and facilities, his plans were stymied by skyrocketing energy costs. Resultant rate increases made consumers conscious of the once nearly invisible workforce. The media went into a feeding frenzy, highlighting the perceived deficiencies and waste on every community newspaper's front page and on every television and radio broadcast. Angered and frustrated, Wonderlich took an aggressive stance inside the company, as well as in external attacks on the media and politicians. Each reaction kept his public relations and HR staffs busy with damage control. Two Field Operations managers died from heart attacks during this period of turmoil.

HR Director Roger Smith, recruited by Wonderlich, came from a staff manager's position with an aerospace company. He had training and experience in organization development and human resource development (HRD). Having a vastly different personality than Wonderlich, Smith assumed an unassigned role of subtly modifying the volatile behavior of his boss. He had built his knowledge of behavior management through extensive reading and public seminars and practiced his new skills on his boss. Smith was "fired" by Wonderlich several times over the years; he just never left.

## Issues and Events

NCEG faced antiquated work practices, aging equipment, poor service reliability, stringent environmental requirements, low employee morale, eroding profits, lowered bond ratings, and canceled stockholder dividends. With rapidly increasing consumer service rates, customer dissatisfaction was the norm. Management's response was to heap controls upon controls, turning the work climate into a 24-hour-a-day, seven-days-a-week, continuous "witch hunt" for people deviating from the rules. Exacerbating the problems, customers literally began vilifying NCEG workers on the street, some even throwing rocks with their curses. This was not a motivating environment for an employee to rise for each day—and many did not. Absenteeism spread, accident rates increased, and grievances mounted.

Smith understood that a major organizational transformation coupled with substantial improvement in quality and productivity was needed to turn around the failing company. Every measurement used to evaluate the company, the traditional financials plus service indexes and critical counts (e.g., number of customer complaints), placed the company at the bottom of the barrel compared with similar utilities. But how could he sell a major change effort in a work climate where "rat packs" (small mobile teams of supervisors) roamed the streets on weekends and nights looking for wrongdoers? Wonderlich ruled his domain with an iron fist and a swift sword. Smith realized that any overt proposal to change organizational culture and management behavior would be rejected and could result in his termination. Instead he "bet" his president that he could turn $8,500 into a return of $20,000. If Wonderlich would allow him to select 12 first-line supervisors, authorize purchase of training materials and 32 hours of classroom training over eight weeks, and release Smith from his day-to-day responsibilities, Smith would demonstrate that this group would produce $20,000 of improvements. For the combined cost of his salary and training materials, Smith said he could generate an ROQI of $2.4 to $1. To provide added incentive, Smith said that if he failed, Wonderlich could fire him. He made no mention of cultural change or the fact that management's behavior would require change if the approach was to be totally successful. Showing measurable dollar payoffs that directly affected the company's bottom line was the prime sales message that enabled Smith to form his pilot group, labeled "Roger's disciples."

## HRD Program Description

Applied Behavior Management (ABM), an organizational and individual change process, was developed to aid NCEG in involving employees in increasing quality, productivity, and profits. ABM focused on improvement of team performance in areas directly linked to the desired outcomes of the organization. ABM improvement projects were expected to produce an ROQI of 3 to 15, although many actual net dollar payoffs exceeded 400 times the investment. Although improvements in quality, productivity, and cost reduction were all encouraged, the program had the strongest emphasis on quality and consequently was labeled Quality Improvement Process.

The ABM process included

- establishing and training a steering group of top management to oversee ABM
- appointing and training a performance improvement administrator (Smith) to coordinate the overall approach
- designing and pilot-testing the approach
- planning for integrating ABM into the organization's culture and developing a supportive climate

- training all levels of management
- coaching each participant individually, on site
- designing and installing a system for tracking and reporting progress and training's contribution to profitability
- evaluating both the process employed and the results obtained.

A carefully worded "invitational" letter (Figure 1) from the president specified what he expected of each participant and explained that participants' progress would be tracked and measured. The system for tracking, measuring, reporting, and reinforcing progress allowed both the participant and all levels of management to continuously monitor and fine-tune the reinforcement and improvement processes.

During the eight weeks of training (four hours per week), each ABM participant planned and implemented a performance improvement project for his or her own work environment, established procedures for performance feedback and positive reinforcement, and monitored and reported progress and payoffs. Work associates helped develop these projects. Dollar payoffs were computed conservatively and generated from bona fide quality or productivity improvements, from cost reductions, or from both improvements and cost reductions.

Only one-tenth of the ABM effort was training. Most effort was spent with operations people facilitating and integrating the ABM process. Trainers were out where the action was—out where they visibly made a measurable impact on the business's success.

The program centered on improving the company's performance in several vital areas: customer service and satisfaction, service quality, productivity, cost containment, employee morale and motivation, public and stockholder relations, and profits. Because the focus was on improving processes and outcomes, the ABM training combined aspects of traditional management training with skills training in how to bring about measurable improvement in performance. This was a total-company effort, so the results were not measured in terms of training's contribution but in terms of the improvements achieved by the participants for the company. The HR department and participants worked in partnership to produce the results.

Of particular note was the program's use of one-to-one coaching. Each participant received personal coaching from his or her instructor for two hours each week, at the work site. This coaching enabled the participant to assimilate the classroom instruction and translate the learning into actions that specifically fit his or her needs and project. In addition, coaching helped many participants to overcome resistance to their projects, helped them to involve their subordinates, and prepared

**Figure 1. Memo from the company president to employees selected to participate in the ABM program.**

---

NORTH COUNTRY ELECTRIC & GAS

**MEMO**

From: Wally Wonderlich, President
To: Pat Overall, Supervisor
Subject: Training

As part of the total company Quality Improvement Process, you have been selected to attend a special training program called

## APPLIED BEHAVIOR MANAGEMENT.

During the eight-week, four-hours-per-week program you will have the opportunity to plan and begin to implement a quality improvement project for your own work area. You will learn skills that will help you involve your direct-reports in the planning and implementation process. And, as long as your quality improvement project stays within the law, company policy, and normal ethical bounds, you and your work associates will have full support of your improvement efforts.

Your class schedule is enclosed. To prepare for your first session, please jot down at least five possible quality improvements that you would like to try for your work area. Four guidelines:

1.   Select project ideas which will not require change in someone else's work practices or in total company systems/policies. Stay within your own sphere of influence.
2.   Select potential projects that will involve most or all of your work associates. We want to ultimately involve everyone in the company.
3.   Select ideas for projects that appear small enough to fully implement within less than a year's time. Look for early successes.
4.   Don't concern yourself, yet, as to whether there will be sufficient resources (time, money, material, machines) to implement the project.

This "homework" is necessary so that each participant has a base from which to practice evaluation of the feasibility of each type project. The project you choose by the end of the first session may come from your list or another project that occurs to you in class. Homework for each of the remaining sessions will include short readings and work on your project plans.

Your manager was consulted in selecting you, but please be sure to clear your class days and times with your manager. I expect you to attend all eight sessions. Absences for declared company emergencies and health reasons are the only excusable reasons I can think of. Participating in our Quality Improvement Process and receiving the training are both "company business" and part of our jobs. I feel personally committed to the Quality Improvement Process and want you to join with me in making it successful.

I'll be personally tracking your progress, both during the training period, and as your improvement project progresses. I wish you every success and will do everything possible to support you.

---

participants to accept their bosses as coaches.

In summary, the ABM approach combined three main elements:

- building and sustaining support systems (e.g., culture change, management commitment and style, steering group, coordinator, employee communication and recognition, tracking, measuring and feedback systems)
- training for all levels of management
- field coaching.

## Training Delivery

Over the three-year period of implementation, Smith and one trainer conducted the training and field coaching. Smith facilitated top management's training, commitment, and support and aided the acceptance of responsibility for the ABM approach by all levels of management. He was the behind-the-scenes "burr in his boss's saddle" and the subtle modifier of Wonderlich's behavior.

Both internal and field supervisors and the next two levels of management, in mixed groups of 12 or 15, received the full eight-week ABM training. Middle management and top management received abbreviated training and instruction in how to support improvement projects. Two hundred management personnel received training, including the president.

All participants received a loose-leaf text and workbook. After the pilot program was completed, groups received selected copies of the work papers of their predecessors. A top management person kicked off each group's training and attended the certificate-awarding ceremony and celebration on the last day. In the classroom sessions, mini-lectures were supplemented by overhead transparencies, workbook exercises, total-group and small-group discussions, and many skill rehearsals. Four films on behavior management were shown and discussed. Each participant started planning his or her improvement project at the first session. Subsequent sessions added the knowledge and skills needed to complete and implement these plans. Field coaching and homework supported the classroom work. The format allowed training to be customized to fit each participant's specific project needs. Also, participants were preselected to obtain a balance between electric and gas supervisors and between internal and field supervisors. Classroom discussion groups were designed to mix people from these different categories so that each participant would gain insights and knowledge from interaction with other class members. (This design was part of the planned cultural change to abolish the interpersonal barriers between different categories of supervisors.) While working on the individual projects, all participants served as team leaders, trainers, and coaches for their work associates.

## Documentation and the ROQI Process

The basic documentation for each ABM project comprised two planning forms: Analysis of Potential for Improved Quality (APIQ; Figure 2) and Probable Opportunities for Quality Solution (POQS; Figure 3).

Each participant used the APIQ worksheet to determine the potential effect of a quality improvement. Each part of the form was important for showing the return.

### Target Outcome

The outcome to be improved was expressed in terms of what was to be achieved (for example, the number of invoices to be processed or sales to be made, or the cost of supplies to be purchased). Plans might call for increasing (productivity) or decreasing (costs) outcomes. Positive expressions were preferred (e.g., increasing days worked rather than reducing absenteeism).

### Target Population

The name and size of the group expected to achieve the outcome was stated.

### Desired Quality Level

Because quality was an important outcome, the desired quality level was expressed as a fixed standard, such as 100 percent accuracy, or as a goal, such as having 99.5 percent of all services meet customer requirements each day or increasing monthly revenue to $25,000. The quality level had to be realistic and achievable. Also, when the conditions needed to achieve the outcome exceeded normal implied conditions, conditions were stated (for example, "five installations per day per crew, as customer orders continue to support this level").

### Basis for Measurement

Of several measurements possible, the one that most clearly and simply measured the attainment of the outcome was selected. For example, in supply, the desired outcome was completed orders for parts, and the desired level of performance was to fill all orders accurately within two hours of receiving them. Possible measurement alternatives were
• number of orders filled

# Figure 2. Analysis of Potential for Improved Quality (APIQ).

| **Project:** | | **Proj. No.** | **Sheet 1** |
|---|---|---|---|

A.  Target Outcome
   - 1. ● increase     what?
   - 2. ● decrease     what?

B.  Target Population
   - ● individual
   - ● group size  (   )

C.  Desired Quality Level
   - ● standard
   - ● goal, expectation

   - ● quantity
   - ● percent of  (   )

D.  Basis for Measurement
   - ● rate (quant./time)
   - ● accuracy
   - ● usability
   - ● completeness
   - ● timeliness/speed
   - ● cost

E.  Baseline (present performance level) in terms comparable to C
   - ● from available records
   - ● from observation
   - ● estimate from other source
   - ● other

F.  Potential for Improved Quality
   - ● (if A1 checked, then C-E=F)
   - ● (if A2 checked, then E-C=F)

G.  Annual Value of PIQ
   (show details of each computation, state assumption, unit rates used, use back of form as needed - more detail is better than less)

| | $ | /yr |
|---|---|---|

H.  POQS (Costs from Sheet 2B)     $

I.  Potential Net Payoff for First Year (G-I=H)     $

Is the project worthy of consideration?   Y   N   Date

By:

## Figure 3. Probable Opportunities for Quality Solutions (POQS).

| Project: | Proj. No. | Sheet 2A |
|---|---|---|

**Re: Target Outcome (Sheet No. 1)**

1. Does there appear to be a value to improving quality?
2. How long has this opportunity existed?
3. Where does the opportunity occur (location)?
4. When does the opportunity occur (situation, time period)?
5. How often does it occur (frequency)?
6. What inconsistencies exist (location, situation, time period, frequency)?
7. Should I proceed to analyze for a solution?

| **Re: Target Population (TP) (Sheet No. 1)** | * | T | K | F | C |
|---|---|---|---|---|---|
| 8. Does TP have time to do the job well? | | x | x | | |
| 9. Does TP have proper facilities in which to work? | | x | | | |
| 10. Does TP have the proper tools to do work? | | x | | | |
| 11. Does TP have the proper procedures, instructions, job aids? | | x | | | |
| 12. Does TP know what they are supposed to do? | | | x | x | |
| 13. Has TP ever done the job correctly? | | | x | x | |
| 14. Could TP do it if their life depended upon it? | | | x | | x |
| 15. If TP could do job in exemplary way, would they? | | | | | x |
| 16. Are there more negative than positive consequences? | | | | | x |
| 17. Does TP know when they are not performing to standard? | | | x | | |
| 18. Do supervisors of TP have requisite knowledge/skills? | | | x | x | x |

| **Areas for Solution** | **Estimate of Costs (First Year)** |
|---|---|

**(*T) Task Considerations**

| | |
|---|---|
| Redesign work/tasks | $ |
| Add, replace, rearrange facilities | $ |
| Add, replace, modify tools | $ |
| Add, delete, rewrite procedures, guides, job aids | $ |
| Other: | $ |

©1990, R.T. Westcott & Associates, 263 Main Street, Old Saybrook, CT 06475

# Figure 3 (continued). Probable Opportunities for Quality Solution (POQS).

| Project: | Proj. No. | Sheet 2A |
|---|---|---|

| Areas for Solution | Estimate of Costs (First Year) |
|---|---|
| **(\*K) Knowledge Considerations** | |
| Needs analysis | $ |
| Determine competencies required of TP | $ |
| Assess knowledge/skill level of TP | $ |
| Provide training for TP (course design, materials, instructor costs, trainee costs, travel, facilities, equipment) | $ |
| Other: | $ |
| | |
| **(\*F) Feedback Considerations** | |
| Analyze feedback requirements | $ |
| Modify present system | $ |
| Design new system | $ |
| Implement new/modified system (training, forms, data collection, summary, communication) | $ |
| Other: | $ |
| | |
| **(\*C) Consequences/Antecedents-Considerations** | |
| Functional analysis of behavior | $ |
| Add, remove, rearrange consequences/antecedents | $ |
| Provide training in behavior management (instructor costs, trainee costs, travel, facilities, equipment) | $ |
| Other: | $ |
| | |
| **Additional Considerations** | |
| Building a training staff (temporary, permanent) | $ |
| Facilities for training staff and for conducting programs | $ |
| Travel & living expenses of staff | $ |
| Overlap of old and new systems | $ |
| Additional maintenance of systems, facilities | $ |
| Consulting services | $ |
| Other: | $ |
| | |
| **Total Estimated Costs for First Year** | $ |
| (transfer to line H on Sheet No. 1) | |

Date:                    By:

- average time to fill an order
- number of orders delivered to loading dock
- percentage of orders filled and delivered correctly within two hours.

The last measurement was preferred because it reflected both timeliness and accuracy, as well as consideration for fluctuations in the number of orders.

### Baseline

The level of quality at the start of the project was determined from records of past work, from observations of work in progress prior to the change, or in the case of completely new work, from industry norms or industrial engineering estimates. Good baseline data are important to computing the value of an improvement. To aid computation, the baseline and standard were expressed in comparable quantitative terms.

### Potential for Improved Quality (PIQ)

This value was the difference between the standard and baseline. Even a seemingly minute difference, such as five minutes saved each day, may be significant if 500 employees are involved (10,833 hours saved overall per year!).

### Annual Value of Potential for Improved Quality

Assuming an average hourly rate of $8.42, the annual value of each of 500 employees saving five minutes per day comes to $91,214. Conservatively, vacation time and holidays might be considered in such calculations; however, most participants were cautioned to cut the potential payoff by up to 50 percent. For time savings to be valid, the time saved had to be used to perform other worthy work, so an even better way to calculate the value of the time savings was to use the value of the work done in the time saved. If overtime was saved, the cost of overtime was used. If costs were reduced, the actual value of the material, supplies, or services was used. In the case of cost avoidance, the cost of fixing a problem, paying a claim, or preventing a legal action was used. The rules were to be conservative (i.e., when in doubt, leave it out), document and label all assumptions and figures carefully (to overcome lapses in memory), and be sure all computations could stand up to an audit.

### POQS

The POQS was used to weigh the alternatives so an appropriate quality improvement strategy would be selected. The 18 questions on the POQS focused on the targeted outcome and population:

- Questions 1 through 6 helped to stimulate thinking beyond just the value of the project.
- The answer to Question 7 indicated whether it was worth continuing the analysis.
- Questions 8 through 18 helped pinpoint whether the quality solution involved some aspect of the task (T), such as tools or procedures; a knowledge deficiency requiring a training solution (K); a need for better performance feedback (F); or a need for a change in the consequences of behavior (C). Each question was given a "yes" or "no" answer, and the appropriate *x* was circled to indicate a deficiency. For example, a "yes" and a circled *x* under F for Question 13 and a "yes" and a circled *x* under C for Question 14 usually indicated that no further training was needed but that better performance feedback and more positive consequences were needed to improve the outcome. A "no" and a circled *x* under F for Question 17 also indicated that the performers did not know what was expected of them nor how well they were doing.

The POQS form also called for costs associated with each potential solution. The list was expandable as needed. Past experience with hundreds of improvement projects showed least need for changing task-related elements (T) and training (K), a substantial need to improve performance feedback systems (F), and a universal need to improve the balance of consequences (C) for performing (to be more positive). There was, therefore, a need for training supervisors and team leaders in how to coach and facilitate improvement.

### Determining the Potential for a Net Payoff

All applicable costs were computed and recorded on an annual basis (unless the improvement applied to a one-time situation). The sum of all costs was then transferred to the APIQ form and deducted from the value of the potential for improved quality. The result was the estimated net payoff for the first year—information used to evaluate the worthiness of the project and decide whether to implement the change. Planners were cautioned not to select a project based on net payoff alone. A first-time planner needed a project that was not too complex, so that results could be achieved quickly. Applying the learned skills to achieve an early, measurable quality improvement was more critical than the magnitude of the dollar payoff.

## Results

Table 1 shows the types of projects implemented by participants. For example, one field supervisor was responsible for three crews of eight persons each. Baseline productivity averaged only five hours per day of on-site work time. The solution was for crews to establish their own work goals and tracking method and to change certain practices (e.g., send one member to secure the work site prior to arrival of the crew, send one member for take-out food rather than having the whole crew go to a restaurant, provide recognition for crew achievements). The result was that productive time increased to 6.8 hours per day, allowing for additional work and earlier completions. The annual payoff was $56,600.

In the area of increased responsibilities, the perceived norm was for a two-person crew to average five new service installations per day, but the actual baseline turned out to be 3.83. The target was to increase to five. Through crew-set goals, better scheduling and performance feedback, and crew recognition for improvement, the target was exceeded, with six installations completed per day. Savings for the first year were $25,220.

All projects involved built-in morale improvement, but one project was specifically planned to lift the morale of the unit. The seven-person typing pool had a reputation for producing "late and lousy work." Standards for quality and quantity existed in the form of "Reasonable Ranges" (R/R) of 95 percent or better. Baseline was 5 percent below the R/R and at a quality level of 80 percent. The solution selected was to implement short-interval scheduling, with hourly work targets set by group collaboration; individual tutoring to bring up deficient skills identified through daily, specific feedback; counseling as needed; and a strong recognition system (devised by one of the typists). As a result of these changes, standards were exceeded, customer satisfaction and image improved dramatically, and two typists and the supervisor ultimately received promotions. The payoff was $27,900 of avoided rework.

As the teams were trained, they implemented projects over a three-year period, and the payoffs mounted. A "snapshot" taken when the last team graduated training, but before these supervisors had implemented projects, showed a documented total payoff of $1,077,750. Implementation costs were $215,500, yielding a net payoff of $862,250 and a benefit-to-cost ratio of 5 to 1. The traditional return formula yields:

$$\frac{\text{net benefits}}{\text{program costs}} = \frac{\$862,250}{\$215,500} = 400\%.$$

Each project leader was cautioned to be very conservative in stating payoff dollars. The emphasis of the ABM approach was to effect improvement, not focus unduly on payoffs. Also, it is important to realize that all costs were taken in the first year, thus substantially raising the potential payoff in subsequent years. Because every participant held full responsibility for the work of his or her crew or unit while attending training, participants' salaries were not considered in costs. Travel time was minimal inasmuch as headquarters was located near most attendees' work locations. The principal program costs were salaries for Smith and the one trainer, costs of training materials, field coaching mileage, and administrative costs. As described earlier, project implementation costs were factored into each project plan.

The benefits to NCEG were several:

- ABM increased employees' involvement and individual empowerment.
- ABM was compatible with and integrated with the continuous quality improvement process.
- ABM contained costs and improved profits, the utility's competitive edge in the marketplace, and the quality of work life.

The aggregate of the dollar payoffs realized through participants'

## Table 1. Sample list of projects implemented.

| Area | Specific goal |
|------|---------------|
| Cost savings, cost avoidance | Reduce expense of tools and supplies |
| | Increase timely collection of accounts receivable |
| | Restock service trucks daily to reduce time lost because of unavailable parts |
| | Increase use of material formerly scrapped |
| | Decrease number of visits to medical department |
| | Reduce auto mileage charges |
| Productivity | Increase number of customer contacts |
| | Increase number of contacts with commercial accounts |
| | Improve productivity of maintenance crews |
| Quality of service | Increase number of meters read accurately |
| | Decrease number and severity of customer complaints |
| | Increase reliability of vehicle repairs and availability of vehicles |
| | Improve timeliness of customer complaint adjustments |
| | Improve follow-through of new accounts to ensure customer satisfaction |
| | Increase responsiveness to requests for new service connection |

improvement projects told the real story about how the training affected profits. Trainers, working side-by-side with line people, helped the utility to achieve its planned outcomes: increased customer satisfaction, better quality, greater productivity, and more profit.

## Reflections

Several key issues emerge from this case study.

### Selling the Concept

Given the existing environment and negative work climate, Smith's concealing the underlying purpose (organizational transformation) by emphasizing ROQI appeared wise. In fact, the transformation took place almost without notice. As NCEG achieved a leading rank among other similar operations, managers began to reflect on the improvements they had achieved: customer complaints reduced to near zero, service quality and productivity at an all-time high, employees involved and motivated, stockholders and the public more satisfied, and profits up. The company became a better place to work.

### Support

Developing early and continuing management support was crucial. Establishing a "cocoon" so that each participant could try out new behavior and new ideas without adverse treatment was a key to success in empowering project leaders and their work associates. Causing the ABM projects to be an agenda item in every staff or crew meeting helped convey support and sustain commitment. Also, Smith took on Wonderlich as his personal "project," meeting with him frequently to try to effect a change in his authoritative, punitive style. The change in the boss's behavior signaled to workers that the ABM approach was more than just another attempt to exploit them.

### Positive Reinforcement for Work Done Well

Positive reinforcement proved to be the largest single success factor. With no monetary reward allowable under the union-management agreement, only nonmonetary recognition was acceptable. It was critical because it cost almost nothing to apply and had a great effect on the largest untapped resource—people. Recognition helped build welcome habits that not only changed management and the whole company but also helped many participants' home lives. A boss needs recognition, too: Smith continually reinforced Wonderlich for his smart decision to implement the improvement effort.

## Sustaining the Effort

The need for continual support from top management became evident when Wonderlich, and then Smith, left NCEG. Within six months, progress-tracking and recognition systems vanished, leaving only vestiges of positive behavior, fading memories, and dusty yellow notebooks on a few bookshelves.

## Questions for Discussion

1.  Given the circumstances, what would you have done differently? Why?
2.  Would the described ROQI-type process be applicable to other management or sales training programs? Why or why not?
3.  Could you and your management accept training being measured by participants' application of training skills to improvement projects, with outcomes computed in dollars of payoff? Why or why not?
4.  Would you, as a trainer, go to the field to assist training participants in applying training content to their specific needs? Why or why not?
5.  What would you have done to try to ensure continuity of management's support of the quality improvement effort?
6.  The ABM program, as described, did not include typical training in using quality tools (e.g., Pareto analysis, cause-and-effect analysis, control charting). Was this a serious deficiency? Why or why not? If so, what would you have added or substituted, and why?
7.  How did the "cocoon" concept address the fading (i.e., memory loss following training) that typically occurs when participants return to the job? Why was this deemed essential in the described environment? What might you have done differently? Why?
8.  Would the outcome likely have been different if separate individuals had fulfilled the roles of quality improvement coordinator, field coach, support systems facilitator, and trainer? How so? Why?
9.  Do you feel that individuals' dignity, self-esteem, and feelings were ignored by the emphasis on obtaining dollar measurements of behavior change? Why or why not?
10. Given the described circumstances, was it right to train only the management? Why or why not?
11. Were the payoffs worth the effort? How might they have been improved?
12. What actions can be taken to ensure long-term program benefit?

## The Author

Russ Westcott, president of R.T. Westcott & Associates in Old

Saybrook, Connecticut, has more than 30 years' business management experience with aerospace companies, financial services, information services, manufacturers, retail stores, government, and utilities. Since 1979, his firm has provided quality and performance improvement consulting services to small businesses. Westcott is active with the American Society for Quality Control, The Quality Consortium, and the National Society for Performance and Instruction.

Westcott's articles on quality topics have appeared in *QNET, ASQC Quality Management Forum, BusinessHartford, BusinessWest, Quality Edge, Middlesex County Business Review,* and the *Business Times.* He can be contacted at the following address: R.T. Westcott & Associates, 263 Main Street, Suite 308, Old Saybrook, CT 06475.

# Performance Management Training

## Yellow Freight System

By Jack Zigon

*Performance management is a critical activity for organizations. The following case shows a human resource development program consisting of a new performance management system coupled with a comprehensive training program. The program results are well documented and impressive, showing the tremendous payoff potential for this type of program.*

## Background

Until 1981, the trucking industry was regulated by the Interstate Commerce Commission. Profits flowed year after year, and price competition was minimal because of set rates and a limited range of offered services. Deregulation brought new realities to the industry: price competition, marketing, and product differentiation. It also brought hundreds of business failures a year to an industry that had seen only growth and prosperity for decades.

Yellow Freight System, one of the largest trucking companies, found itself competing with smaller companies on the basis of price and was losing money for the first time in many years. This financial shock caused soul-searching and strategy reformulation at the highest levels of the corporation. Top management concluded that only the very largest companies with the best performing employees would survive deregulation. This resulted in a program of route expansion and reorganization into a hub-and-spoke transportation system. A full-scale employee training program was needed.

## Organizational Profile

Yellow Freight System moves commodities by truck over long distances. It transports goods between manufacturing plants and warehouses, and delivers goods to distributors, dealers, and retail stores. Yellow specializes in small, less-than-truckload shipments that weigh 5,000 to 10,000 pounds and are more than 450 miles from their destination. In 1981, Yellow had 450 locations and 22,000 employees, generating sales of $950 million annually; it was the third largest trucking company in the United States. (It is now the country's largest trucking company, with more than 600 locations and revenues in excess of $2 billion.)

The company was organized into five regions with two to three hubs each. A hub, or breakbulk, was a central sorting facility that collected freight from feeder terminals and consolidated it into trailers by destination. The more trailers that could be filled with freight going to a single, distant destination, the more quickly that freight could be moved to that destination with fewer intermediate stops for unloading and reloading the trailers. If done well, this reduction in freight handling also meant a lower cost per shipment.

Yellow is a union carrier, with its employees represented by the Teamsters. All the largest common carriers operated with the same master labor agreement. Over 60 percent of Yellow's expenses were employee costs of payroll and benefits. Improvement in the productivity of the labor force had the potential to drop immediately to the bottom line.

Regulation and the high profits it supported had lulled the industry into a false sense of security. Revenue and profit were determined by regulation and not by close attention to cost accounting and financial management. Deregulation removed the price controls that had guaranteed profitability. Smaller carriers took to discounting published tariff rates as a way of taking market share from the larger carriers, such as Yellow, Consolidated Freightways, and Roadway Express.

Although this strategy worked well from a market share standpoint, the unsophisticated carriers lowered their revenue per shipment below their cost per shipment, causing them to lose money on each shipment. And to make things worse, they figured that they could make up for the losses by increasing their volume of shipments! Hundreds of carriers went out of business each year in this business climate. Tremendous price pressures were placed on the carriers who wanted to remain in business for the long haul.

Yellow is a publicly traded company, but the majority of stock is owned by the family of the chairman, George Powell Sr. A shy man, he created a family business that was quick to provide security to its employees and reluctant to introduce changes such as commission pay systems for its sales representatives. This kindness policy extended to handling of poor performance; for example, rather than fire a vice-president whose skills no longer matched the demands of the deregulated environment, Yellow instead demoted this individual four times until he found his new productive niche in sales. Although employee loyalty was high in this environment of employee protection, the company suffered with the least talented sales force in the industry. The very best sales producers went to the positions in other companies and industries where commissions could result in much higher total compensation. Yellow had to find a way to produce extraordinary results from the very ordinary individuals it was left with.

## Needs Analysis

Yellow's board of directors decided that the entire workforce needed to be trained to take advantage of the realities of the deregulated environment. The head of human resource was directed to hire a manager of human resource development (HRD), who could provide state-of-the-art employee development that would help differentiate Yellow from its competitors.

The HRD manager's first step was to define the new department's mission as "helping management manage and improve employee performance." A needs analysis was conducted with the chairman of the board, president, and various vice-presidents and area managers. The results of these interviews suggested that branch managers, sales representatives, and frontline supervisors needed to be trained. Unfortunately, there was no consensus as to which group was *most* in need of training. The HRD department suggested a performance audit to identify the group with the greatest potential for improving performance. Top management agreed.

A sample of employees from each of the three groups was identified based on functional and political considerations. Individuals were drawn from each major geographic region, from terminals of different sizes, from every job function, from all levels of management, and with high, average, and low levels of job performance. This type of sample allowed each group in the company to feel it had been represented. It also allowed the HRD department to observe exemplary and poor performers, thus providing excellent information on why some employees performed better than others.

Performance measures and standards were identified for each of the three groups. Actual performance data were collected (where available) and the value of the average performer's results was compared with the value of the exemplar's performance. A performance improvement potential was defined as the gap between the performance of the exemplar and the average of the group. The largest gaps coupled with the largest number of performers pointed to the areas with the greatest potential return on investment. The HRD department also searched for causes for these performance gaps and interviewed employees and managers to develop additional causes and statements regarding how to close the gaps. After six to eight weeks of study, the findings of the audit were summarized.

The main finding was that, although job responsibilities were not consistent from location to location for any given job title, the work that had to get done was very consistent. The job title assigned to the work varied a great deal because of location size.

Stakes were calculated for each major performance measure. The equation for calculating stakes was as follows:

stakes = (exemplar − average) x (dollar value of gap) x (number of occurrences/year).

The stakes that came out of the performance audit are listed in Table 1.

## Table 1. Performance improvement priorities.

| Job title | Measure* | Annual stakes (in millions of dollars) |
|---|---|---|
| Branch manager | Cost/bill | 44 |
| Sales representative | Bill count growth | 30 |
| Break supervisor | Breakbulk cost/bill | 11 |
| Dock supervisor | End-of-line dock cost/bill | 10 |
| Pickup and delivery supervisor | Pickup and delivery cost/bill | 8 |
| Office supervisor | Office cost/bill | 6 |
| Supervisor | Claims ratio | 2 |

*A bill is a freight shipment.

Although stakes for the various supervisor categories added up to $37 million per year, the branch manager position had the advantage of being relatively homogeneous and still having $7 million per year more in potential performance improvements. Thus, the three-way "tie" was broken, giving branch managers first priority, sales representatives second priority, and supervisors third priority for training.

But prioritizing training populations was only the first step. The HRD department went on to summarize the causes of the observed performance gaps:

- Area and branch managers had clear measures and standards for their jobs, but employees below them lacked individual performance measures and standards.
- Area and branch managers received a great deal of performance feedback, but employees below them lacked feedback on their individual performance. Their feedback system was a "no news is good news" feedback system.
- The main reward for doing a good job was getting to keep your job.
- Training was usually a short period of observing someone doing the job, with a long period of on-the-job, trial-and-error self-teaching.

Based on these findings, HRD made two recommendations:

- Upgrade the performance appraisal system of the company by creating performance standards, feedback systems, and rewards contingent upon performance for every job. Provide training to support the new system.
- Provide training in the technical skills and knowledge to cut down on the time needed to master every job.

## HRD Program Description

Yellow's new performance appraisal system was initially designed as a performance management system. This meant that it was designed first as a tool for supervisors to use when managing employee performance, and second as a tool for evaluation and compensation. An appraisal system that is mainly a tool for the human resource department to approve salary increases is usually tolerated by management as a necessary evil, and these underlying negative feelings come out when the system is being revised. But creating a management tool that helps supervisors meet their performance goals also helps to alleviate these feelings.

The performance management portion of the program taught managers how to write accomplishment-based performance standards, design feedback systems, troubleshoot performance problems, and reward employees. These analytical skills will not produce performance improvements unless supervisors are able to communicate well, however. To make sure the new program would succeed, Yellow provided additional training in the areas of interpersonal skills, communicating expectations, and coaching. The interpersonal skills covered listening, observing and interpreting employees' behavior, communicating an understanding of content and feelings expressed by an employee, and using these skills naturally. Communicating expectations focused on how to negotiate agreement with an employee on performance standards. Coaching covered how to decide if coaching were needed, and how to work with an employee to get agreement on the problem, its causes, and what would be done to correct it.

The presenters of the program were high-performing line managers on two-year assignment to the HRD department. These individuals were handpicked by the division vice-presidents and were promised that they would return to higher operations positions than the ones they left if they performed well as trainers. As it turned out, most were promoted two levels higher than the positions they left. This made recruiting future trainers a very simple task.

The participants in Phase I of the program included approximately 1,100 managers—everyone who conduced performance appraisals, from the division vice-presidents to the second-level supervisors. Phase II of the program covered the remaining 1,000 frontline supervisors. In Phase III, which is not included in this case study, sales representatives received training in product knowledge, territory management, and consultative selling skills.

The training was delivered using a combination of self-paced training, group-paced role plays, and job aids. All training was criterion-referenced. Creating performance standards and designing feedback systems were taught using self-paced reading materials. Each participant finished this portion of the training by creating a set of performance standards for his or her position. To reduce the time required to write performance standards, a large collection of example standards was created and provided to each trainee. Topics such as interpersonal skills, negotiation, and coaching were taught with a combination of self-paced reading, videotaped models, group-paced discussions, three-person role plays, and videotaped feedback.

## Models and Techniques

The model that guided both the program's content and its implementation was Gilbert's (1978) performance engineering model, shown as Table 2. Although Gilbert's model is excellent for use with HRD professionals, it needed to be revised to work with Yellow's managers, as indicated by Figure 1.

Yellow's managers could identify immediately with the new model because it shows freight being moved. It has a dynamic visual message: If any link in the chain is weak, the chain will not work, and the freight does not move. The model pictures the manager and employee working together. It loses the idea of the first four links coming from the environment and the last three the employee, but it is easier than Gilbert's model to sell and explain to line managers because of its inherent "common sense." This model was used to guide the rest of the program's implementation and installation.

## Expectations

The program engineered expectations in several ways. A videotaped message from the chairman of the board and vice-presidents of all the operating divisions was played at the start of each training workshop. The chairman said that Yellow needed this program to stay competitive. He endorsed it and expected everyone to use it. The vice-presidents said that they had been through the program, they intended to use it, and they expected their employees to use it, too.

Each trainee was directed to apply the program's skills on the job. Performance standards for using these skills were built into each trainee's performance appraisal objectives. At the beginning of the program, an

## Table 2. Gilbert's Performance Engineering Model.

| Environmental supports | Information | Instrumentation | Motivation |
|---|---|---|---|
| | DATA<br>Feedback<br>Expectations<br>Guidelines | INSTRUMENTS<br>Tools and materials | INCENTIVES<br>Financial incentives<br><br>Other incentives<br><br>Career Opportunities |
| **Person's repertory of behavior** | KNOWLEDGE<br>Training<br>Placement | CAPACITY<br>Flexible schedule<br>Prosthesis<br>Physical shaping<br>Adaptation<br>Selection | MOTIVES<br>Assessment of desire to work<br><br>Recruitment |

## Figure 1. Performance model for Yellow Freight System.

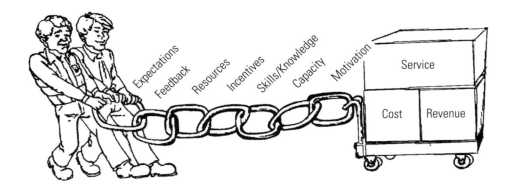

article from the employee newsletter and a letter from the chairman of the board were sent to every employee, restating what was on the videotape. Delivery progressed from the top down. Before employees went through the training, they saw their bosses using the skills.

At the end of a training session, all trainees created contracts that described how they would put the skills to use back on the job. Each contract specified when the trainee would have his or her employees oriented to the system, would have performance standards and feedback systems set up, and would begin using rewards and coaching.

### Feedback

Feedback was used in a variety of ways to implement the program. During the workshop, trainees received evaluative feedback in the form of results of criterion tests and exercises, and corrective feedback verbally from trainers and peers, as well as from watching videotapes of their own performance. Trainers followed up by helping trainees apply the skills and giving corrective feedback, and by checking the quality of the trainees' performance standards and feedback systems. The immediate supervisors also followed up the trainees' use of the skills. Because the performance standards spelled out the expectation that the skills were to be used, the supervisors gave the employees feedback on how well the skills were actually practiced.

In response to an initial low use of rewards, later trainees created a feedback report that increased their use of rewards. They planned weekly or monthly schedules for using their rewards, then monitored their own performance against those checklists. Trainees sent testimonials to top management communicating how they felt about the training. Because top management needed feedback on their decision to fund programs like this one, the trainees were instructed at the end of the training to send messages to management describing their reactions, both good and bad. Top management got weekly feedback on the field's reactions to the program.

Monthly one-page status reports were sent to top management to provide information on the progress of the project. An evaluation of the results of the program was sent to top management as soon as the data were obtained. The monthly employee newsletter carried a regular feature telling how many people had been trained, describing how managers felt about the program, and describing results managers had produced with the skills.

## Resources

The proper resources were obtained to ensure the program's success. Job aids were used during training to speed up performance to criterion and as observers' checklists for recording and guiding feedback. After training, job aids were used to help trainees use the skills correctly, without relying on recall from memory. Sample performance standards sped up the creation of the performance standards and improved consistency by listing accomplishments, measures, and sample standards for each function in field operations. Managers customized the standards as needed. Samples of feedback reports helped managers quickly put together reports to support the performance standards.

As follow-up, trainers were available to help trainees use the skills they had learned and to document results, at least three times. The monthly newsletter ran articles summarizing the content of the workshop and included job aids that acted as a preview for people who had not been trained, and as a review for those who had received training. The self-instructional workshop materials allowed the trainees to review the skills on their own after training.

## Incentives

Tangible and intangible incentives can serve as powerful reinforcers of training. In this program, no less than 11 forms of incentives were used:

- The HRD department paid all trainee expenses to eliminate any financial disincentive to managers' sending trainees to the program.
- Verbal praise was used liberally throughout the workshop, as imme-

diately as possible and always in proportion to the performance.

- A graduation ceremony was held after a trainee passed eight out of 10 criterion tests. A certificate of completion signed by the chairman of the board and a vice-president was presented, amid applause.
- A personal letter was sent from the trainee's vice-president congratulating the trainee on successfully using the skills. The HRD department produced the letter on the vice-president's personal stationary, the vice-president signed it, and it was sent to the employee's home.
- Every trainee received either a suede portfolio or a gold lapel pin as a reward for using the skills.
- Articles in the monthly newsletter named reward recipients, described their successes, and printed trainees' reactions to the training.
- Top management received thank-you messages from trainees the Monday morning after a workshop ended.
- Departments that supported HRD's efforts received verbal praise and were also rewarded with memos to their bosses, doughnuts for extraordinary work (delivered as soon as possible), and a party at the end of the program. At the party, each person's contributions were described publicly.
- Managers who had reviewed the training materials to be sure they were realistic and clear received memos thanking them and were listed by name on the inside front cover of the final printed training materials.
- Trainers received a promotion and pay raise to enter the job, and usually got double-jump promotions after their tours of duty.
- Trainers were rewarded with perks based on performance, including hotel suites to the best trainers and personalized portfolios. The entire group was sent to the conference of the National Society for Performance and Instruction to receive the national award the program had earned.

## Analysis and Results

Total costs for the first phase of the program totaled about $1.7 million, as shown in Table 3.

This program was evaluated at four levels: reaction, learning, use, and performance change. The data reported here cover only Phase I of the training, which involved the managers from the vice-president level to second-level supervisors. Reaction data were collected using a paper questionnaire at the end of the five-day training program. Trainees were asked to rate the effectiveness of the trainer and the program on a 5-point scale. Mean scores were calculated for each question for each group and for all trainees.

Learning data were collected throughout the training program using 10 criterion-referenced performance tests and simulations. Eight of these tests had to be passed to pass the entire course. The percentage of trainees who passed eight out of 10 tests was the primary statistic calculated.

Use data were collected by asking trainees to produce evidence of having used what they had learned in the program. Each trainee was asked to send the trainer copies of performance standards, feedback reports, notes from a coaching session, and evidence of rewarding employees contingent on performance. A simple yes/no tally summarized which trainees had demonstrated that they were using what they had learned in the program. Table 4 shows a summary of the results for these three evaluation levels.

Routinely kept management reports and follow-up interviews with trainees at six and 12 months after their training were used to collect the performance data. Specifically, terminal managers were asked:

## Table 3. Phase I costs.

| Category | Description | Costs ($) |
|----------|-------------|-----------|
| Trainee salaries | 1,046 managers x 5 days training x average salary of $140/day | 732,200 |
| Travel, food, and hotel for trainees | Travel, room, and board for 5 days | 420,000 |
| HRD overhead | Total cost of salaries and benefits for HRD manager, performance technologists, and secretary; equipment and prorated office costs | 200,000 |
| Trainer salaries | 6 trainers x 1 year x $30,000/year | 180,000 |
| Materials | Production and reproduction of print and video materials | 180,000 |
| **Total costs** | | **1,712,200** |

- what changes in terminal or employee performance (if any) they had seen since they began using performance management skills
- what these changes were worth to Yellow in dollars (if possible)
- what percentage of the improvement (if any) they thought was due to their use of the skills taught in the program.

**Table 4. Summary of evaluation results.**

| Level of expectation | Results |
|---|---|
| Reaction | During Phase I, 1,046 managers completed the program. On the average, they rated the program 4.9 out of 5.0 on a 5-point Likert scale when asked "how useful and relevant" the training had been. |
| Learning | Of the 1,046 managers, 1,043 managers met the completion requirement of 8 out of 10 criterion tests passed, for a success rate of 99.7%. |
| Use | Of the 1,046 managers, 924, or 88%, produced evidence that they were using the skills on the job. |

These data provided a very conservative estimate of the impact of the program in a form that was believable to top management. Table 5 shows a sample of the results from this follow-up.

The total dollar value was calculated for the number of months the improvement had actually been observed. No results were extrapolated beyond the months observed. It was up to the trainees to decide how much credit to give the program for any observed performance improvements. Field trainers were strictly instructed to accept any percentage a manager chose to give, although if the trainer felt the percentage was too high, he would discuss the data with the trainee to come up with a more conservative figure.

Data from 249 terminals (about 49 percent of the total system) in all five divisions were collected. About 92 percent of the terminals contacted said that they had some performance improvements they felt were due to performance management skills. The other 8 percent either had no improvement or did not feel that any improvement was due to use of performance management skills. The total value of improvements that could be translated into dollars was about

# Table 5. Sample of results.

| Terminal in division I | Improvement | Percentage of improvement attributed to performance management skills | Dollar value* |
|---|---|---|---|
| A | To reduce high cost per bill due to poor planning on pickup and delivery and low sales, manager installed job models and feedback systems, coached supervisors and drivers, and praised all employees for improved performance. Cost per bill decreased an average of $1.30. | 25 | 6,928 (C) |
| B | In new terminal with cost per bill running high, manager installed job models and used coaching and rewards for supervisory, clerical, and sales staff. Terminal's profits increased from $43,253 to $49,024. | 10 | 27,680 (R) |
| C | Terminal had low bill count and high cost per bill. Manager installed job models and feedback systems, and used interpersonal skills. Cost per bill decreased an average of $1.79, over same period before the program. | 5 | 800 (C) |
| D | Terminal had low bill count, which contributed to a high cost per bill. Manager installed job models and feedback systems, and used rewards and coaching with office staff, supervisors, and sales representatives. Cost per bill decreased an average of $0.92; number of bills increased from 7,765 to 9,405 per month. | 25 | 9,856 (C) |
|  | To improve sales growth, sales manager created job models, coached sales representatives, and used interpersonal skills with representatives and customers. Number of bills increased from 7,290 to | 10 | 245,058 (R) |

*(R) indicates a revenue gain; (C) indicates decreased costs.

**Table 5 (continued). Sample of results.**

| Terminal in division I | Improvement | Percentage of improvement attributed to performance management skills | Dollar value* |
|---|---|---|---|
| | 9,765 per month; total bill count increased from 65,614 to 87,892 per month; at an average revenue of $110 per bill, the 22,278 additional bills brought in $2,450,580 in extra revenue. | | |
| E | Terminal had low bill count and high cost per bill. Manager installed job models and had his sales manager and operations manager install job models, also. All managers used rewards, coaching, and interpersonal skills. Cost per bill decreased from $22.49 to $21.00; number of bills increased from 11,716 to 12,974 per month. | 50 | 56,060 (C) |
| F | Terminal had rising cost per bill with a fluctuating bill count. Manager used job models and feedback reports. Cost per bill decreased from $17.13 to $15.46; number of bills rose from 6,160 to 7,357 per month. | 10 | 5,754 (C) |

*(R) indicates a revenue gain; (C) indicates decreased costs.

$20,791,000. Based on this figure and costs of $1.7 million, the ratio of benefits to costs was 12 to 1. The traditional formula for the return yields a return on investment of 1,115 percent.

The total value of the program was actually much higher than the $20.8 million, however. First, this figure did not include the dollar value of anecdotal results, such as reducing grievances filed by one employee from 27 to zero. In this case, no dollar value could be calculated, but there was general agreement that this change saved money in supervisory time, legal fees, and general employee morale. Second, this figure includes only three to six months' data from about half of the field locations involved in the training. If the performance improvements continued for only 12 months and were replicated in all 500 terminals, the $20.8 million could quadruple.

The full extent of the results will never be known, because data collection was stopped at this point for political reasons. Until very recently, people at the field terminals saw corporate headquarters as nonhelpful. Management wanted to turn around this attitude. Although collection of hard performance improvement data was needed for program evaluation and return-on-investment calculations, data that showed a staff function improving productivity, lowering costs, and improving sales made it appear that the staff function was taking credit for results that only field operations could produce. The president of Yellow Freight therefore asked the manager of HRD to stop collecting results data.

## Summary and Recommendations

This case illustrates how one trucking company responded to external deregulatory pressures and trained all managers and supervisors how to manage more effectively and improve the performance of their employees. Based on performance audit results, the greatest potential return on training investment was identified. Observations of exemplary and average performers led to the conclusion that the differences between the two groups' performance were due to unclear expectations, poor feedback, and dysfunctional incentives. A performance management system was designed and installed to address the causes of the performance gap. Results showed that an overwhelming percentage of the trainees felt that the program was useful and that they met the learning objectives and were using the skills taught. Performance changes that could be turned into dollars totaled more than $20 million in one year.

The following conclusions can be drawn from this experience:

- Performance appraisal and performance management systems have tremendous return-on-investment potential. Because they address the most common causes of employees' performance deficiencies (unclear expectations, poor feedback, and dysfunctional incentives), they are the solution to hundreds (or thousands) of small problems that can sap the competitiveness of any company.
- Effective performance management depends on a combination of technical and soft skills. Supervisors must know how to define performance standards and design feedback systems. But if they lack interpersonal, negotiation, and coaching skills, the system will fail.

- Evaluation of the effectiveness of performance management training is a natural extension of the program itself. Because the training program teaches how to define performance measures and collect performance data, measurable changes in performance are easy to observe.
- Individual and team performance must be measured to avoid one conflicting with the other. Although models for adequately measuring team performance did not exist in this organization at the time of this work, the problems of team measures conflicting with individual measures did. With a merit pay system reinforcing only individual contributions, it was difficult to get managers to pay attention to teamwork.

## Questions for Discussion

1. Was the needs analysis for the program adequate? Explain.
2. Discuss the model for calculating the stages. Are there other equally effective approaches? Explain.
3. In an opening video tape, the chairman of the board endorsed the program and created expectation for each manager to use it. Is this practice helpful?
4. The program was evaluated at four levels. Contrast the levels with those of Kirkpatrick and address the adequacy of the data collection at each level.
5. The dollar value of the performance improvement is a very large number, resulting in a high ROI. Is this figure credible? Explain.
6. The data was collected for six months and from only half the locations. If data were collected for twelve months and from all locations, the $20.8 million could quadruple. Is this believable? Please comment.
7. Is it possible to isolate the effect of training versus the other factors contributing to performance improvement such as the program design, incentives, etc. Explain.
8. This case states that after a 12:1 return on investment was realized, the president asked the manager of human resource development to stop collecting results data. Why do you suppose this action was taken and what is your reaction to it?

## The Author

Jack Zigon is president of Zigon Performance Group, a management consulting firm specializing in the design and installation of custom performance management and performance appraisal systems. His latest work has resulted in a state-of-the-art model for measuring the performance of self-managed and cross-functional work teams. He has developed 11 performance appraisal systems for companies such as

Hallmark Cards, General Dynamics/Lockheed, Yellow Freight System, United Telephone, Air Products and Chemicals, and R.L. Polk and Company. His projects have won four national awards, and he is a frequent speaker at conferences of the National Society for Performance and Instruction, American Society for Training and Development, Society for Human Resource Management, and American Compensation Association. Zigon can be contacted at the following address: 604 Crum Creek Road, Media, PA 19063-1646.

## Reference

Gilbert, T.F. (1978). *Human competence: engineering worthy performance.* New York: McGraw-Hill.

# About the Editor

Jack Phillips has more than 25 years of professional and managerial experience, most of it in the human resource development and management field. Currently he serves on the management faculty of Middle Tennessee State University, where he teaches human resource courses at the graduate and undergraduate levels. Through Performance Resources Organization, he consults with clients in manufacturing, service, and government organizations in the United States and abroad. Consulting assignments include a variety of human resource accountability programs, ranging from measurement and evaluation to productivity and quality enhancement programs, with active clients in the United States, Canada, Mexico, Venezuela, Malaysia, Indonesia, South Africa, and Europe.

A frequent contributor to management literature, Phillips has written *Handbook of Training Evaluation and Measurement Methods* (Gulf Publishing, 2d ed., 1991), *The Development of a Human Resource Effectiveness Index* (University of Michigan Press, 1988), *Recruiting, Training and Retaining New Employees* (Jossey-Bass, 1987), and *Improving Supervisors' Effectiveness* (Jossey-Bass, 1985), which won an award from the Society for Human Resource Management in 1986. Phillips has written more than 75 articles for professional, business, and trade publications.